ARISTOTLE

The Art of Rhetoric

Translated with an Introduction and Notes by
H. C. LAWSON-TANCRED

D0017756

PENGUIN BOOKS

PENGUIN BOOKS

Published by the Penguin Group
Penguin Books Ltd, 80 Strand, London WC2R ORL, England
Penguin Group (USA) Inc., 375 Hudson Street, New York, New York 10014, USA
Penguin Books Australia Ltd, 250 Camberwell Road, Camberwell, Victoria 3124, Australia
Penguin Books Canada Ltd, 10 Alcorn Avenue, Toronto, Ontario, Canada M4V 3B2
Penguin Books India (P) Ltd, 11 Community Centre, Panchsheel Park, New Delhi – 110 017, India
Penguin Books (NZ) Ltd, Cnr Rosedale and Airborne Roads, Albany, Auckland, New Zealand
Penguin Books (South Africa) (Pty) Ltd, 24 Sturdee Avenue, Rosebank 2196, South Africa

Penguin Books Ltd, Registered Offices: 80 Strand, London WC2R ORL, England

www.penguin.com

First published 1991
Reprinted with updated Bibliography 2004
18

Translation, Introduction and Notes copyright © H. C. Lawson-Tancred, 1991, 2004
All rights reserved

The moral right of the translator has been asserted

Printed in England by Clays Ltd, St Ives plc
Set in Bembo (Lasercomp)

ISBN-13: 978-0-140-44510-7
ISBN-10: 0-140-44510-2

PENGUIN ⬤ CLASSICS

THE ART OF RHETORIC

ARISTOTLE was born in Stageira, in the dominion of the kings of Macedonia, in 384 BC. For twenty years he studied at Athens in the Academy of Plato, on whose death in 347 he left, and, some time later, became tutor of the young Alexander the Great. When Alexander succeeded to the throne of Macedonia in 336, Aristotle returned to Athens and established his school and research institute, the Lyceum, to which his great erudition attracted a large number of scholars. After Alexander's death in 323, anti-Macedonian feeling drove Aristotle out of Athens, and he fled to Chalcis in Euboea, where he died in 322. His writings, which were of extraordinary range, profoundly affected the whole course of ancient and medieval philosophy, and they are still eagerly studied and debated by philosophers today. Very many of them have survived and among the most famous are the *Ethics* and the *Politics*, both of which are published in Penguin Classics, together with *The Athenian Constitution, De Anima, The Art of Rhetoric, Poetics* and the *Metaphysics*.

HUGH LAWSON-TANCRED was born in 1955 and educated at Eton and Balliol College, Oxford. He is a Departmental Fellow in the Department of Philosophy at Birkbeck College in the University of London. He has published extensively on Aristotle and Plato and is currently engaged in research in computational linguistics. He translates widely from the Slavonic and Scandinavian languages. His translations of Aristotle's *The Art of Rhetoric* and *De Anima* are also published in Penguin Classics. He is married with a daughter and two sons and lives in north London and Somerset.

In Piam Memoriam
E.M.L.-T.

CONTENTS

PART TWO: EMOTION AND CHARACTER

PREFACE

The translation of Aristotle must be reckoned amongst the greatest, but also amongst the driest, of the pleasures that the study of the Classics affords the scholar. There is hardly a paragraph that he wrote which does not contain some stimulating or arresting thought, some consideration of a familiar problem from a new perspective, or some fruitful discovery of a new problem where all previously seemed to be blandly clear. The freshness of the intellectual content is unvarying, for all that its relevance to the contemporary debate may constantly change. Even, therefore, those treatises that are less than central to the whole corpus are thoroughly deserving of the attentions of the translator, and the present work is a conspicuous example. *The Art of Rhetoric* (henceforth *Rhetoric*) could fairly be claimed to be the ancestor of a whole line of texts which defined the academic syllabus for the ordinary educated Greek and Roman. This work, we might say, founded the middle-brow culture of antiquity.

It has certainly been a most rewarding and enjoyable experience to work on the *Rhetoric*, and my labours will not have been in vain if some portion of that enjoyment is shared by at least some of my readers. It is not, indeed, an immediately accessible text and no ingenuity could make it so, but I hope that those who persist with it will find that the depth of Aristotle's understanding of the subject and the originality of his philosophical conception of rhetoric have a compulsion every bit as powerful as the subtlest dialectic or the most rigorous argumentation. One word of warning, however, would be appropriate. The style of exposition is relentlessly piecemeal and draws heavily on citations from a wide literature – citations which are often both hard for us wholly to grasp in the first place and moreover presented in a disconcertingly elliptic and compressed manner. My policy with such difficulties has been to pursue the course usual in this series and offer, I hope, adequate information in the notes for the essential point of the reference to be intelligible to the non-specialist reader, without aspiring to give full documentation of all aspects of the original context from which it is drawn. This volume should therefore be intelligible throughout in itself, but invite supplementation in many places from the copious material available in standard works of reference.

Many people have assisted me with this translation, and I am indebted to too many scholars for it to be possible to list them, but I would like especially to thank for their encouragement at all stages A. J. Radice and E. C. Jenkyns, though I must remove the poison from the chalice by speedily exempting them from complicity in such no doubt numerous errors as even their diligence may have failed to eliminate. In the matter of the diligent elimination of mistakes, I would also like to express my great gratitude to Kate Parker, whose copy-editing services to this orthographically complicated text have been of an exceptional order.

HUGH LAWSON-TANCRED

INTRODUCTION

I. THE IMPORTANCE OF ANCIENT RHETORIC

Can there be a science of persuasion? It would be hard to deny that the ability to persuade, convince, cajole or win round is one of the most useful skills in human life. It is a capacity that shows its importance equally easily in the market, the court, the council chamber and the bedroom. It seems a crucial knack to be mastered by anyone aspiring to influence the private or public activities of men and women, for whatever ends. Yet at the same time it would appear to be – and is so held by popular supposition – not something that can be transmitted from a master to his disciples, not something that can be acquired as the result of a patient period of study, not something that can be reliably achieved by following a rigorous method. It seems rather to be a gift dispensed among mortals with capricious favouritism, whose results can only otherwise be achieved by fluke and good fortune. It is certainly natural to think that oratory, like musical or sporting prowess, is a natural endowment, open only to the envy, not for the emulation, of those denied it. The twentieth century has seen only too many cases of the natural, untutored orator capable of wielding often demonic influence over a malleable crowd. All too often the voice of reason, decency and common sense has been left impotent by a deficiency in that magical art of persuasion which seems to remain the perquisite only of a charmed few. On other occasions, a speaker with no credentials or proven record of persuasive utterance may by happy chance hit on the one line of attack that will bring him or her success. Many, contemplating these varied outcomes of oratorical exercises, would be tempted to throw their hands up in despair and pronounce the art of oratory to be a wholly unscientific and unsystematic affair, in which it would be vain to look for valuable instruction.

This approach was not that of the ancient Greeks. If there are two definitive features of ancient Greek civilization, they are loquacity and competition. Even in the earliest phase of the classical culture – the heroic age of early archaic Greece, the age of Homer and the first lyric poets – it is obvious that an importance was attached to prominence in debate second only to that ascribed to the victorious warrior himself. The capacity for forceful and cogent self-expression was from the very first enshrined as a central social value, and enormous importance was attached to it by those who sought to achieve pre-eminence in these early societies. This is made clear in almost every page of the *Iliad* itself. A central episode in the poem is the attempt by three leading Greek heroes to recall to the field the greatest of their warriors, Achilles, who has taken to sulking in his tent after a row with the king, Agamemnon, that is fraught with catastrophic consequences for the Greek forces.[1] Thus at the very heart of the story there lies a rhetorical contest of great *gravitas*. (It is, in fact, a noteworthy feature of the poem how relatively little Homer, in writing an heroic epic, finds it necessary to concentrate on the actual course of the fighting. Scenes of physical violence are interspersed with episodes of human or divine persuasion.) Throughout antiquity the attempt of the great heroes Odysseus, Phoenix and Ajax to woo Achilles back to the fighting was held up as a paradigm of rhetorical excellence, often cited in later discussion of various aspects of the art and more than once by Aristotle in the present work. No less memorable is the passage in the eleventh book[2] where the old and wise hero Nestor seeks to urge the young and impressionable Patroclus to use his special friendship with Achilles to spare the Greeks. Other examples from the poem could be multiplied at random and echoed from the *Odyssey*, and we should not forget that these were at all times the works that the élite chose to set before their sons as models for their behaviour.

From the earliest times, then, the ability to persuade carried a high social prestige in the Greek world. To say this, however, is not to claim that it was the object of theoretical study. Homer regards the rhetorical skill of Nestor or Odysseus as no less a natural endowment than the extraordinary physical strength of Diomedes, Hector and Achilles. It is wholly consistent with the aristocratic tenor of the *Iliad* that the heroes are naturally in a class apart both in their mental and in their physical attributes, though it is noteworthy that when one of the ordinary soldiers, Thersites, does attempt to offer his thoughts to the aristocrats, he is given a perfectly respectable speech even though he is in all other respects made out to be a buffoon.[3] The oratory of archaic Greece was instinctive and unlearned, which indeed reflects a simple underlying circumstance. It was a truism of later antiquity that rhetoric and democracy were coeval. In the societies of the early archaic age, the prevalent systems of government were either aristocracies or tyrannies. Neither of these was conducive to the flowering of public debate. There is no great mystery in the fact that it took the rise of democracies and otherwise open societies at Athens and elsewhere to create the climate in which public eloquence became a political indispensability. When power was to be secured either by brute force or by the inheritance of authority from ancestors, there was little need for the politician to find convincing reasons for the citizens to accept his policies. Indeed to have offered them such reasons might well have been to risk undermining his other credentials by implying their insufficiency.

It was the coming of the true democracies that changed this and created the threshold over which systematic rhetorical practice was to enter Greek life. When at Athens, in the years around 460 BC, the popular assembly finally wrested full power from the other institutions of the state, it became vital for those aspiring to the control of that city to use all forms of popular persuasion that were to hand. The aristocrats still willing to secure their position were determined to employ any methods to resist those who sought still further to erode their traditional prestige, and the protagonists of the people, in their turn, knew well how to fan the flames of dissatisfaction. The two great figures of the first generation of Athenian democratic life, the age immediately following the pivotal constitutional reforms of Cleisthenes, were Aristides and Themistocles – the one standing for the dignity and integrity valued by the aristocrats, the other for the brilliance and thrusting energy of the new men. In the next generation, according to the time-honoured tradition, a synthesis of their skills was effected by the unique political talents of Pericles.

Even if we lacked specific testimony to the effect, we would be entitled to suppose that Pericles did not rely entirely on his mother wit to control the Athenians for thirty almost uninterrupted years. His association with the great natural philosopher Anaxagoras[4] led to his incorporating in his political speeches some of the jargon and conceptual subtlety that had developed even in the infancy of natural philosophy. This points clearly to the growing recognition among Athenian and other Greek politicians that success in oratory was too important a matter to be left entirely to chance. Thus, by the middle years of the fifth century, imperial Athens was ready to receive the weanling science of rhetoric, which had been born and nurtured in the West of the Greek world, in the colonial city of Syracuse. The peculiar circumstances arising out of the fall of the Syracusan tyranny seem to have produced the first practitioners of the art of rhetorical instruction.[5] It was at this point that the transition was first made to the conception that rhetoric was a teachable skill, that it could, usually in return for a fee, be passed from one skilled performer on to others, who might thereby achieve successes in their practical life that would otherwise have eluded them. Within a generation the institution of rhetorical training was established at Athens. It became something of a craze. The idea spread rapidly through the political élite that the worst consequences of opening up the constitution to mass accountability, in both the assembly and the law courts, could be mitigated by the mastery of these new arts from abroad. The man, it was thought, who possessed a systematic understanding of the art of rhetoric could, in the phrase coined by Aristophanes in his well-known satire on the whole business in the *Clouds*, 'make the weaker argument the stronger'.[6] A rhetorical revolution was under way – the effect of the early teachers of oratory at Athens was to produce in audiences an expectation of a similar level of performance from all speakers, thus raising the required standard of articulacy in the already intimidating assemblies of the city, and rhetorical training rapidly came to be in effect the equivalent of a modern university degree for those who sought prominence in Athenian public life.

The developments of the 420s paved the way for the full flowering of Attic oratory. Thucydides, writing his history of the Peloponnesian War in the period between his exile in 423 and his death probably soon after the fall of Athens in 404,[7] includes, amid his otherwise sparse narrative, a number of highly wrought and elaborate rhetorical exercises, betraying no little rhetorical training and, despite his claim to be composing a possession for all time,[8] pandering to the contemporary demand for rhetorical elaboration. By the end of the century the wealthy metic Lysias, impoverished by the fall of the city, had taken to the profession of a *logographos*, a writer of speeches for others to use (Greek practice, unlike Roman, required the litigant to present his own case in court). The emergence around this time of the *logographoi* is of great significance for the rise of rhetorical theory. Now for the first time there was a class of men whose primary occupation and means of livelihood was the production of effective speeches, often on topics in which they were not directly involved themselves. It was vitally important for them to reflect on how to render their productions convincing, and from this time onwards a secondary industry develops which seeks to supply both professional and amateur speakers with the technical underpinning essential for consistent success. This is the tradition of those composing the 'Arts' of rhetoric, to which Aristotle makes frequent reference in this work and indeed of which it was itself later accepted as the supreme example. The age of the 'Arts' of rhetoric stretches from about 400 to 320 BC and was brought to an end almost as much by the magisterial summary of Aristotle as by the rise of Macedonian power.

The present work is, then, the masterpiece of one particular literary genre that flourished in the fourth century BC in Greece, that of the rhetorical manual, and it is a remarkable fact that it should have fallen to Aristotle to write it. It is natural enough to experience astonishment at the breadth of Aristotle's achievement. Few men have reached such eminence, or exercised such influence, in so diverse a range of fields. Even if we allow, as we should, that much of the research and indeed many of the ideas that went into the great treatises should be at least in part credited to the scholars of the Lyceum that he founded, it remains remarkable that so much should have flowed from the pen of a single man. Yet quite apart from Aristotle's prodigious output, his addressing the task of summarizing rhetorical theory is remarkable for an entirely different reason. We have seen that rhetoric became something of an obsession among the Athenian political élite in the last decades of the fifth century BC. This, however, should be qualified with an important reservation. The intellectual and social élite was far from being absolutely at one in its response to the challenge of the 'Open Society'. Many accepted it as inevitable and resolved to make the best of a bad job, but there remained a minority who dreamed of a radical change to a better system. Of these, by the early fourth century, the most profound example was the extraordinary figure of Plato. The monstrous injustice of the condemnation of Socrates convinced Plato that democracy at Athens would only ever be capable of spreading misery and suffering or of giving place to some still worse régime, and from that time on (399 BC) he devoted his energies to working out and promoting his radical alternative conception of the state. This of course reaches its finest theoretical enunciation in the *Republic* of *c.*375 and its dismal practical applications in the two trips to Sicily in 366 and 361. The reason for the foundation of the Academy, which can be tentatively dated to shortly after 390, when Plato returned from a decade of travel, was not just to promote the general study of philosophy but also to produce a new generation of revolutionaries who would put the new politics into practice in the cities of Greece.[9] Plato was also determined, in his vindication of the memory of Socrates himself as a saint of reason, to expose the absurdities and weaknesses of the whole democratic system of government. An important element in the latter task was the exposure of the absurdity of rhetoric. Though Plato would firmly have rejected Aristophanes' suggestion that Socrates was in any way responsible for the growing obsession with the rhetoric of the late fifth century, he would equally firmly have agreed with his assessment of its disastrous social consequences, and in two dialogues in particular, the *Gorgias* and the *Phaedrus*, he sets out his own fundamentally hostile approach to rhetoric. Now it was at the Academy at precisely this time (367) that the seventeen-year-old son of the Macedonian court physician arrived to begin his studies in philosophy.

The question of Aristotle's general relations with Platonism has been the subject of a great deal of discussion since 1923, when Werner Jaeger published his account of the philosopher's gradual evolution away from the Academy.[10] What is perhaps most widely agreed is that for at least the first of the two decades in which Aristotle was a member of the Academy he was a fairly loyal Platonist, his ideas reflecting the changes and developments taking place in Plato's own thought but never opposing his fundamental outlook. It is thus reasonable to suppose that such was also his attitude to rhetoric, and that view is substantiated by what we know of the fragments of the early dialogue the *Gryllus*, probably written about 360 BC. This, then, produces the puzzle. How can a man who, for a significant phase of his formation, shared his master's opposition to rhetoric have in maturity composed a masterpiece of the formal study of rhetoric? This question can, in fact, be given an historical answer and it reveals the importance of the present work. The answer is in reality relatively uncontroversial. Aristotle cultivated an interest in rhetoric to counterbalance the effectiveness of rhetoric as a form of tertiary education as established by his rival Isocrates.[11]

The fact that the Athenian élite was much more attracted to the school of Isocrates (436–338 BC) than to the Academy did not fail to make its mark on Aristotle. He had left Athens in the year after the death of Plato, motivated probably both by pique at his non-selection as the successor to the Scholarchy and by fears of rising anti-Macedonian sentiment, and taken himself to the northern Aegean to engage in the foundation of the science of empirical biology. Twelve years later, he returned to Athens, now made safe by the victory of Philip of Macedon at the battle of Chaeroneia, and, perhaps with the direct support of Philip,[12] established his own school, with aims that were clearly distinct from those of both Isocrates and Plato. The hallmark of the new school was to be its catholicity. All branches of learning were to be studied, including those only recently put on the map by Aristotle himself. Evidently, with such a remit the art of rhetoric could be neglected neither on ideological nor on practical grounds, and this too was to be absorbed into the curriculum and given its place in the hierarchy of sciences.

However, although the systematic study of rhetoric was now to be countenanced, this constituted a renunciation of Aristotle's Platonist background and he was at least resolved that it should be studied in a form that emphasized its most general and philosophical aspects; in other words, rhetoric was to be surveyed from the standpoint of philosophy.

The notion of philosophical rhetoric or of a philosophy of rhetoric may not strike us as extraordinary, but it must have seemed strange to the men of the fourth century, and it is from this combination that both the difficulties and the greatness of the present work are derived. The difficulties are real, but the greatness should also not be missed. For in making the subject of rhetoric safe for philosophy Aristotle was obliged to treat it in a manner that for the first time thoroughly investigated its underpinnings in the other areas of human life in which it plays a role. In other words, the mature Aristotelian approach to rhetoric involved the philosopher in three major topics otherwise not covered in the corpus of his works: the detailed psychology of the emotions, the use of informal reasoning and the aesthetics of prose style. Whereas previous exponents of the art of rhetorical theory had concentrated on what were in effect only tricks and devices for *ad hoc* success, Aristotle sought to grasp the very roots of persuasion itself, which required him to ponder the nature of character and emotion and also the method of demonstration in the absence of deductive certainty. Thus persuasiveness becomes for the first time a fully systematic and even scientific exercise; it can indeed be taught, but only by a deep grasp of some of the most central features of human nature. Thus the study of rhetoric, instead of being a philosophical outcast, transcends its humble and practical origins to become an important component in the general study of man.

2. THE HISTORICAL BACKGROUND TO THE *RHETORIC*

Athenian democracy, as presented to us in the pseudo-Aristotelian *Constitution of the Athenians*, is a remarkable political system. But just how democratic should we consider it to be? Sovereignty unquestionably rested with the assembly of the people, the Ecclesia (or

Assembly), which was open to all adult male citizens. But it is true that when statistical allowance is made for women, metics and slaves, those entitled to attend the Assembly only compose some 20 to 25 per cent of the total adult population, and that when allowance is made for the inconvenience or indeed effective impossibility of regular attendance for residents of the remoter parts of Attica, which were far from uninhabited, it can be seen that for practical purposes the sovereign body, or *demos*, formed a remarkably tight oligarchy of city-dwelling, enfranchised male adults. The fact that a quorum for an ostracism[13] was a mere six thousand out of a total Attic population of perhaps some three hundred thousand is sufficient indication of the unrepresentative character of the *demos*, whose regular membership in the years around the Peloponnesian War will have probably been something between ten and fifteen thousand. For all that, the power of the Assembly was very great, justifying the modern description of the democracy as 'radical'. The famous debates recorded by Thucydides give us a remarkable taste of its meetings, compounded of the heady feeling of imperial power and the latent violence of the excited crowd. It is not hard to see how in this stimulating environment the arts of persuasion made rapid progress.

Decisions of the Assembly brooked neither obstruction nor delay, and the task of executing them fell to the Council of Five Hundred, the Boule, which sat regularly in the Agora, the market square just north of the Acropolis. The Council, unlike the Assembly, was an elective body – fifty men being returned by each of the ten Attic tribes – whose function was in some ways similar to that of a modern constituency.[14] However, unlike representatives returned by a modern constituency, those sent by the tribes to the Council had no real power at all, but only the onerous responsibility of seeing that the Assembly was well supplied with all the information that it needed and that its decisions were carried out with promptness and exactitude. The business of enacting the particular requirements of the *demos* was further delegated by the Council to ordinary Athenian citizens appointed to the various magistracies by the unusual method of lot selection, a method that Aristotle actually considered to be the hallmark of democracy.[15] These appointees were as answerable to the Council as the Council members themselves were to the Assembly, and individual magistrates, on leaving office, would often have had to put their case with force and clarity when subjected by the Council to the mandatory rendering of accounts that was known in Athens as the *euthunae*. Thus the Council provided another audience for displays of rhetorical skill.

Both the Assembly and the Council were places in which men might have to justify their actions, but the Assembly was also a theatre for deliberative rhetoric – the task of urging the city to one course of action rather than another. The difference between these two rhetorical functions, between vindication and exhortation, was soon realized to be central and was later to be the subject of much theory. But the stage on which the business of self-justification, or of the denigration of one's enemies, was most at home was the law court, which enjoyed an extraordinarily wide scope at Athens in the fifth and fourth centuries BC. The classical Athenian judiciary system originated at the beginning of the sixth century with Solon, who made two important contributions. He thoroughly revised and greatly extended the written code of laws that he had inherited from Dracon, a reactionary politician of the previous generation, and he instituted the first popular appeal court, the Heliaea, named after the sanctuary of Apollo Heliaeus in which it met. This was popular in the sense that it was open to all citizens, unlike the aristocratic Areopagus, and it also differed greatly from the Areopagus in having a jury that was huge by modern standards. Probably even at the start of its existence and certainly by the end of the sixth century BC, the juries in the Heliaea were regularly five hundred strong. Thus, as has often been remarked, there was something distinctly theatrical about appearing before this court. Moreover, the principle of the large jury, and of the relatively powerless presiding magistrate, became even more central to the Athenian system when, in the democratic 'revolution' of the 460s, popular law courts on the model of the Heliaea replaced the earlier magistrate courts as the sessions of first instance, rather than merely of appeal. From then on, any citizen under prosecution would have to be ready to defend himself before a large, partisan and under-regulated jury. This predicament was no doubt parlous enough, but it was made worse by two remarkable features of the Athenian system. The first was that prosecutions were no state monopoly, as, effectively, in our system, but available to all who could establish a prima-facie case.[16] The inevitable result was the rise of the 'political prosecution', which well before the end of the fifth century had replaced the crude method of ostracism as the favoured means for conducting tests of political strength. This development was in turn helped by the second feature of Athenian juries, already the subject of satire by 423 (the date of Aristophanes' *Wasps*), which was an over-zealous readiness to convict, especially, perhaps, when the defendant came from the more comfortable strata of Athens' diverse society. Thus all those who lived in the limelight of public opinion ran the constant risk of finding themselves before their fellow citizens, in highly unpredictable mood, possibly needing to refute the most extravagant allegations against them mustered by their political or private enemies. It is easy to see how, as soon as this system really began to bite, by the generation of Pericles, those who still aspired to a public career should have begun to devote large amounts of time, energy and money to the cultivation of the elusive skill of winning over mass audiences. What is perhaps more surprising is that so few of the Athenian aristocracy before the time of Plato seem to have abandoned the political aspirations traditional among their class. The fact that they did not do so created a firm and steady demand for others who could provide a reliable method for achieving persuasion.

Those who sought to meet the demand for oratorical expertise were the varied collection of freelance intellectuals known to philosophical history as the sophists. Unfortunately, our tradition of information about the sophists was poisoned almost at source by Plato and the Academy, who saw them as partly responsible for the discrediting and thus for the demise of Socrates and as the propagators of shallow and irresponsible theories, with which their name has ever since been associated. It is not hard to see the root of Plato's dislike for the sophists. They were indeed a disparate group, with widely varying interests and no single common 'core curriculum' to expound, but if they were united by anything it was in the professed usefulness to their pupils of what they taught, and specifically its usefulness for purposes of political influence in democratic cities. The rise of the sophists at Athens, in which many of them came to reside, was crucially and inextricably bound up with the profound change in the character of Athenian politics that had occurred in the middle of the fifth century BC. Both sophistry and democracy alike displeased Plato, who witnessed in his twenties two traumatic events: the brief but bloody oligarchy of the thirty tyrants, imposed on Athens by the Spartans after the fall of the city at the end of the Peloponnesian War, and the judicial murder of Socrates, a mere four years after the restoration of the democracy. The latter convinced him that no existing form of constitution could promote anything but misery and evil, and that a city could be well run only if it were under the exclusive control of those who shared his own metaphysical vision of reality. Sophistry, for its part, represented all that was worst about democracy in Plato's eyes, especially the cynical emphasis it placed on the shameless exploitation of the techniques of mass persuasion.

Yet one of the first intellectuals whom we know to have had a practical influence on a major politician was not a sophist. Anaxagoras of Clazomenae was a natural philosopher with an idiosyncratic theory of the origin of the cosmos.[17] He was also, apparently, a close collaborator with Pericles, whose oratory seems to have acquired its peculiar distinction from his transfer to the realm of public policy of the nice distinctions spawned by Presocratic physics. However, it was soon discovered that intellectual acuity could be more directly brought to bear on the problem of persuasion than by adapting the jargon of physics and philosophy. The key figure of the 420s is the Sicilian Gorgias, who has indeed a strong claim to be considered the true father of the systematic study of the techniques of rhetoric; and there can be little doubt, although not enough of his work has survived for us to be absolutely sure, that his stay in Athens had a seminal influence on the development of Attic oratory at the beginning of its golden age. One indication of this, indeed, is his appearance as the eponymous interlocutor of Plato's most sustained attack on rhetoric and the outlook that it encourages. Yet Gorgias is himself treated with considerable respect (as is Protagoras in the work named after him), while it is his over-zealous pupil

Polus who receives most of the scorn of Socrates, and the sinister figure of Callicles is introduced to illustrate the deleterious effect of an excessive capacity to persuade on the morals of the members of the Athenian political class. What also transpires from the *Gorgias*, however, apart from the author's distaste for its subject, is the emergence of the rudiments of a technical vocabulary to denote the different types of effect that contribute to a successful exercise of persuasion, and in this we are given a foretaste of the clearly defined and well-established art of rhetoric that had its origins in the next century and was to develop throughout the Hellenistic age.

After Gorgias two men of very different temperaments, interests and inclinations contested his successor's crown. One of these is the underrated figure of Isocrates. He lived to the enormous age of ninety-eight and his life spans much of the period in which rhetoric developed during the fifth century BC as well as the fourth. He emerged most clearly after the foundation of the Academy by Plato, to whose approach his was in many ways the antithesis. Plato had founded the Academy in the years immediately after his ten-year absence from Athens, probably in the early 380s. From the start the institution was devoted to two purposes: the apologetic vindication of the reputation of Socrates, which Plato seems to have regarded as a duty of intellectual *pietas* and which motivated so many of the early dialogues, including the marvellous tetralogy on the days of Socrates' death; and the repudiation of all forms of enquiry, whether practical or theoretical, that might distract the student from the proper business of philosophy – the contemplation of the entirely rational and formal structure of reality revealed by the dialectic method. From this apparently unpromising approach, the new school claimed, could emerge solutions to all the political difficulties currently baffling the Greek cities, as well as the blueprint for a new and better system of organization for human society. All this was wholeheartedly rejected by the followers of Isocrates, who accepted unashamedly the general intellectual outlook of the sophistic movement. Isocrates saw nothing at all wrong with the pursuit of political influence by the use of techniques of persuasion. Indeed, this was for him, as for the men of the late fifth century, the natural objective of the respectable man, the *spoudaios* ('serious man') and *kalos te k'agathos* ('gentleman'). The only disagreement that Isocrates had with the sophists and Gorgias was that they had been insufficiently thorough and scientific in developing the techniques of persuasion. In particular, they had neglected stylistic matters, concentrating too much on parataxis, the balance of elements in a sentence, rather than on true syntaxis, the composition of extended sentences whose elaborate and constantly varied structure should beautifully echo the diverse turns taken by the thought expressed.[18] To illustrate his point Isocrates effectively invented a whole new genre of rhetoric. This was the so-called 'epideictic' or 'display' rhetoric, which now took its place in the canons of the art alongside the established branches of 'forensic' and 'deliberative'. It is true that this was not quite a new thing, as there had been earlier examples, such as Gorgias' partly extant encomium on Helen, but there had certainly been nothing before to compare with such full-length masterpieces of rhetorical elaboration as the *Panegyricus*, *Panathenaicus* and *Philippus* of Isocrates' maturity. In epideictic oratory we see a unique blend of the theoretical and the practical, for the speeches are virtuoso pieces designed not for a particular occasion but to serve as models to be variously copied by those engaged in actual persuasion, as well, no doubt, as to stand in their own right as autonomous works of art.

Isocrates was certainly building on the foundation left by Gorgias, and showing the way in which rhetoric could become a fully fledged and wholly credible subject. However, with an irony which we have already noted,[19] it was not Isocrates who was to provide the most permanently influential account of the theory of public persuasion, but the intellectual successor of his great rival – the author of the present work. Aristotle, the one-time Academician, is the true heir of Gorgias.

3. RHETORIC AS *TECHNE*

We have seen that the Platonic tradition, inheriting as it did so much of the perspective of the dissident Athenian aristocrats of the fifth century BC, was profoundly suspicious of the whole activity of rhetoric, and that Plato himself only turned to it with some ambivalence relatively late in his career, though then, admittedly, in one of his most impressive dialogues. After the developments of the mid fourth century, however, the Lyceum could not permit itself the luxury of spurning rhetoric. Isocrates and others had established rhetoric as a legitimate basis for further education and in so doing they were setting a trend that was to last for a millennium. Aristotle was prudent enough to realize that this challenge could not simply be ignored and that it was therefore necessary for him to evolve his own Peripatetic doctrine of rhetoric.

It is to this task that the present treatise is devoted. There are, indeed, signs that the work was not composed at a single time. Most notably, the attitude adopted to the unashamed use of emotional manipulation in rhetoric shifts during the course of the work. In the introductory section of Book I in the traditional division (see 'The Translation', p. 58), we have, as it were, the high Platonic rejection of persuasion by the emotions, while, by contrast, Book II is wholly devoted to expounding the art of it. However, these inconsistencies should be seen as superficial. The underlying tenor of the work is strikingly coherent. What Aristotle is offering is a manual of persuasion in the established manner, but one which is presented in the context of a genuinely philosophical conception of rhetoric. He is at pains to integrate the activity of rhetoric within his general hierarchy of intellectual activity. It must be assigned its place alongside those sciences and arts to which the Platonic tradition attached greater significance. This task is achieved by the recognition of rhetoric as a *techne*. For Aristotle, the word *techne* has a quite specific significance.[20] The concept of a *techne* is correlated with that of an *episteme*: what an *episteme* is in the field of theoretical speculation, a *techne* is in the domain of practical reasoning. The central characteristic of an *episteme* is that it evolves its propositions from intuitively given principles (*archae*) by the use of the syllogistic method, as set out in the *Posterior Analytics* and, notoriously, not exactly followed in Aristotle's own contributions to biology and the other empirical sciences.[21] Thus it is the function of an *episteme* to provide, for some domain of knowledge, a comprehensively detailed account of all salient aspects of the domain, which yet derives by logical steps from certain and indubitable premises. Thus the possession of an *episteme* puts us in a uniquely advantageous position in regard to a given subject-matter, and it is the task of enquiry to provide us with this perspective on as much of nature as will turn out to be possible. When we have acquired an *episteme* of the whole of nature, then the scientific task will be complete, a possibility that Aristotle, quaintly to our eyes, seems readily to have entertained.

· With this theoretical concept of an *episteme* the practical concept of a *techne* is correlated. It too takes self-evident premisses as its starting point and proceeds by the syllogistic method. But it aims, not at the production of theorems for the contemplation of the rational mind, but at that of functions for the execution of the rational agent. It is perhaps worth stressing that Aristotle's conception of rationality does admit of its application to practice in this way, in view of the widespread supposition that his conception of intellectual activity was excessively biased towards the contemplative and indeed that in this respect he bequeathed a significant and unfortunate legacy to subsequent generations of Greek scientists. Aristotle has a very clear and satisfying conception of the practical use of the mind, that is to say its use in the realization of specific targets or objectives, but where he, like the whole of Greek science, strays from modern ideals is in his exclusive choice of non-mechanical objectives. We have in the corpus two examples of a fully fledged *techne* – that of the *Poetics* for the composition of tragic drama and that of the *Rhetoric* for the performance of oratory.

By classifying rhetoric, then, as a *techne*, Aristotle was locating it on his philosophical landscape and at the same time imputing to it a structure of its own. However, this structure, as he makes immediately clear, is unusually complex. The whole function of rhetoric can be divined by reflection on its central purpose. This, we are told at the start, is the detection in any given subject-matter of its persuasive aspects. It is this universality of rhetoric that gives it its affinity with dialectic, as opposed, say, to an affinity with poetry or drama, the latter of which at least has a remarkably specific function for Aristotle.[22] However, although a science of persuasive aspects might initially seem hopelessly general, it turns out, fortuitously, that there are in fact only three kinds of such aspect, or, to put the same point another way, that there are only three kinds of proof available to the rhetorician. These three kinds of proof are those achieved by argument, those by character and those by emotion, and this trichotomy dominates much of the work. The division requires, naturally enough, that the orator understand both the principles of argument and the basis of character and emotion: this, of course, is to say that he must be both a logician and a psychologist. Rhetoric can then be seen as precisely a mixture of these two disciplines. There are, however, further structural complications. Psychology is indeed the science both of character and of emotion and it is convenient that these two areas of proof fall under the same discipline. Argumentation, however, though essentially logical, is also greatly characterized by the subject-matter that it concerns. Hence, there cannot for the rhetorician be a general science of argument in the way that there can be a general science of emotion and character, namely psychology. The character of a rhetorical argument will be determined by the character of the persuasion that is being essayed. Thus within the rhetorical study of argument, as one of the kinds of proof, we find a further division and this also turns out to be a trichotomy. For persuasion can have only three objectives: the establishment of the justice of its given subject-matter, the establishment of its admirability or the establishment of its advisability. These three tasks of persuasion determine, indeed, the three genres of rhetoric, which are the forensic, epideictic (or laudatory) and deliberative (or political) branches of the subject.

The tasks, therefore, of the orator are to find aspects of the subject that can be employed in arguments designed to establish the features that need to be stressed and that can be used to induce the appropriate emotional state in the listener and to create the appropriate impression of character. The problem in all these areas is not the construction of the arguments after the discovery of the premises but rather the initial discovery of these premises. For this activity rhetorical tradition has the technical concept of *invention*, and invention can be said to be the primary subject of the *Rhetoric*. The great contribution of the theoretician, the rhetorician, to the practical business of oratory is the provision of the premises on which rhetorical proofs can be built. How this is to be done is shown at great length in the present work, more perhaps than in any other production of ancient or modern rhetorical theory. The

Rhetoric might indeed be called an encyclopaedia of invention, and although this imposes upon it a somewhat monotonous structure, the sheer energy of the quest for the premisses of persuasion has a unique exhilaration.

The first eight Sections of the work, in the arrangement adopted in this translation (see 'The Translation', p. 58), are devoted to the study of the various aspects of invention, logical and psychological, and the remaining two are devoted to style and composition. Of those concerned specifically with invention, Sections Three, Four and Five deal with demonstrative invention, the invention of premisses that can support logical arguments, rather than psychological ones, to which Sections Six and Seven are devoted. The Sections on demonstrative invention are devoted each to one genre of rhetoric: Three focuses on deliberative, Four on epideictic and Five on litigious rhetoric. They are of very uneven length, the treatment of litigation being by some way the longest, while the order of presentation bears out Aristotle's claim that deliberative rhetoric is the most important and worthy branch. Each Section thus presents the principal aspects of any subject-matter that will be needed for the successful carrying out of each of these forms of persuasion.

We have seen that the Sections on demonstrative invention are concerned primarily with the invention of the premisses of the various types of demonstrative proof rather than with the structure of the argument, but we should not conclude that Aristotle entirely neglects the characteristic structure of a rhetorical argument. On the contrary, he produces an explicit account of the contrast between logical and rhetorical argumentation. He first draws a distinction between those elements of a demonstrative proof which are in a sense external to the speech, of which the most obvious examples are witnesses and evidence in litigation, and those that are intrinsic to it, as being the productions of the orator himself. He then passes to the exposition of how the intrinsically produced premisses, the products of rhetorical invention, can be used in two complementary ways. Just as in the dialectic there is the possibility of arguing either by the rigid deductions of the syllogistic method or by the use of more loosely inductive methods, so in rhetoric there is a peculiarly rhetorical form of syllogism known as the *enthymeme*, and it is also possible to argue inductively by the use of examples (*paradeigmata*). These two forms of argument, the enthymeme and the paradigm, are the constituents of the whole demonstrative art of the rhetorician. They form, as has been said, a schematic parallel with the argumentative forms of the dialectic, but they differ from the simple syllogism and induction of logic in ways which are determined by their characteristically applying to subject-matter that is vague and contingent. All this Aristotle sets out at some length in Section Two, which is devoted to the study of the structure of rhetorical argument.

The concept of the enthymeme is a characteristic Aristotelian explanatory device, doing useful work in an area which had not previously been subjected to philosophical examination. The enthymeme differs in two ways from the syllogism. In the first place, it is characterized by the suppression of premises whose contribution to the argument is in some way obvious and which it would be pedantic to include in a speech (as it might not be in a more formal demonstration).[23] In the second place, while the syllogisms of logic, dialectic and science are directed at the production of conclusions as indubitably true as the premises, the enthymemes of rhetoric are characteristically derived from premises which are true *for the most part* and inevitably tend to produce conclusions of the same status.[24] Aristotle manages skilfully to prevent the enthymeme from being indistinguishable from the syllogisms of such specific sciences as politics, while keeping it from being absolutely universal. Enthymemes are tied to subject-matter, arising as they do out of premises that are only available in connection with the subject that is in fact being discussed. In this respect, they contrast with the third form of rhetorical argument, the topic.

Topics are the subject of Section Eight. Unlike enthymemes, they are arguments of a quite general kind, applicable with equal propriety to any possible subject-matter. This inevitably makes their character somewhat schematic, but this does not invalidate them from constituting a genuine form of rhetorical argument. The clearest of topics are the group that are connected with possibility, and these Aristotle exhaustively surveys in Chapter 2.19. The topics had been the subject of an earlier work and they retained their importance in the rhetorical tradition of pedagogy right down until the time of Quintilian. The modern reader is likely to find the discussion of the topics in this work, however, a rather arid read, though it is noteworthy that Aristotle does relieve the possible monotony by the insertion of a lively subsection on the use of maxims (Chapter 2.21).

The bulk of the discussion of demonstrative invention, however, concerns subject-matter that is restricted to one of the genres – the deliberative. This can be well illustrated by Section Three. The treatment throughout is philosophical in character. Aristotle is concerned to produce a general account of what it is to engage in deliberation, on the tacit assumption that successful deliberation presupposes such an account. Deliberation, he asserts, is designed to promote the happiness or the expediency of those on whose behalf it is conducted. Thus, to understand what aspects of a subject may be relevant to a deliberative demonstrative proof, it is vital that we have a grasp of the constituents of human happiness. This is entirely in the spirit of the *Nicomachean Ethics*, the central thesis of which is that ethics studies the pursuit of happiness. Indeed, the section of the *Rhetoric* that is devoted to the survey of the concept of happiness in its relation to deliberative demonstration is an invaluable supplement to the study of the concept of happiness in the *Ethics*. One respect in which it complements the discussion in the *Ethics* lies in the fact that the approaches adopted in the two works are so different. In the *Ethics* we have something that comes close to being a conceptual analysis of the notion of happiness. In the *Rhetoric*, by contrast, the approach is simpler, seeking rather to identify the various constituent components of happiness without evolving a theory of their interconnection or of the structure of the concept as a whole.

A similar point could be made about the treatment of pleasure in the Section devoted to the premisses of forensic demonstrative proof. Pleasure is also a concept penetratingly analysed in the *Ethics*. In the *Rhetoric*, again, although a definition is offered, the treatment is much more that of a survey of the actual constituents of pleasure, which are of course useful to the forensic orator in establishing the motives of his adversary. Thus, with both concepts, happiness and pleasure, the treatment in the present work provides useful background material to the portrait of the concepts offered in the *Ethics*.

Those who have read the *Ethics* will certainly miss the well-structured study of the interrelation of the elements of the concepts, but while the treatment of the concepts in the *Rhetoric* is, in a sense, one-dimensional, at the same time it is extraordinarily rich in concrete illustrations of the various aspects of happiness and pleasure. It is thus of great value as much for the light it throws on the actual application of these concepts in Aristotle's time as for the evidence it provides for the Aristotelian analysis of the concepts.

The part of the work devoted to demonstration provides a remarkable and unique study of the application of logical argument to a range of philosophically interesting subject-matters. From it there emerges a clear account of the nature of logical invention. This is evidently of value in the overall structure of the account being offered of rhetoric as a whole, but it also has an intrinsic interest for anyone concerned to examine the source of effective arguments connected with any material that is to be defended or attacked in particular, rather than general, questions.

4. PSYCHOLOGY IN THE *RHETORIC*

The first Sections of the discussion of invention in the *Rhetoric* concern demonstrative invention, distributed according to the three genres of rhetoric (deliberative, epideictic and litigious), all of which require their special and proper material. The next two Sections of the work deal with the invention of material for the other two kinds of persuasion, those by emotion (Six) and character (Seven). These both come within the ambit of psychology, and indeed, just as the Sections on demonstration valuably supplement Aristotle's ethical theory, so do these Sections valuably supplement his no less sophisticated and original psychology.

The first half of the second book (see 'The Translation', p. 58). is, then, devoted to the study of the emotions. Indeed, it is the only major discussion of this topic in the entire extant corpus of Aristotle.[25] This alone secures for it a certain importance, but the importance can be exaggerated. This is because of the restricted perspective from which the emotions are studied. Aristotle remains loyal to the standpoint imposed upon him by the scope of this work. His interest in the emotions remains partly that of the orator who seeks to produce or control them, and not entirely that of the psychologist or philosopher who seeks to offer a scientific account of their relation to human cognition and behaviour. Aristotle is offering a survey of the circumstances of production of various emotions. He is not, for instance, concerned with the question of how it is that anger produces its characteristic effects in the angry person, or with the philosophical characterization of the mental state of anger. He is concerned to explain what the standard circumstances are in which a person's anger is, in the normal way, aroused or calmed, and to some extent with the question of the compatibility of states of anger with other emotional states, such as that of fear. We can, therefore, say that Aristotle is not here producing a fully philosophical account of the *intentionality* of anger, of what it is for anger to concern a particular object, so much as offering a survey of the terrain of anger.[26]

This approach might induce us to withhold the description 'philosophical' from the discussion of the emotions, but it should by no means blind us to its wealth of psychological insight. For the accounts of the main emotions are meticulously attentive to the circumstances in which they characteristically arise and so contribute substantially to our grasp of the content of emotional states. In the case of every emotion, Aristotle standardly holds that for it to arise it is necessary that the following three conditions are satisfied: first, the subject must be in an appropriate state of mind to experience the emotion; second, there must be a stimulus of the right kind to induce the emotion; and, third, the object of the emotion must be of the appropriate kind. Readers of contemporary Anglo-American analytical philosophy will be at home with this approach. For in the analytical tradition of philosophy of mind it is common practice to seek to throw light on the use of some mental term by investigating the circumstances in which it would naturally be applied. Aristotle's approach to the interrelation of linguistic practices and psychological concepts has, in fact, often been praised for its anticipation of twentieth-century methods. The present schema for the analysis of the emotions is a case in point. Aristotle isolates three distinct contributory factors to the actual occurrence of an emotional state. First, the subject must be suitably predisposed. Emotions, though they are notoriously not under the straightforward control of the will, do not on the other hand merely happen to people. In the case of anger, then, there must be a predisposition, which Aristotle defines further by saying that the subject must be in a certain state of desire. A necessary prerequisite of being angry, in this view, is that the subject has some aspiration or need which can be blocked or frustrated, the blocking or frustration being a key factor in the development of the anger. Moreover, the anger must be occasioned by the appropriate *stimulus*. Only about certain things can one get angry. The stimuli of anger are to be distinguished carefully from those of, for instance, hate and fear (with which Aristotle claims that anger is incompatible). Is there, then, some common feature which is always present in the stimuli of anger? Aristotle suggests that there is indeed such a common feature and that this is the notion of a real or imagined *insult*. Finally, it is not with everybody that one can be angry. We cannot be angry with those who are too strong for us to be able to contemplate the prospect of revenge, nor can we be angry with those weaker than ourselves, when they give manifest signs of contrition for what they have done. More interestingly still, we cannot be angry with those who appear to have done what they have done out of their own anger. For these people do not display the element of giving insult that is integral to the authentic stimulus of anger. We are also told that it is impossible to be angry with a group or class, but only with an individual. Regrettably, this interesting suggestion is not really followed through as far as it might be in the text.[27]

The case of anger would, then, seem to show the operation of the classificatory schema in a good light.[28] But one might still raise the objection that the natures of the stimuli and of the object are insufficiently distinct. The picture offered is that the subject is first, not through the agency of the object, in the appropriate state, that then the object performs an act which, as the stimulus, triggers the anger, and that he then, from the subject's perception of his responsibility, becomes fully the object of the subject's anger. There is, however, a serious danger of overlap in the accounts of the stimulus and of the object. The object is very likely, for instance, to be defined simply as whoever has produced the stimulus, thus rendering unnecessary any further description of the object in his own right. And indeed that is more or less what happens in the later items in the list of emotions, so that the schema cannot really be said to have lasted the course.

The whole discussion of emotions is, I would suggest, not primarily valuable for the schematic approach that it adopts. It is a very reasonable and worthwhile task to outline the circumstances in which various emotional states occur. Supposedly, Aristotle is most interested in occurrences that can be construed as the product of rhetorical skill, but his broadening of the discussion away from these is certainly in character with the whole work and will hardly be objected to by the reader. What is less obviously useful is the operation of the tripartite schema, but since this is in any case tacitly dropped in the course of the account and since it cannot be said to have a seriously distorting effect, it would be unnecessary to complain about it at excessively great length. It would similarly be unreasonable to take issue with the apparent clash between the tripartite schema and the definitional approach. The definitional approach leads naturally to a subdivision of the defining clause, the *definiens*, and the separate treatment of each of these elements. Thus, in the case of anger, we discuss the notion of insult, which itself turns out to have subspecies, before we see how insult is an element in the stimulus which occasions anger, and so on.

What, on the other hand, is valuable about the discussion of the emotions is the wealth of particular insights that Aristotle has to offer in almost all cases. The treatment of anger is illustrative of both the strengths and the weaknesses of his approach. He is clearly preoccupied with the idea that anger is closely connected with insult. Indeed he does not acknowledge the possibility that anger might occur in the absence of any kind of insult or slight. That anger should not occur in other circumstances does not seem plausible, however. To be angry that one's train is repeatedly late, or with the pronouncements of a politician or other public figure, is not obviously to perceive any kind of insult on the part of those with whom we are angry. It would be thought eccentric to complain that the station staff are deliberately making the train late in order to convey to the passengers the low opinion that they have of them.

It is more reasonable to suggest that the source of our anger in these circumstances is the thought that some duty or service owing to us has not been performed, but this is a different feeling from the sense that one has been insulted or shown disrespect.

The fact is that Aristotle's account of anger is very much geared to the rather hierarchic society in which he lives. Aristotle is certainly no egalitarian and he will not have imbibed either from his early upbringing in Pella or from the society of the Academy, or yet from the friendship with Hermias and the years on Assos, any particularly enlightened attitudes to his social inferiors.[29] Amongst his own pupils, he will no doubt have been accorded a kingly status, and in his dealings with the political forces he may well have enjoyed a prestige comparable to that of a Renaissance cardinal.[30] We should remember that he was a firm advocate of the principle of slavery,[31] and the comments that he offers in this Section on the emotions are rich in references to this central institution in Greek life. The discussion of anger is much preoccupied with the appropriate deference owed by inferiors to their betters. The angry man is, characteristically for Aristotle, the man whose servants have failed to perform some task for him or who has been insulted in some way by a social inferior. Indeed, at one point he suggests that it is in effect impossible to feel anger with a superior, as it is impossible to combine the emotions of anger and fear. These aspects of the treatment are both limiting and unattractive. On the other hand, he does offer insights such as that anger is distinguished from hate in being capable of being directed only against an individual, not against a class, and that while anger seeks the pleasure of revenge, hate seeks merely the annihilation of its object.[32]

Another objection that could be raised against the treatment of the emotions is an only too familiar criticism of ancient Greek social philosophy, namely that there is too great an emphasis on a symmetry not really demanded by the subject-matter. It is a fair remark to make that the Greek mind was in general over-attracted to logical balances and that this all too often led to an obsession with symmetry in philosophy, which only serves to obscure the real points at issue. This is an objection to which Aristotle is as liable as any of the Greeks, and it applies to some extent to the discussion of

the emotions in the *Rhetoric*. The discussion of anger is balanced by
that of calming, but this is certainly not unjustified by the context,
as it is clearly a primary function of the orator to be able to remove
the anger that has been inspired in the audience by his opponent's
use of the very techniques, it may be, that have just been outlined.
On the subject of calming, too, Aristotle has some of his most
interesting remarks to offer. He points out, for instance, that the
desire for revenge against one individual can be forestalled by the
achievement of revenge against another, even though the anger
against the former may originally have been greater. He then moves
on to friendship, balanced by enmity, and fear, balanced by confidence, and then to shame, contrasted more loosely with favour, and
pity, which stands in approximately the same relation to indignation.
He concludes with an account of envy and jealousy, which have a
certain affinity with indignation and which are notoriously hard to
distinguish from each other. By and large, for all its artificial symmetry, his treatment of these emotions reflects well their special
features.

Friendship is a theme which is discussed elsewhere in the corpus,
especially in the *Ethics*, but the angle there is rather on friendship as
a moral phenomenon, from which perspective its various species are
distinguished. Here in the *Rhetoric*, friendship is given the familiar
tripartite treatment, with the above-mentioned reservations applying
to the extent to which the three elements of the schema are really
distinguished. To turn from the discussion of friendship in the *Ethics*
to the discussion of the same topic in the present work is to be
confronted with a notable change of tone. In the *Ethics*, friendship is
divided into three species: those of friendship based on interest, of
friendship based on pleasure and of friendship based on contemplation.[33] These are ranked in ascending order of moral merit. In
connection with each species, there is an attempt to examine what
exactly the state of mind is that supports each kind of friendship.
This is as much as to say that the discussion is analytical, in that it seeks
to support the conceptual underpinning of the notion, or rather of
the various notions, of friendship. The discussion in the *Rhetoric* is
very different. As with anger, Aristotle is not primarily interested in
the task of offering an analysis of the concept of anger itself, although

he does present a definition, which stresses the importance of the idea of a real or apparent slight or insult. Rather than that, we are given a kind of route map through the concept of friendship. The leading thought is that the friend is someone who shares the same wishes as oneself. This is not quite what the definition stresses, where the friend is found to be the one who wishes the good for oneself purely on the basis of its being good for oneself and without any ulterior aspirations of his own being therewith connected. However, in the bulk of the discussion itself the guiding idea is that the friend will be one with whom one will have no serious difference of opinion or objective. It is thus possible to be friends with rivals for political office, where both may have a chance of success, but not with economic competitors, who threaten each other's advantages too directly. The principle that people wish for the same thing as their friends is also the explanation of why it is that one's enemies' enemies are one's friends. It is also possible to befriend those who, though not yet one's friends, are desirable as friends for their possession of some attractive characteristic. One is disposed to friendship, for instance, with the virtuous and with the famous.

In dealing with the emotions of indignation, envy and jealousy, Aristotle can be credited with especial acumen. Indignation is presented in the context of pity, to which it to some extent forms the opposite. Pity consists in the feeling that another has suffered unjustly; indignation, by contrast, consists in the idea that another has done undeservedly well. One of the features of indignation that distinguishes it from both envy and jealousy is the fact that one's indignation at the sight of undeserved success will not be diminished by one's own prosperity, but this will be the case with envy and jealousy. The hallmark of envy, which marks it off from indignation, is that one characteristically feels envy only for an equal. It is those whom we feel are entitled only to the same degree of prosperity as ourselves, of whom we are envious. This, of course, coincides with one of the insights of the received wisdom of our own time, by which each class concentrates its envy on that immediately above it.[34] Similarly, the object of envy proper must be near to hand. We do not envy those who lived in the remote past or, less probably for a Greek, those who may be presumed to be destined to live in some far-off future; nor do we, as Aristotle puts it, envy those who live beyond the Pillars of Hercules. Aristotle is also convincing on the distinction between envy and emulation. Both emotions are indeed excited by the prospect of the supposedly undeserved success of our equals, but each issues in quite a different response. The envious man feels only negatively towards the success of his neighbour, and only the ending of that success will satisfy him and quieten his envy. The emulous man, on the other hand, is stirred by the prospect of his equal's good fortune into seeking to achieve the same himself. He is indeed pained at the prospect of the success of the other, but his solution to the pain consists in the strategy of producing similar good fortune in himself. Another form that can be taken by emulation is that of the jealous preservation of inherited or acquired advantages. If one belongs to a famous city, then one is emulous in that one seeks to maintain and defend the reputation of that city, and so too with a distinguished family. It is a feature of the virtuous man to feel emulous, of the base one to feel jealous. Indeed, the subject of emulation in Aristotle's mind has much in common with the subject of anger. It is the man of a certain status who is anxious that this status be neither outshone nor impaired by any of his fellow citizens, and that he receive the general regard and estimation that is his due from all and sundry. We see here only too clearly the shadow of the *aner megalopsychos* ('man of great soul') of the fifth book of the *Ethics*, a character who has been described as 'an appalling picture'.[35]

In general, the discussion of the emotions only pays lip-service to the overall purpose of the work, which is to equip the orator with the practical means of producing emotion. It is no doubt true that to produce an emotion, or any other mental state, it is necessary to have a grasp of what, in the normal way, that emotion is or involves, but one's understanding should be geared to the practical, rather than theoretical, purpose, and above all should be directed towards the type of figure who is to be present in one's audience, not some abstractly conceived subject. With the discussion in the *Rhetoric*, it is evident that Aristotle rather loses sight of the practical objective. He is engaging in an exercise of social anthropology, like that in the third book of the *Ethics*, where he is studying the virtues of character. He is clearly interested in setting out the observations that have accrued in the Lyceum about the circumstances in which various emotions occur, and has been mainly attentive to those of his own social position and class. In including them in this text he has not striven overmuch to modify the form of his reflections. One excuse that can be made for this is the absence of a direct precedent for a discussion of psychology in the context of persuasion. As we have seen, the *Rhetoric* is in various ways a bridge between rhetoric and philosophy. The inclusion of the psychological material of the discussion of the emotions is in itself revolutionary for a rhetorical manual. We should, then, not complain too vociferously that the actual treatment is both rather one-dimensional, disappointingly for the philosopher, and at the same time rather theoretically orientated, disappointingly for the rhetorician.

Very much the same sort of criticism can be levelled at the discussion of character that follows. This should be devoted to the demonstration of how the orator is to project himself as having the three characteristics necessary for persuasion: intelligence, virtue and goodwill. However, in the first chapter of the second book, we have been told that virtue and intelligence have already been covered and that goodwill will be discussed in the context of the emotions. There is also a danger of overlap between the presentation of character and the general business of epideictic oratory, given that, as Aristotle tells us, and as is indeed obvious in itself, the presentation of one's own character does not differ greatly from the presentation of the character of the subject of an epideictic speech. (It is of course the case that in the latter instance one concentrates entirely on description, whereas one's own character must come across *through* the things that one says; it must be shown, not stated. An objection might well be raised that Aristotle takes too little interest in this important difference.) These considerations might have given grounds for the exclusion of all direct discussion of the subject of character projection, though it is explicitly recognized as a specific form of persuasion. However, Aristotle is independently interested in the question of the characters and he is keen here to include a discussion of them and of their relation to circumstance, which is of undeniable interest, for all that it is even less relevant to the task immediately in hand than the discussion of the emotions.

There are, in his analysis, two primary determinants of character formation: age and social or material condition. As regards age and its effects on character, Aristotle offers a survey of the characteristics of the three principal ages of man that is almost Jacquesian in its humanity and richness. It has to be said that Aristotle is dealing primarily in stock types; he does not make much allowance for the possibility of the survival, say, of some youthful traits into old age, nor of the respects in which the young may be prematurely developed. He is also, as usual, too keen to bring out a certain untoward symmetry in the characters of the age groups, with the features of the old all too often echoing those of the young, and with the mean being suspiciously well struck by those of middle years. Against these complaints, it might plausibly be said in his defence that he is not seeking to produce a comprehensive and exact survey of the determinants of personality, but rather to elaborate the standard prototypes that the orator can use in his speech in the reasonable hope that his audience will recognize and respond to them. The intention is that the audience will be made to feel that the character described or presented is sympathetic or antipathetic to them on the basis of the similarity of his and their traits and characteristics. If the speaker's hearers are old, then he must endeavour to represent himself as having the characteristics that old men possess and thus, in Aristotle's view, admire, and so also with the other age groups. Conversely, his opponent must be made out to possess the follies of youth or the vices of age, depending again on the composition and temperament of the audience.

The discussions of the age groups are enjoyable essays in their own right and, as with the rest of the text, they offer interesting insights into human nature. Most striking, perhaps, in general conception is the discussion of the effects on character of social and material position. Aristotle considers three kinds of circumstance which might affect a man's character, namely birth, wealth and power, and he shows a considerable degree of sensitivity and acumen in examining the effects that these are likely to have on the character of agents. In both the discussion of the ages and in that of the effects of good or bad fortune on men, it would seem fair to detect the influence of the comic theatre, which was moving at this time progressively towards the depiction of ordinary human nature in stock characters. (The comic playwright Menander was, apparently, a pupil of Aristotle's disciple Theophrastus.) Very possibly this form of characterization might have been a topic of discussion in the lost section of the *Poetics* that dealt with comedy.[36] Certainly, the whole discussion is very much orientated towards the presentation of archetypes. Whether or not this is an effective approach in comic drama, it seems reasonable to find it at least prudent in oratory; for it is reassuring for an audience to be offered a picture of human nature that they find readily intelligible and provocative of a response. The business of persuasion must necessarily be conservative in its conception of humanity. Too much is at stake for it to be able to risk daring innovation.

In the middle part of the work, therefore, Aristotle presents his account of the two methods of persuasion which he himself added to the oratorical repertoire to supplement the use of demonstration: emotional manipulation and the representation of character. It is not obvious that he succeeds in his avowed intent of raising these to the level of systematic methods of proof. He certainly has insights to offer about the creation of both emotional and ethical impressions but he does not fully distinguish between them, and the suggestions remain rather *ad hoc* in nature. The discussion of emotion has greater stature than that of character and comes closer to illustrating the use of philosophy to underpin rhetoric. Fortenbaugh[37] has, indeed, seen the Section on the emotions as resolving a major debate within the Academy as to the rationality of emotion, and it is by no means impossible that it was reflection on this issue that originally led Aristotle to introduce emotional manipulation as a form of proof co-ordinate with rhetorical demonstration. If he thereby achieved nothing else, he certainly took some steps towards establishing the serious study of the cognitive role of the emotions in determining action, which is today a major area of psychology and of the philosophy of mind.

5. STYLE AND COMPOSITION

The style of all Aristotle's own extant treatises, including the present work, is of a severity that precludes elegance. Yet we know from ample ancient testimony that his works intended for a wider audience were graced by literary charms as well as intellectual acumen.[38] It is thus by no means out of place that a whole Section (Nine) of the *Rhetoric* should be devoted to the study of oratorical style. This Section, indeed, amounts to the first systematic study of the nature of prose style in the history of Western literary criticism, indeed the first true study of literary style as a universal vehicle for thought, given that the *Poetics* does not concern itself with the variation of expression appropriate to the different elements in drama and epic. Aristotle's own awareness that he is breaking new ground is at least suggested by the fact that he prefaces his investigation of the elements of style with a historical, and characteristically dismissive, survey of his predecessors in this area. Style, he tells us, has made its way from the stage into the courts; in this respect it resembles the art of delivery, but Aristotle does not deal with the latter here. The study of style, however, further parallels that of delivery in that both are, though to varying degrees, functional in character. Just as we would not tolerate an orator who engaged in exotic techniques of delivery entirely for their own sake, without considering their aptitude to the matter in hand, so do we also take a disapproving view of those who engage quite gratuitously in stylistic flourishes. It is very much in the spirit of this approach that Aristotle assures us that a principal virtue of style is propriety. By this he means that the manner of the expression must always suit the content of what is being put across, in such a way as to maximize the impact that it has on the audience. There can be no criterion by which excellences of rhetorical style can be assessed other than that by which any feature of a rhetorical composition is to be assessed – the degree to which it gains the conviction of the hearers. Style is largely, though not wholly, a means to an end, and the concept of style for its own sake is not explicitly formulated by Aristotle.

This purely functional conception of style dominates the entire discussion. The areas reviewed are clarity, linguistic purity, propriety, amplitude, rhythm, syntax, wit, imagery, simile and metaphor. It is obvious, however, that it is in the last two areas that Aristotle is most interested. Unfortunately, the discussion is no model of orderly exposition, and the treatment of the simile is rather unnaturally separated from that of metaphor. The overall treatment, however, is given coherence by the pervasive view that the primary concern of the stylist is to evoke a tone at once close to, and in interesting contrast with, that of his subject-matter. The ideal, in fact, is a kind of controlled exoticism. The discussion for the most part is confined to the more abstract and universal features of style, and there is not much discrimination of the appropriate styles for each genre of oratory or even for each section of the speech. Such discrimination became a major preoccupation of later authorities on prose style in rhetoric, but this cannot be said to be anticipated in the *Rhetoric*. For all its limitations, however, the Section offers some valuable insights into the stylistic aspects of persuasion in antiquity, and there is no doubt that study of it can enhance our enjoyment of Greek writers not only in the field of rhetoric but also in those of philosophy and history.

The introductory chapter to the discussion, and to the third book as it stands in our texts, is something of a rag-bag. Aristotle announces that he has hitherto been concerned with the prime business of the rhetorician, the invention of the various types of proof, logical, emotional and ethical. For a complete survey of the whole art of rhetoric what now remain to be considered are three things: putting into appropriate language the points that the procedure of invention has unearthed, the arrangement of these into a whole speech, lasting perhaps several hours, and the effective and convincing delivery of the whole work in actual performance. Of these three aspects, Aristotle briefly and dismissively reviews the last in the course of the introductory chapter. He only faintly conceals that he does not consider it a fit subject for philosophical reflection. Perhaps more surprisingly, it would seem that it had also been neglected by the sophistic tradition, against which Aristotle is reacting in so many ways. At any rate, he only mentions one recognized authority on the subject of good delivery, namely Thrasymachus in his *On Arousing Pity*. Even he, we are told, only dealt with the subject in passing. This testimony is revealing, as Aristotle has a penchant for recording the history of a subject even when he disagrees with many of the views that he is relating, or indeed even when he has a low opinion, as here, of the subject whose history he is presenting.[39] It is thus hardly surprising that the subject of delivery is not revisited in the course of the discussion of those aspects of rhetoric that have to do with presentation rather than with content. Much more attention, however, is devoted to style and arrangement; and of these the more substantial and interesting discussion is devoted to style.

The discussion of style occupies Chapters 2–12 of Book III (in the traditional division – see 'The Translation', p. 58). Aristotle undeniably has a clear, significant and suggestive account to offer, but unfortunately, as with other areas of the work, there is controversy about the coherence of the discussion as we have it and dispute as to whether the composition reveals various levels. The basic conception of oratorical style that is set out in these chapters is as follows: the orator must not only find the right thing to say to his brief, but he must also present it in an attractive manner in order to retain the interest of the listener, who is likely both to be of a dubiously serious character and to feel that the subject-matter does not directly affect his own interests. The most crucial way in which the listener's attention can be retained – and this is the *summum bonum* of good style – is by clarity. The orator must first and foremost be clear, so that the listener can at all times understand exactly what is being narrated or argued. However, it is also undeniably the case that poets and dramatists have shown that clarity is not the only way to fascinate an audience. For many of them have achieved great success despite considerable obscurity, and indeed often despite the inanity of what they have had to say. How so? Because they have spoken ornately. They have decorated their thoughts with elegance, vivacity, wit, colour, rhythm and a long list of other embellishments. And all these undeniably have an effect. Thus the orator must seek to employ them as well; his style, too, must be ornate. Should he then simply cast his speeches into prose verse? That cannot be right, and this is because of the third crucial feature of good style, which is propriety. The speaker's words must be suitable to the occasion and to the matter in hand, and for the orator these will naturally differ from those for the poet. Thus there are three cardinal virtues of good oratorical style: clarity, decoration and propriety. All good style essentially consists in the combination and reconciliation of these three aspects, which is no easy task. But it is also possible to subdivide these elements further. Clarity, for instance, consists in the restrained choice of diction and also in linguistic and grammatical purity. Ornament consists in the use of metaphor, simile and figure and in amplitude, rhythm and sentence structure. Propriety consists in aptitude both to the subject-matter under discussion and to the particular genre of oratory in which one is speaking. All these are treated at considerable length in the course of the discussion. Chapter 3.2 is devoted to clarity and metaphor, Chapter 3.3 to the misuse of metaphor, Chapter 3.4 to the closely related subject of the simile, Chapter 3.5 to linguistic purity, Chapter 3.6 to amplitude, Chapter 3.7 to propriety, Chapter 3.8 to prose rhythm, Chapter 3.9 to sentence structure, Chapters 3.10 and 3.11 to the figures of the metaphor and Chapter 3.12 to generic variation. This might seem to constitute a fairly thorough coverage of all the main aspects of style, and at the same time coherence is secured by the logical and clear account of the function of style in oratory outlined above. How, then, does there come to be controversy about the status of the discussion?

The trouble with the discussion of style is not that it is incomplete or incoherent, but rather that the order of presentation is hopelessly muddled. One might think that a natural order for Aristotle to follow would be the exposition of the central concept of clarity first and then that of the closely related requirement of linguistic purity. From this he would proceed to the treatment of the various aspects of ornament, beginning with metaphor, passing to simile and figure and then moving on to rhythm and sentence structure. Finally, as a counterpart to the discussion of ornament, would come that of propriety, both to subject-matter and to genre. In fact, however, the arrangement of the material that we find is far less orderly. We embark in Chapters 3.2–4 on a discussion of both clarity and ornament, and then in Chapter 3.5 we are suddenly brought back to what is at the very least a closely related subject to clarity – linguistic purity – from which we pass to amplitude, whose affinities lie with the discussion of metaphor from which it is separated by the treatment of linguistic purity. We then move to propriety, rhythm and syntax, then back to ornament for Chapters 3.10–11, and finish with a return to the topic of propriety, this time considered generically. By any standards, this is disconcerting.

The two most convincing explanations of this difficulty come from Cope and Kennedy.[40] Cope, indeed, sees no insuperable problem about the arrangement of the discussion. For him the key is to regard the first three chapters (3.2–4) as dealing with the stylistic aspects of individual words, and the following eight (Chapters 3.5–12) as dealing with those of the composition of whole sentences. Thus the discussion of linguistic purity is really a discussion of syntactic correctness, and amplitude, rhythm and structure concern the sentence as a whole, not the word, while metaphor is concerned only with the word. The treatment of simile poses something of a difficulty for this account, as does that of generic propriety, which seems to relate as much to the word as to the sentence. However, Cope's schema has the merit of preserving the unity of the discussion. Kennedy, on the other hand, despairs of preserving its integrity. For him, the chapters on purity, amplitude and propriety constitute an interruption to the flow of the rest of the discussion. Not only do they disrupt the evolution of the account, but they also represent an earlier and simpler stage of Aristotle's conception of style. They are in fact very close in character, he claims, to the account of style given in the anonymous, but certainly sophistic, *Rhetorica ad Alexandrum*, and they constitute Aristotle's still not fully developed account of style, dating from a period when he had yet to see the shortcomings of the sophistic approach. Most significantly, they overlap, and are inconsistent, with the material in the first four chapters, and they differ radically from them in not showing the same grasp of the central importance of metaphor, an understanding of which was only achieved by Aristotle himself after the completion of the *Poetics*. The study of metaphor in the *Poetics* made the philosopher realize its equally great importance for oratory, and in the light of it he reviewed his account of style in the *Rhetoric*. As an exercise in psychogenetics, this has a considerable amount to recommend it, but it does not follow from this that the discussion, as we have it, is a mere scrap-book. There is not in fact the degree of inconsistency between the old and new chapters that

Kennedy finds, and it is very reasonable to suppose that Aristotle decided that, since the new discussion complemented, without superseding, the old, both could reasonably be included, even if at the cost of some disruption to the structure of the account.

Kennedy is, however, undeniably right to stress the importance of metaphor to Aristotle's whole conception of good prose style. Metaphor constitutes one of the three main areas of discussion of the merits of style, and there are also two subsidiary areas. The main areas of the discussion are those of dictional ornament, which is covered in Chapters 3.2, 10 and 11, of rhythmical and periodic structure, covered in Chapters 3.8 and 9, and of amplitude, covered in Chapter 3.6. Indeed, the subjects of clarity and amplitude come close to merging, in that they both treat of the arrangement of the sentence in such a way as most clearly to convey the sense, as opposed to the discussion of period structure itself, which is looked on as something to be arranged in aesthetically pleasing form by its own canons.

Of these areas, those of clarity and purity can be dealt with most briefly. There has been a considerable amount of discussion as to whether these two concepts, *saphēneia* ('clarity') and *hellēnizein* ('purity'), are really distinct from one another.[41] At the very least they overlap, but Cope may be right to suggest that *saphēneia* has more to do with the correct choice of words, *hellēnizein* more with their lucid and grammatically sound ordering. The view of dictional clarity offered plainly derives from the treatment of the same subject in the *Poetics*. In the *Poetics*, nine different types of word are distinguished, and each of their properties is discussed. The merits of some are to provide clarity, of others a certain exoticism. Good style in poetry, we are told, consists in the judicious balancing of the two functions. The situation with prose, as discussed here in the *Rhetoric*, is very similar, with the complication that the criteria of prose propriety require a rather chaster approach to ornament. Some exoticisms that are permissible in verse are inadmissible in oratory. Clarity, in any case, arises out of the use of only one type of word, the proper noun or verb. The principle of clarity amounts to the principle of calling a spade a spade, of choosing for each concept conveyed in the argument or narration that expression which will least distract the minds of the audience from the point and thus least obstruct the operation of whatever type of proof is in play. This, it might be commented, is not a very sophisticated requirement to make of the role of style, and indeed Aristotle effectively acknowledges as much by his very light treatment of it. A few brief examples suffice to make clear what it is that he has in mind, and it is evidently a subject on which he expects little controversy. This low importance assigned to the discussion of clarity was one of Aristotle's many legacies to the rhetorical tradition, finding a notable echo, for instance, in Cicero's *De Oratore*, where Crassus, invited on the third day of the discussion to speak on the subject of style, says, after some preamble:

What style of speaking, then, is better – I shall discuss delivery later – than that we should speak in good Latin, with clarity and ornament, and that we should speak with propriety and congruence to that of which we are treating? And of these two subjects which I have mentioned first, I do not imagine that an account will be expected from me of pure and lucid language. One does not try to teach eloquence to a man who cannot even speak, nor expect that one who cannot speak good Latin is going to speak with ornament, nor that one who does not even say things we can understand is capable of saying something for us to admire![42]

Aristotle is a little more expansive on the subject of *hellēnizein* (see Chapter 3.5). There are, he tells us, five elements of this. Of these, two – the avoidance of errors of grammatical 'agreement' between genders and between the numbers of nouns and adjectives – are of application only to languages more inflected than English, and in any case seem more at home in the grammar book than in a treatise on rhetorical technique. Two of the other recommendations – the avoidance of obscurity by the use of nouns rather than of descriptions and the avoidance of ambiguous terms – are close to what has already been said in Chapter 3.2 under the heading of clarity. Indeed, these two sections of Chapter 3.5 are those that give most support to Kennedy's view that Chapter 3.2 is merely a more sophisticated revision of this chapter in the light of the work done on style in the *Poetics*. As with the discussion of clarity, they offer advice which might be felt to be uncontroversial, supported by crisp exemplification. It must also be said, as against Kennedy, that Chapter 3.5 reads perfectly satisfactorily as an amplification of the very brief discussion of clarity in Chapter 3.2 and certainly exists in no state of tension with it, as he at various points implies.[43] The final section of the discussion of *hellēnizein* deals with the avoidance of confusing connections in the structure of sentences, and again Aristotle's examples, though directly pertaining to the connective apparatus of classical Greek, are admirably clear and relevant.

Slightly less familiar ground is broken by the discussion of amplitude (*onkos*). Here, in possible tension with the strictures of the discussion of purity, we are advised to substitute a descriptive phrase for a mere noun in the search for amplification of our point, and to do the reverse, earlier recommended for clarity, only in the search for its diminution or belittlement. Other sources of amplification include the avoidance of obscenity, the use of metaphor and the variation of number, all of course with a constant eye on the dangers of lapsing into poetry. A further device of amplification is the description of something in terms of properties that it does not have – a kind of privative periphrasis. A curious feature of the discussion is that Aristotle does not make it wholly clear, and indeed may not have been himself too scrupulous in distinguishing, whether he is talking about amplitude in the sense of raising the dignity of the topic of discussion or in that of merely increasing its bulk. His practical advice would seem to point towards both effects.

Saphēneia, *hellēnizein* and *onkos* can fairly be called subsidiary aspects of the general discussion of style. They are not developed at great length and they do not raise issues that are likely to have provoked bitter controversy at the time of composition, or are indeed any more likely to do so today. Nor do they offer Aristotle the opportunity to do what is most significant in his treatment of style, namely trace the psychological roots of stylistic effectiveness. This is not the case with his treatment of the three major areas of style: metaphor, structure and propriety. Indeed the discussions of metaphor and propriety really form a single discussion of the general concept of prose style, viewed, as it were, from two complementary angles.

Kennedy is at least partly right to claim that metaphor is the central concept of Aristotle's whole approach to style. He is also very probably right to stress the originality of Aristotle's treatment. Aristotle is in no sense the inventor of metaphor and in the *Poetics* metaphor appears among the general list of established word-types. Nor perhaps is he distinctive in selecting metaphor as the naturally appropriate ornament of prose style. His originality lies, characteristically, in his attempt to ground the stylistic operation of metaphor in his general psychology. This may appear to be done with relative crudity in the present work, but it was the first time that anything like this had been attempted, and it is a very eloquent indication of the resolutely philosophical character of the *Rhetoric*. Kennedy singles out the following passage from Chapter 3.10 for approval:

To learn easily is by nature pleasant to all. Words contain meaning. As a result, whichever words impart new knowledge to us are the pleasantest. But foreign words are not understood and we already know proper words; so it is a metaphor that most *produces* knowledge.[44]

This stress on the role of cognitive pleasure in aesthetics is of course familiar to readers of the *Poetics*, but it is worth observing that the *Rhetoric* shows that it is not confined merely to the specific doctrine of *mimesis*, which is central to Aristotle's theory of poetry and drama.[45] As for the role of metaphor in the present work, it is also revealed by the following excerpt from Chapter 3.2:

For an unusual replacement for the word makes the style seem more lofty. Men in fact are affected in the same way as by foreigners and compatriots.[46]

The stress is therefore on the charm of unfamiliarity. There lies behind Aristotle's whole account of style the unargued assumption that the essence of literary pleasure is the combination of the familiar with the exotic; when this combination is submitted to the further discipline of propriety, the result in prose is metaphorical expression. It has, however, to be stressed that Aristotle's notion of metaphor is by our standards a very wide one. The meaning of the Greek word is simply 'exchange', and in Aristotle's usage it covers any substitution of one effectively synonymous expression for another. He covers separately the subject of similes, which he distinguishes in the conventional way from metaphor, but it is really under the heading of the simile that he deals with what we would most normally call metaphorical language. In the discussion of metaphor itself he deals with such phenomena as euphemism and the use of diminutives. On the other hand, he stresses that not all forms of metaphor are equally appropriate for prose. Here he directly draws from the discussion of metaphor in the *Poetics*, where four types are distinguished. The type appropriate for prose is that of analogy, which is also that which we most easily recognize, and Aristotle provides the usual full illustration of successful and unsuccessful prose deployments of the metaphor by analogy. Chapter 3.3 is wholly given over to the discussion of metaphors that fall flat, and the reason that is by far the most common explanation of the failure is that they stray across into the field of poetry and are thus too extravagant and bombastic for prose. The discussion, however, is not rigorously ordered and even in Chapter 3.2 Aristotle is already discussing the faults of metaphor. It is not always clear exactly what is wrong with those metaphors of which he disapproves. For instance, he does not really make clear why it was wrong for Dionysius the Brazen to call poetry the 'scream of Calliope'. Whatever may be wrong with the sentiment, the expression does not seem in itself to be unreasonable. However, Aristotle's account here is almost certainly obscured by textual problems.[47] More puzzling, and not extenuable in the same way, is the criticism of Alcidamas' calling philosophy 'the bulwark of the laws' and the *Odyssey* 'a beautiful mirror of human life'. This last judgement contrasts most clearly with his approval for Pericles' famous comment that Aegina was the 'eyesore of the Peiraeus'. Aristotle is also much preoccupied with a number of rather obscure expressions, which seem to have enjoyed a certain *renommée* in his time, but which are now not easily appreciated or even understood. He regards, for instance, the remark that a shield is a 'jug of Ares' as being a paradigm of the analogous metaphor, and also approves the use of metaphor to indicate things for which there exists no obvious natural term, giving as an example a strange line about 'man fixing bronze on man', which uses the term 'fixing' metaphorically.[48] Other examples, however, are telling and convincing, such as his taking Euripides to task for describing sailors as 'ruling the oar'. In general, what transpires from the whole account is a sound feel for the concept of style and ornament rather than any very systematic theory, though the unifying thought is certainly the psychological insight that the charm of metaphor, and with it that of ornament in general, is primarily cognitive. This stress on the rational character of stylistic charm is an important part of the general reappraisal of rhetoric from the point of view of the philosopher. It is true that in the *Phaedrus* and the *Gorgias* Plato does not directly discuss rhetorical style, though it is certainly parodied both in Lysias' speech in the former and in the words of the young acolyte Polus in the latter, but he would no doubt have held, and the Academy with him, that it was part of the meretricious and bogus charms of the whole rhetorical exercise with which the rigorous logic of the dialectic method so clearly contrasts.[49] Aristotle, on the other hand, is keen to stress that style too has its rational side and need not be regarded as in some way unworthy of human nature.

Aristotle also has some pertinent comments to make on the notion of propriety. The expression of the speech must be suited both ethically, that is, to the character being projected at this point in the speech by the speaker, and generically, that is, of course, to the genre to which the whole speech belongs. The latter was a subject of very great elaboration by later rhetoricians, but Aristotle's account only contains the germ of these distinctions. What is most notable is that the rules of epideictic oratory are already beginning to mark it off from the forms of oratory which seek practical results. It is interesting that there is no Academic or Peripatetic discussion of the art of style in the dialogue, much less in such forms as history or the treatise. Prose literature in antiquity never entirely freed itself from its rhetorical roots, but the evolution, often under political pressures, of the branch of epideictic oratory did a great deal towards assisting at the birth of a tradition of general prose eloquence. It is also possible to argue that the discussion of ethical propriety had a certain influence on the treatment of character in comic drama and thus eventually in the ancient novel. At any rate there are many points of affinity between Aristotle's discussion here of the expressions appropriate to each type and the specific investigations of character which constitute the best-known surviving work of Theophrastus.

Just as striking is the pioneering work done in Chapters 3.8 and 9 on the formal properties of the sentence, its rhythmical and periodic structure. It is important that these two aspects are considered in their own right, not merely as adjuncts to the business of persuasion. There is, asserts Aristotle, a certain peculiar pleasure that we derive from hearing a well-structured sentence with a good rhythm, and this can be studied on its own terms, quite apart from the overall function of the passage which it decorates. This is one of the sections of the whole discussion where Aristotle seems to have most clearly a concept of what we might call the autonomy of style, a concept that was not to come fully into its own until several centuries later. As far as rhythm goes, the bench-mark is once again set by poetry. The science of prosody and metrics had been well developed by the time that Aristotle wrote the *Poetics* and he makes few contributions to it, beyond stressing the greater naturalness of the iambic than of the other forms of metre. Here in the *Rhetoric*, he emphasizes that the object of prose is rhythm without metre. The rigidity of metric exactitude is quite inappropriate to a speech and produces the worst of all results, an artificial effect. On the other hand, mere flatness is ugly and offends the ear, thus risking a possibly disastrous alienation of the audience. The solution suggested is rhythm without metre, and this in practice means an extensive use of the paean,[50] a metrical unit that is in fact much used in the best Greek oratorical prose.

The discussion of style is in general a worthy contribution to the whole work. It has been suggested that it constitutes in some sense an afterthought, and, together with the discussion of the arrangement of the whole speech, it certainly deals with those parts of the art of rhetoric traditionally covered by the sophistic treatises. It is also true that Aristotle appears specifically to be distancing himself from that tradition in the opening Section of the whole work. However, it would not be fair to claim that the discussion of style is incompatible with the bulk of the text. It is in many ways in harmony with its approach, if not with its substance. At no point does Aristotle give the impression that he is merely handing on the established tricks of the trade. Rather he is constantly seeking to show the value and rationality of the study and practice of good style, just as elsewhere he is concerned to show the legitimacy of rhetorical demonstrative proofs or the rationality of the emotional response. What we find in the discussion is perhaps rather the germ of a theory than the theory itself, but the task of elaboration and completion was taken up with relish by the subsequent rhetorical tradition. As in many other areas, what begin as hints and pregnant suggestions in Aristotle end up as large bodies of theory in the later classical writers on rhetoric. At the same time, however, a certain scholasticism creeps in, and few of the later writers show the same readiness as Aristotle to examine the psychological grounding of the various effects open to the stylist. Above all, Aristotle can be said in this work and in the *Poetics*, with which there are many good points of contact, to have first mooted the concept of the autonomy of style – the notion that good writing may have canons of its own which cannot be deduced exclusively from a mere consideration of the function of the passage being written, although, by the doctrine of propriety, they at the same time are strictly conditioned by that function. The consequences of this for the later development of ancient literature would be hard to overestimate.

By comparison, the treatment of the arrangement of the speech as a whole is much more perfunctory, although this was an important subject for the sophistic tradition as well as for later writers. Even here, however, Aristotle has one or two surprises to offer. It is certainly apparent that the conventional divisions of the oratorical speech mentioned here pre-date Aristotle. Indeed Kennedy sees a certain development even within the course of this section of Aristotle's text.[51] In Chapter 3.13 Aristotle suggests that there are really only two sections of a speech: the narration of the facts and the proof of the case. Elsewhere, however, he conforms to the more conventional analysis into four sections, with the narration being preceded by an introduction and the proof being capped by an epilogue. Kennedy, with his predilection for psychogenetics, sees this as evidence of different stages of composition, but the real explanation may have more to do with relative expository interests. In Chapter 3.13, the philosopher is concerned to examine the two fundamental functions of the speech, that of presenting an account of the facts relevant to the case or proposal, and that of giving the reasons, obvious or apparent, why the case should be accepted as true or the proposal accepted as beneficial; by contrast, from Chapter 3.14 on, he is seeking to give a more comprehensive survey of all the different elements in the speech, and for this the four-part division is required. This division is itself wholly functional, the purpose of the introduction being to dispel the slanders that the opponent will have raised against the speaker and thus to secure a fair hearing for his own narration, and the purpose of the epilogue being, obviously enough, to round off the proofs, to recapitulate the entire substance of the speech in especially lucid and forceful form and to make a last, powerful appeal to the emotions of the audience. These strictly functional considerations also govern what Aristotle has to say on each section of the speech, all of which contrast in character with the discussion of style. The contrast, however, is surely justified. Style is an aspect of rhetoric for whose partly autonomous treatment a convincing case can be made out, and indeed it is included in the subject primarily because of this pressure from outside. A theory of arrangement, however, would be absurd if not conditioned throughout by the criteria for the inclusion in the speech in the first place of each of the sections to be discussed. In any case, Aristotle does not feel excluded from the right to make comments on different sections of the speech, whose scope transcends the consideration merely of that section's role within the economy of the speech as a whole.

As previously stated, in the first section of the discussion of arrangement (Chapter 3.13), Aristotle insists that the basic function of the narrative is to perform the two tasks of narration and proof; these can be subdivided, but it would be wrong to see any other aspects of the speech as being of equal importance with these two. The section also betrays a general impatience with the scholastic pedantry of some of the sophistic refinements of speech-part definition, and in general it would be unreasonable to see it, with Kennedy, as clashing in substantial doctrine with the rest of the discussion, but rather as insisting on the basic functional concepts that should dominate the arrangement, whatever the superficial structural elaboration might be. Here, indeed, we see Aristotle's philosophical temperament, as so often elsewhere in the work, getting to grips with the received wisdom of the sophistic tradition. The bulk of the subsequent discussion, in which the four sections of the speech are analysed, with extensive digressions on the subjects of slander and the refutation of slander and on interrogation, is indeed in many ways informed by the sophistic tradition and covers ground which was no doubt familiar even then and certainly became very much more so in later antiquity. However, even here the material is rich in original insights and a comparison with the corresponding sections of the *Rhetorica ad Alexandrum* reveals that Aristotle never lapses into the mere transmission of received wisdom.[52]

The chapter on introductions (3.14) draws an interesting analogy between the rhetorical introduction and the prelude to a piece of music. What they have in common is that both must state the keynote of the composition to follow, but at the same time both should feel free to indulge in virtuoso elaboration, often of material not closely connected to the bulk of the subject-matter later to be covered. Aristotle cites with approval the case of Isocrates' *Helen*, in the introduction to which, having made mention of Helen, his main theme, the orator immediately digresses to a splenetic attack on the sophists. The point of this exercise seems to be to clear the air for the main task of the introduction, which is to win the audience round to sympathize with the point of view of the speech as a whole, and in the case of forensic oratory to induce the hearer to acknowledge the speaker's moral supremacy over his adversary. Furthermore, the discussion is enriched by a sensitivity to the requirements of the different genres of speech. In the epideictic introduction, the task is to make the hearer feel that he too in some measure shares in the praise that is to be cast on the main subject of the speech, or perhaps that his enemies share in some of the disapprise. The introductions to forensic speeches, by contrast, are tantalizingly compared to the prologues of the dramatic stage, though the point of this analogy is never made wholly clear. The essential point of similarity, however, seems to be the plausible one that the introduction must specify the subject-matter as narrowly as is done on the stage, so that the audience start off with a feeling that they know exactly what areas are to be covered in the narration and argument that are to come. These are the positive aspects of the function of the introduction, those which it must perform if, as it were, all other things are equal. In forensic oratory in particular, however, though also in the other genres to a lesser degree, all other things will not be equal, because the adversary will have sought to blacken the reputation of the speaker before he even opens his mouth. It is therefore a primarily important negative function of the forensic introduction to disarm the prejudice that will have been built up against the speaker by his adversary, and it is therefore in this part of the speech that the various topics for establishing the moral merit of one's own character are particularly to be deployed. After a perfunctory comment that this section of the discussion is only included in response to the constraints imposed by the baseness of the hearer of the speech, who needs to be protected from the machinations of the adversary, Aristotle launches into a discussion of the means both of guarding against, and of inflicting, slander in a forensic context, and this provides the content of the third section of the treatment of arrangement (Chapter 3.15). The subject of slander is not, of course, confined to the introduction (indeed, Aristotle explicitly says that the inflicting of slander is the business of the conclusion) but the subject is fitted in at this point. It is evidently one that does not especially interest the philosopher, as the expository technique is here at its barest and the reliance on copious exemplification rather than on psychological grounding is at its most extreme. Nevertheless, a formidable array of techniques for the creation or removal of slander is certainly built up.

The subject of narration is one that offers Aristotle (in Chapter 3.16) more scope for the deployment of his characteristic psychologizing method. He mocks the requirement, which he claims to be something of a cliché, that good narrative must be rapid, in favour of the assumption that the speed of the narrative must be wholly conditioned by the internal logic of the material, and produces three main theses about the art of narrative. The narrative must be distributed across the whole speech; otherwise there will be a danger of the other elements' sinking into monotony, of the audience's switching off after they have heard the story. The narrative must be ethical in character and it must also be emotional. Both these last two claims are highly significant not only for the later development of oratorical narrative but also for that of prose narrative as a whole in the ancient period. The notion of the ethical detail, the telling observation that reveals much of the character to whom it is attributed, is outlined with remarkable clarity by Aristotle and he has many interesting and suggestive examples to offer of successful uses of this device. It was of course hardly a brand-new concept for the culture that had produced the *Odyssey*, but Aristotle is here seeking to give a formal theoretical grounding to a concept that had had practical application both in verse and in prose narrative before his time. He is also sensitive to the interaction of emotional and more strictly ethical effects. Less convincing for us, perhaps, is the discussion of the propriety of the different forms of narrative to the different genres of speech, but here too the treatment seems well in line with the account of these genres in the earlier part of the work.

It is, however, in the discussion of proof and refutation, and of the appended topics of interrogation and mockery, that Aristotle is most at home. Having investigated in considerable detail the various forms of rhetorical proof, he now has many useful insights to offer on the arrangement of them into a coherent and mutually reinforcing structure. Some of the discussion is devoted to the so-called *staseis*, the bases of proof, which are appropriate to the different genres of speech.[53] In the discussion of these, Aristotle is to a great extent recapitulating material that has been covered before.[54] The more interesting section of the treatment concerns the legitimate and most effective combinations of proof and refutation. It is also more or less certain to be the case that these points are original, as they draw largely on his own division of the forms of argument. For instance, he asserts interestingly that example is better suited to deliberative oratory and enthymeme to forensic, on the grounds, primarily, that the former has to do with the past, the latter with the future. He also urges that enthymemes be not delivered too obviously *seriatim*, but interspersed with other forms of argument, to prevent their having a mutually enfeebling effect. Enthymeme, furthermore, cannot be well combined with the moral slogan or maxim, nor with the arousal of emotion, since the psychological process in which the arousal of emotion consists is incompatible with that whereby the mind engages in the type of reasoning characteristic of the grasp of an enthymeme. In display oratory, a way of breaking up the flow of enthymemes is the use of laudatory digressions, which are, of course, in keeping with the character of this kind of speech. The enthymeme and the example can also be used in the attack on the adversary's points as well as in the defence of the speaker's own, and for this refutational deployment there are rules similar to those for the positive use of the arguments. For instance, if the adversary's case is strong then it is prudent to deal with it before proceeding to the establishment of one's own, while if it is weak the reverse is the case. There are also some points both of assertion and of refutation which are best established by the use of the device of prosopopoeia or personification, either real or fictitious. All this amounts to a stimulating and penetrative essay on the art of the combination of persuasive techniques, which is fully comparable in both originality and merit with the presentation and discussion of the means of proof themselves in the first book. It is, however, relatively neglected by the commentators, Kennedy only devoting a single page, for instance, to the whole of the discussion of arrangement.[55] Certainly, there could be no better place than the section on the use of proof in the economy of the speech to illustrate Aristotle's admirable ability to breathe genuine philosophical life into the potentially dry bones of sophistic rhetorical convention.

To the discussion of the economy of proof there is appended a brief survey of the techniques of cross-questioning and of humour (Chapter 3.18), but in this, as in the discussion of the creation and rebuttal of slander, Aristotle seems less engaged. The survey of the techniques of conclusion with which the work ends is also relatively perfunctory. This does little, however, to blunt the impact of the survey of arrangement as a whole. The section of the work with which the discussion is most naturally compared is the treatment of the non-technical proofs at the end of the first book, but whereas that might be dismissed as something included by Aristotle for completeness rather than for its intrinsic interest (at least to himself), the same could not fairly be said of the account of arrangement.

There is true critical sensitivity in the discussion of the possible combinations of the effects available to the orator, and most notably an emerging sense of the difference between the techniques of narration and of argumentative exposition. When we consider how young prose literature was in the Greek world at the time when this section was written, we cannot help but be impressed by the maturity and perceptiveness of the discussion. We are especially, I think, unlikely to conclude, as some commentators have done,[56] that the third book is either spurious or a mere afterthought, or, more improbably still, an early work which was appended to the main treatise in a rather unharmonious forced marriage. There is nothing in the discussions either of style or of arrangement that does not well complement the substantial accounts of the modes of proof that have been advanced in the first two books; and at various sections, notably in the discussion of the economy of proof, the treatment of presentation in the third book does much to enhance the effectiveness of the accounts of the forms of proof themselves in the first two. It is, for instance, not from the first book that we learn that the enthymeme cannot easily be combined with the appeal to the emotions. And the explanation of this fact also gives us a vivid feel for the readiness with which Aristotle looks below the mere surface of the phenomena of persuasion to focus on the rationality that underlies this whole, profoundly human, activity. It is almost as though Aristotle feels the challenge of the sophists to convert their most unpromising rules of thumb into psychologically plausible theses; if that was part of his intention, then we should, I feel, credit him with outstanding success.

6. THE RHETORICAL LEGACY OF ARISTOTLE

There can be no doubt that Aristotle's division of the art of persuasion into three subsidiary techniques – that of projecting an impression, of 'coming over well', that of lucidly expounding the facts and that of creating a suitable disposition in the audience – remained central to the subsequent theory and practice of the subject. However, as with so many of Aristotle's contributions to the social sciences – and the *Rhetoric* might loosely be so described – its immediate influence was unfortunately circumscribed by the decline of the system for which it was intended and within which it found its natural scope and justification. Within five years of the death of Aristotle, Athens had come under the mild tyranny of Demetrius of Phalerum,[57] and the great democratic experiment, which had been so rich in both triumph and disaster, finally came to an end. Aristotle cannot be entirely absolved from blame for this. Although, in the *Politics*, he advocates a limited democracy such as had long been the ideal of the Athenian upper classes,[58] yet he was in practice a loyal servant of Macedonian imperialism, in the name of which the Lyceum was very probably founded in 335 BC, and there is no reason to suppose that any influence he may ever have enjoyed over the young Alexander was exercised in the interests of democracy, however limited.[59] Moreover, Demetrius was himself a product of Aristotle's Peripatetic School, now under the leadership of the founder's friend, pupil and successor, Theophrastus. Whatever the responsibility of the Lyceum may have been for the corrosion of democratic values at the end of the fourth century, it is clear that the collapse of open constitutions was profoundly inimical to the development of the art of oratory. Henceforth, in the Greek-speaking world, only one of the three established genres of rhetoric could survive. The assemblies were silent and with them true deliberative rhetoric, and the courts were strictly controlled, thus curbing the scope of the forensic orators. Only epideictic oratory was left, and this was in constant danger of degenerating into mere panegyric. For reasons that are only too clear, the Hellenistic age, roughly the period from Aristotle to Cicero, so rich in science, architecture, scholarship and philosophy, was as barren of great oratory as it was of great poetry. This was of course not a quantitative barrenness but an emotional, moral and intellectual jejunity, incompatible with that linguistic inspiration that had redeemed the output of the classical orators from mere virtuosity and flamboyance.

It is thus no exaggeration to say that the ancient science of rhetoric was saved from continuing decline by the literary revival that saw out the Roman Republic. If we consider the state of Rome in 150 BC, we soon see how ready she was to accept the venerable but decayed art. For three and a half centuries public policy had been determined by the co-operation of two institutions both admirably suited to the rhetorically gifted, albeit in different ways. The great magistrates had aired their ideas before the Senate of some three to five hundred aristocrats and, on receipt of a favourable response from them, had then addressed the assembled people gathering in an open *contio* or public meeting. Here there had been no general discussion, as at Athens, but the crowd would still have had to be won round, often to accept policies far from obviously in their interests. In both these environments, that of a seasoned élite of military and political specialists and that of the raw but canny populace, the art of persuasion could be deployed to great effect. Yet it seems clear that up to the middle of the second century BC very little serious thought had been devoted at Rome to the mastery of techniques long understood elsewhere, as is suggested by Cato the Elder's notorious definition of the orator as merely a *vir bonus dicendi peritus* (a 'good man with experience of speaking'). Rome was thus very much a cultural vacuum, with the perfect environment for the growth of rhetoric but as yet no native flowering. It is thus not at all surprising that her political life went through a profound change as a result of the arrival in the city of a whole series of Greek embassies during the period of her effective take-over of the Hellenic world. Some of the ambassadors seem to have elected to stay in Rome and help found there a local rhetorical tradition, thus neatly reversing the process that had brought Gorgias and others to Greece three centuries earlier. It is quite clear that by the end of the second century the native Roman genius for forceful expression had already begun to adapt itself to the sophistications of Greek technique.

There can be no doubt that the years from 149 to 81 BC, the period from the establishment of a permanent Extortion Court at Rome to the first oratorical triumph of the 26-year-old Cicero, was one of extremely rapid development as the Romans moved confidently into an area where the Greeks seemed less than inimitable. Yet, however great the achievements of the period may have been, it is the universal consensus of later generations, who had access to all the relevant texts, that Cicero completely outshone his predecessors – whence, of course, his almost sole survival from the great host of republican orators. Indeed, he also excelled beyond the orators of his own day who, like himself, benefited from the work of the great pioneers. (Conspicuous among these was L. Hortensius Hortalus, for many years Cicero's sparring partner but very thinly represented by quotations in later writers.) Moreover, if his own letters are to be trusted on these matters, Cicero achieved extraordinary degrees of success with his greatest speeches, which excited the sort of mass hysteria confined in our day to popular-music concerts. A pleasantry of his in the correspondence with Atticus is that there is no need to describe the reception of a particularly well chosen *mot* or pithy punchline, as the reader will undoubtedly have heard it for himself even in Greece![60] But this phenomenal success was not achieved without a profound mastery of the theory of rhetoric as expounded in the Greek schools of his day, and in his later life Cicero turned to the exposition of much of this material in a form that he thought would make it acceptable to young men eager to emulate his own glory. It is fortunate for us that he did so, as this enables us to form a particularly clear and vivid picture of the state of rhetorical theory after the Hellenistic period and in the golden age of Latin oratory.

The work in which Cicero most completely sets forth his ideas is the great dialogue the *De Oratore*, written in an unusually Aristotelianizing, rather than Platonizing, style; but a very useful compendium to the main conclusions of the *De Oratore* is provided by the similarly named, but much shorter, *Orator* of approximately the same date (*c*.50 BC). In this work, which purports to be written in response to an approach from M. Brutus, Cicero addresses the question of what it is that a complete orator, one deserving the ultimate accolade of *eloquens*, must have. He thus considers himself to be in search of the *figura dicendi*, a kind of Platonic ideal of the orator, and he modestly expresses the hope that by offering such a model he will not put off too many aspiring orators by the apparent impossibility of imitation. A markedly new feature of Cicero's conception of the orator is that he must have a philosophical grounding; for, as he puts it, the philosophical schools are as useful to the orator as the *palaestra* ('gymnasium') is to the actor. Philosophy, as conducted by the practitioners of Cicero's day, offered the perfect sparring-ground in which the orator could sharpen his dialectic weapons, and it was consequently a matter of some surprise to Cicero that no one had yet managed to achieve pre-eminence in both fields. Doubtless, he felt sure that posterity would regard his own work as fitting this ambitious bill. In any case, a further discussion to which he feels committed – in addition to that as to whether, or to what extent, the orator must also be a philosopher – is the question, in many ways central to the rhetorical education of his day, of which of two traditions to follow, the Attic or the Asiatic. The two great institutional centres of the study of rhetoric in the first century BC were the cities of Athens and Rhodes. The credentials of Athens were not to be impugned, and Cicero was fortunate to visit the city before the catastrophic effects of her occupation by his compatriot, the dictator L. Cornelius Sulla, after which she went through at least a generation of relative decline.[61] The claims of Rhodes were not of the same vintage, but the island had steered a shrewd course through the Hellenistic turmoil, not least by her judicious use of the Roman connection, and by the time of the great sage and polymath Posidonius in the early first century, she had achieved parity with Athens as a centre of intellectual activity. These two cities were, not unnaturally, associated with contrasting and even rival conceptions of oratory. The Asiatic tradition stressed virtuosity and exuberance even if at the cost of formal elegance, while the Atticists stressed restraint, purity and symmetry both at the level of the sentence and at that of the speech as a whole. Cicero cannot be neatly assigned to either category, but it is clear that he tended more towards the Asiatics (he had received his early training at Rhodes), and, as a certain snob-value seems to have attached to the severity of the Attic style, Cicero not infrequently, and in the *Orator* conspicuously, is at pains to stress that true Atticism, as exhibited by the older masters, is eminently compatible with bright colouring and striking effects.

Having resolved the questions of the relation between oratory and philosophy and of that between the Attic and Asiatic styles, he briskly dismisses the epideictic genre as being more suitable to festivals and games than to the courts and the forum, and passes to his own triparite division of the business of oratory into the problems of what to say, when to say each thing and how to say it.

The first problem is that of *invention*, also Aristotle's primary concern, and the perfect orator, whom Cicero is adumbrating, will resolve it with a thorough knowledge of the *argumentorum et rationum loca* ('topics of inference and demonstration') – direct descendants of the topics of Aristotle. However, the discrimination with which the orator will select from among these abstracts of argument belongs properly rather to his *prudentia* (practical wisdom) than to his oratorical skill as such. More surprisingly, Cicero also assigns to *prudentia* the task of ordering the material which has been selected and enriched with its sprinkling of commonplaces. This leaves as the real business of oratory the crucial question of *how* to make each point. This specialization of the conception of oratory away from Aristotle's wide study of everything in any way connected with the making of speeches to progressively narrower matters of style is the real key to the development of the science after the *Rhetoric*. Cicero also divides the manner of the speech into two aspects, that of delivery and that of style. Unlike Aristotle, he is by no means contemptuous of the former and has here some interesting remarks to make, but his real interest is, of course, in style. It is this technique of expression that is the true eloquence that he has been asked to define. He begins by a categoric separation of it from the stylistic merits of both philosophers and poets. With regard to the latter, he repudiates the notion of prose poets, and specifies that what is common to the two performers – stylistic judgement and selective diction – is overshadowed by what separates them. Thus he comes at last to the specifically rhetorical man of eloquence. 'The eloquent speaker,' he tells us, 'is he who in the forum and in the courts will speak in such a way as to achieve proof, delight and influence.'[62] And of these three the last is the most vital. It is, says Cicero, the single thing most responsible for advocatorial success, and just as the orator must be subtle in proof and moderate in charm, so must he be vehement in exerting influence. Thus the whole art of rhetoric consists in the effective varying and mixture of these three natural levels of speech, but always so arranged that the vehemence of the influencing passages will be given full scope to have its effect.

Having established this natural division of rhetorical skill, Cicero launches into a fascinatingly detailed study of how each level of speaking can be given its characteristic and appropriate form. He does this by making copious reference to the great practitioners of the past, of whom he seems, so far as we can judge, a fair and perceptive critic. It is obvious, indeed, from this work alone that he is steeped in the available writings of his predecessors. Moreover, there is something highly suggestive in his adoption of this strategy of exposition, which stands in such marked contrast to that of Aristotle. For Cicero's approach is very much that of the practical orator. His conception of his task is much more straightforward than was Aristotle's, who, from the perspective of philosophy, saw the task of rhetoric not as the production of persuasion but as the discovery of the latently persuasive in any subject. Cicero has his sights set un-waveringly on victory and is reluctant to make recommendations that are not backed by clear evidence of actual success in practice, of a proven track-record. This surely marks the final emergence of the science of rhetoric as a central, perhaps the central, activity of classical citizenship. The cadences of the familiar stylistic figures and tropes have become by Cicero's age as well established in the ears of his audience as the structure of the diatonic scale in those of musical audiences in the Europe of the nineteenth and early twentieth centuries. If to read Aristotle is to feel present at the birth of a system-atic conception of public speaking, then to read Cicero's rhetorical treatises is to be made aware of an abundantly flowering tradition, whose very richness defies easy taxonomy or glib categorization.

In the age of Cicero we do indeed see the theory and practice of rhetoric reach its peak, not so much in that the greatest individual orators flourished at that time, but rather in that by the first century BC oratory had at last achieved a centrality within ancient culture that it had never enjoyed before. Moreover, this situation was to last right up to the beginnings of the decline of the West in the early third century AD. Our last chance to inspect it is in the writings of Pliny, Tacitus and, above all, Quintilian. Pliny frequently discusses technical rhetorical issues in his correspondence as well as offering reports on the speeches he has attended. Among the minor works of Tacitus there is an early work entitled *De Oratoribus*, in which the prestige of oratory is defended against the claims made for other activities, notably dramatic poetry, and the relative merits of the orators of the past and the present are assessed. However, the centre stage for this period must be reserved for Quintilian, whose massive *Institutio Oratoria* takes us through every stage of the orator's education from the cradle to his entry into his career. Even a cursory look at this magnificent work would extend this introduction excessively, but its very existence is a worthy monument to the final triumph of rhetoric as the very core of later ancient culture.

I hope that I have said enough in the foregoing pages to win some sympathy for the claim that Aristotle's *Rhetoric* is a masterly attempt to bridge the gap between rhetoric and philosophy. As it has been a commonplace to remark since antiquity, there are few things that are more to be deplored in Greek culture, and notably in the legacy of Plato, than the wholly forced and unnatural division between these two sister studies. It is at least arguable that the evolution of both moral philosophy and the psychological and social sciences would have been permanently hindered had it not been for the reintegration of those studies of human nature which Platonic obsessiveness had driven into different camps. For this a very large measure of the credit must go to the present work, a judgement of which we can be the more confident for the fact that it seems to have been universally accepted by the later tradition of rhetorical exposition, for whom the *Rhetoric* was little short of a Bible.[63]

It would be impossible, within the confines of this introduction, to do more than hint at the profundity of the debt of Aristotle's posterity to this work. The two most eloquent of the Latin writers on rhetorical technique – and thus by far the most influential on the modern era – were Cicero and Quintilian, and both are enormously indebted to Aristotle for their whole conception of the science of rhetoric and its role in civil society. Cicero, it is true, is writing at a time when the works of Aristotle may have been only recently rediscovered, and he may not have known the *Rhetoric* at first hand, but his deep belief that rhetoric, so far from being in any way antagonistic to philosophy, is in fact a continuation of it by other means reflects the influence of the *Rhetoric* on the Greek tradition in which he was schooled. Quintilian is writing under the assumption that the mastery of rhetoric is the mastery of the key to civilized and educated living, and he makes frequent reference to, and use of, Aristotelian ideas and arguments.[64]

Since these classical writers, there has been a continuing, uneasy, but consistently fruitful interaction between these two disciplines, which has been admirably traced in Hugo Vickers's readable and entertaining *In Defence of Rhetoric*. It would seem safe to say that the extensive evidence that he assembles of the pervasively benign influence of rhetorical disciplines on various aspects of Western culture prompts the suggestion that rhetoric is at its most productive when it leads naturally to reflection on the states of mind that it is intended to provoke, states both of rational contemplation and of strong emotional reaction and of the instinctive response to the nebulous dimension of character. If that is so, the credit for the fact that this seeking for the psychological roots of rhetorical effects has so often been successfully carried out must in large measure redound to the author of the present treatise. For it is surely the most conspicuous merit of the *Rhetoric*, and one that will guarantee it a position of importance as long as the study of persuasive technique is of interest to psychologists, that it never allows us to forget that in engaging in persuasion we are having to contend with the human mind, a cognitive engine of extraordinary sophistication, which requires in its handling a degree of flexibility greater than that of the objects of any other of the practical sciences. The *Rhetoric* truly deserves to stand alongside the *Poetics* as a profound contribution to the permanent duty of philosophy to vindicate the rationality of art.

7. THE TRANSLATION

The greatness of the work is, therefore, not in doubt; but it does not follow that this greatness will be immediately apparent to every student. For even more than in other works of Aristotle, the style of writing and the manner of exposition suggest lecture notes rather than a polished treatise. Predominantly, the *Rhetoric* relies on the technique of massive exemplification, though this is certainly not without its structure. Moreover, many of the examples elude even the best attempts at translation, while others have to be rendered in a partly speculative manner. This has presented some difficulties for a version to meet the needs of the present series. My policy has been to err on the side of readability, favouring those interpretations of dubious citations that seem least likely to break the flow of the reader's concentration. I have of course annotated those passages where I have permitted myself this degree of licence.

The overall structure of the text has also been subjected to some reworking, in the hopes of producing a format more intelligible to the modern reader. This has involved changes both on the large and on the small scale. On the large scale, the whole work is divided conventionally into three books, of, respectively, fifteen, twenty-six and nineteen chapters. Both the division into books and that into chapters are post-Aristotelian. The text is also very commonly referred to, like all the works of Aristotle, by the pages of the modern edition of Bekker. I have retained the traditional chapter division and I have also included reference to the Bekker pages in the margin of the translation. However, following occasional Penguin practice, I have departed from the arrangement of the chapters into the three traditional books.

The expository structure of the work is one of ten Sections, of which one forms an introduction and the other nine fit into three larger Parts, not corresponding exactly with the traditional book divisions. My policy has been to retain the traditional numbering of the chapters, so that, for instance, the traditional 'Book II, Chapter 17' is referred to in the translation as '2.17', but I have arranged them into the ten expository Sections of the work, and the expository sections into the three larger Parts: *Demonstration, Emotion and Character* and *Universal Aspects*. This has the merit, in my assessment, of presenting the material in the most natural and intelligible arrangement, though the structure of the work has been the source of controversy and I would by no means wish to claim that my arrangement is a definitive maximization of its coherence. However, the non-match between the Parts of my translation and the traditional division into books does mean that, on this arrangement, the first integer of the chapter number may not correspond to the number of the Part in which it appears. I very much hope that this discrepancy will not be a source of confusion, and that the arrangement will be recognized as an attempt to compromise between the interests of those wishing to refer to the text from other works and those wishing to read it as a continuous whole.

There has also been reorganization on a smaller scale, within the chapters themselves. It cannot be too much emphasized, as will indeed be obvious to readers, that this text is not intended for the most part as a piece of continuous literary exposition, but rather as the structured presentation of a wealth of particular points. The overall purpose of the work is to provide the reader not with a direct discussion of the nature of rhetoric but with the material with which to make an effective speech, though the presentation of this material both presupposes and illustrates an analysis of the nature of the task itself. The work is thus almost, in our terms, a manual, and to present it as a continuous piece of prose exposition would have been both to distort its nature and to have produced a text that would have been effectively unreadable. Instead, I have attempted to arrange the work in such a way that it should be best able to perform the role originally intended for it, that of a readily accessible encyclopaedia of rhetorical devices.

As Aristotle reaches each area of the subject, he first explains what that area is and why it is relevant to rhetoric, and he next explains what its elements are. He then proceeds to work through the elements. These in turn are first explained and then illustrated. A clear illustration is the treatment of the emotions in Section Six. First the general nature of the emotions is explained and why they are useful for the orator. Then we embark on a survey of the individual emotions, beginning with anger. These emotions are first analysed succinctly and then very fully illustrated from the speaker's perspective. Anger, for instance, is shown to be indisseverably connected with the supposition that one has been undeservedly insulted, so that first the notion of an insult is analysed and then the circumstances in which men usually consider themselves to have been insulted are illustrated at great length, according to the tripartite scheme under which the orator considers the emotions – that of the condition of those who have them, the stimuli that arouse them and the usual objects of them.

The most sensible way to present an exposition of this kind has seemed to me to be to highlight the key concepts in the analytical phases and then to indent when the illustration begins, marking each new illustration with a conventional list-item 'bullet'. It is true that this applies a little better to the first eight Sections of the work than to the last two, which are rather more discursive in character, but even they have some recourse to the illustrative method. This arrangement makes most sense to me, attempting to consider the text from the perspective of a modern reader. Obviously, the wording of Aristotle's text itself makes no reference to this policy of indentation and there are a few inconcinnities in the transitions to the indented lists, but these, I hope, should not prove excessively distracting for the reader.

Once the reader develops a feel for the unfamiliar style of exposition, he or she will, I hope, rapidly form the view that it is in fact well suited for a work that bridges the gap between manual and essay, and that the manner of treatment does not constitute a lasting block to sharing that assessment of the content of the work to which this introduction has been intended to lead.

THE ART OF RHETORIC

SECTION ONE: INTRODUCTORY

CHAPTER I.I. THE NATURE OF RHETORIC

The work opens with a suitably general introduction, setting the art of rhetoric within its broader intellectual framework. At the same time, the pursuit of this activity, controversial in Academic circles, is defended, though with fulsome pretensions to scrupulous probity which are to a considerable extent undermined by the subsequent treatment. Rhetoric, then, is a general activity, not tied to any specific subject-matter, so that Aristotle is right to dub it the counterpart of dialectic and logic. Yet it has the same identifiable objective in all cases, which, being achievable both by chance and by practice, must also be susceptible of the methodical approach of an art. Aristotle is, of course, not the first to claim that rhetoric is an art, but he is concerned at once to show that his predecessors in the composition of technical manuals of the subject have completely failed to grasp the true core of the activity that they are expounding. They have failed, that is, to concentrate on the central notion of proof, preferring to treat of the formal structure of the speech and of the psychological aspects of successful persuasion. (This distribution of their interest, Aristotle also, without obvious plausibility, claims, explains their preference for the discussion of forensic over political oratory.) By contrast, the present work will set proof and specifically demonstrative proof at the very heart of the exposition, as Aristotle's introduction is at pains to make clear.

The central business of the rhetorician is to instruct the orator in the production of demonstrative proofs. It is this that justifies the definition of rhetoric not, as in earlier studies, as the artificer of persuasion, but as the technique of discovering the persuasive aspects of any given subject-matter, and it is this too that justifies the close parallel frequently drawn with

65

dialectic. This clear emphasis on the rational dimension of oratory is a striking and impressive feature of the Rhetoric and there is no reason to doubt that it had never been so clearly made before in a rhetorical manual. However, it has to be said at once that the substance of the text does not altogether conform to the lofty claims of the introduction; for whereas the introduction appears almost to equate proof with quasi-logical demonstration, we are shortly to be told that there are in fact three forms of proof — by demonstration, by emotion and by character — and the last two of these, to be dealt with in Part Two of the work, are only too similar to the extrinsic interests of the previous writers which are here denounced. Furthermore, in the final Part, the discussion of oratorical prose style is followed by a treatment of the structure of the speech, a subject also disparaged here.

Despite this inconsistency over the extension of the concept of proof and over the true province of the rhetorician, the introduction does make clear that the work intends to give logical invention a more central and extensive treatment than it has ever before received, and it ends, after a conventional defence of the study of rhetoric, by anticipating the formal definition of Section Two.

CHAPTER I. I

1354a **Rhetoric is the counterpart of dialectic.** For both treat of such things as are in a way common for all to grasp and belong to no delimited science. Accordingly, indeed, all men engage in them both after a fashion. For all men attempt in some measure both to conduct investigations and to furnish explanations, both to defend and to prosecute. Amongst the general public, then, some perform these tasks haphazardly, others by custom and out of habit, and since they admit of being carried out in both ways, it is apparent that it would also be possible to do them by a method. For it is possible to study the reason for success both of those who succeed by habituation and of those who do so by chance, and anything that is just of this kind everyone would agree to be the province of an art.[1]

In fact, however, those who have composed treatises on the art of speaking have not concocted any real part of it, so to speak (for the *proofs* alone are intrinsic to the art and all other features merely ancillary, while they have said nothing about *enthymemes*, the flesh and blood of proof, and have for the most part concerned themselves with things extrinsic to the business). For prejudice, pity, anger and similar psychological affections are not relevant to the case itself but related to the judge, so that if it was the rule with all courts as it actually is in some of the cities, and especially in those of sound constitution, these writers would have nothing to say; for all men either believe that the laws should proscribe such things or actually have such laws and ban speaking off the point, as in the Areopagus, and this is a commendable regulation. For speakers ought not to distract the judge by driving him to anger, envy or compassion – that would be rather as if one were deliberately to make crooked a ruler that one was intending to use. Moreover, it is clear that the business of the litigant is none other than to demonstrate the past or present occurrence or non-occurrence of the events, and the question whether they are serious or trivial, just or unjust, in so far as the lawgiver has not decreed, it is surely for the judge himself to decide and not to learn from the parties.

It is, then, especially appropriate that properly established laws should themselves determine as much as they can, leaving as little as possible to those judging, first because it is easier to find one man or a few of sound outlook and the capacity to frame laws and give judgement rather than many,[2] and secondly because the institution *1354b* of laws is done by men who survey a wide sweep of time, whereas judgements are of the moment, so that it is hard for those judging to make a fair award of justice and advantage, but above all, because the judgement of the lawgiver is not particular but concerns what is probable and general, whereas those in the Assembly or the juries judge particular and current matters, and often favour, hatred or personal interest are involved, so that they are no longer adequately able to consider the truth, and private feelings of pleasure and pain overcloud their judgement. So, as we have said, about other aspects the judge should be made as little responsible as possible, but the question whether or not the alleged facts have occurred, will occur or are occurring must be left with the judges, as it is not possible that the lawgiver should foresee these things.

If all this is so, then it is clear that things extrinsic to the business

67

are the subject-matter of those who define such other aspects as what the introduction or narration and each of the other sections should contain, since they are contriving nothing else in them than the bringing of the judge into a certain state and reveal nothing about the properly technical proofs, whereas it is from the latter that one might become a master of enthymeme.[3] It is because of this that, while there is the same method for political and forensic oratory, and the business of political oratory is a nobler one and more worthy of a citizen than the oratory of contracts, they say nothing about the former but all seek to devise a technique for the courts, just because it is less a part of the task to speak outside the subject-matter in political oratory, which is less invidious than litigious oratory, being more general. In the former, the listener is assessing his own interests, so that there is no need to do other than demonstrate that the situation is as the giver of the advice is claiming. In forensic speaking on the other hand, this is not sufficient; rather it is part of the task to capture the hearer's sympathy, since his judgement concerns the affairs of other men, with the result that with an eye to their own advantage and listening for pleasure they bestow 1355a rewards on the litigants rather than truly judge. For this reason also in many cities, as I said before, the law forbids speaking off the point, while in political oratory the audience are themselves a sufficient guard against it.

It is, then, clear that the method intrinsic to the art has to do with proofs, and that proof is a kind of *demonstration* (for it is when we suppose a demonstration to have been given that our credence is greatest). Now the enthymeme is rhetorical demonstration, and it is, to speak generally, the most powerful of proofs. Since this is a kind of syllogism, and it belongs to dialectic[4] to survey equally all kinds of *syllogism*, syllogism both in its entirety and in its parts, it is apparent that whoever is best able to study from what elements and in what manner the syllogism is produced will also be the greatest master of enthymeme, assuming he further grasps the characteristic subject-matter of the enthymeme and its differences from logical syllogisms. For it lies within the province of the same capacity to discern both truth and verisimilitude, in addition to the fact that truth is not beyond human nature and men do, for the most part, achieve it. Hence to be capable of speculation with regard to received opinions belongs to the very man who has a similar capacity with regard to the truth.

We have shown that other writers have produced a technique for things external to the question, and why they show a marked inclination towards forensic speaking. Yet rhetoric is a useful skill. This is because truth and justice are naturally superior to their opposites, so that if the event of judgements is unseemly, then they must be self-defeating, which merits reproof. It is also because, with some audiences, even if we should possess the most precise understanding of a question, we would more easily achieve persuasion by speaking rhetorically. Scientific explanations belong to education, and, since this is impossible in this case, proofs and arguments must be contrived from the commonplaces, as we said in the *Topics*[5] when discussing the address to the multitude. Furthermore, we need the capacity effectively to urge contradictory positions, as also with the syllogism, not so that we may adopt either of the two (it is quite wrong to persuade men to evil), but that we should be aware how the case stands and be able, if our adversary deploys his arguments unjustly, to refute them. So, while none of the other sciences produces opposing arguments, this is done only by dialectic and rhetoric, being both concerned in the same way with opposition. (On the other hand, there subject-matter is not of one kind, but it is rather in all cases the true and naturally superior position that is more easily argued and, to put it bluntly, more persuasive.) On top *1355b* of this, there would be absurdity in a stigma's attaching to the incapacity for bodily, but not to that for rational, self-defence, given that reason is a more particular human property than the use of the body. And even if someone who misuses this sort of verbal capacity might do the greatest possible damage, this is a problem common to all good things except virtue and applies particularly to the most advantageous, such as strength, health, wealth and strategic expertise – if one used these well one might do the greatest possible good and if badly the greatest possible harm.

It is, then, established that rhetoric is not concerned with any single delimited kind of subject but is like dialectic and that it is a useful art. It is also clear that its function is *not* persuasion. It is rather the *detection of the persuasive aspects of each matter* and this is in line with all other skills.[6] (It is not the function of medicine to produce health but to bring the patient to the degree of well-being that is possible; for those that cannot attain to health can nevertheless be well looked after.) It is further clear that it is for the same art to detect what is persuasive and what is apparently persuasive, just as it belongs to dialectic to perceive both the real and the apparent syllogism, since sophistry resides not in the capacity but the choice of its use. The difference, however, is that in rhetoric there will be the orator by understanding and the orator by choice, whereas a man may be a sophist by choice but he will be a dialectician not by preference but by capacity.[7]

Let us then try to talk about the method itself. Let us ask by what means and from what fundamentals we will be able to achieve our objectives. Let us, as it were, go back to the beginning, define rhetoric and proceed from there.

PART ONE: DEMONSTRATION

SECTION TWO: THE GENRES OF ORATORY

CHAPTER I.2. THE DEFINITION OF RHETORIC

The Section begins with the formal definition of rhetoric anticipated in the introduction and immediately passes to a new distinction between intrinsic and extrinsic proofs. Here the distinction is between proofs which the speaker must create for himself and those which require only skilful exploitation. The latter are in fact dealt with eventually in a kind of appendix to the discussion of forensic rhetoric. Aristotle is obviously right to relegate them to an ancillary role, but what is most notable about this Section is the tripartite division of proof itself into that by character, disposition and argument. This makes firmly against the apparent position of the introductory Section, but paves the way for the discussion of emotion and character in Part Two. We are even told here at one point that proof by character, though neglected by other writers, is in fact the sovereign form of proof. And the importance of emotional and ethical proofs is underlined by the remark that rhetoric is an offshoot of logic and ethics.

Aristotle moves promptly to the preliminary definition of demonstrative proof. Its salient characteristic is that it divides into the two subspecies of enthymeme and example, and the parallelism here with dialectic is spelt out in detail. In fact, Aristotle will have little to say about examples in this part of the work and soon passes to his main subject, the premises of rhetorical syllogisms or enthymemes. The distinctive hallmark of the premiss of the enthymeme is that it is probable rather than necessary, and for such a premiss Aristotle uses the key term 'topic'. The bulk of the discussion of rhetorical demonstration thus takes the form of an investigation of the topics appropriate to various exercises of persuasion. The most general division within the topics themselves is that between general and special topics, the latter being of course connected, unlike the former, with some particular subject-matter. This being the case, the discussion of the special topics, which forms the bulk of the discussion of demonstration, is divided among the three basic species of oratory which Aristotle proceeds to explain. The discussion of the general topics has to wait, in some ways inconsistently, until after the treatment of emotion and character. This arrangement may of course reflect the circumstances of composition of the work, but it is also possible that Aristotle thought their discussion relevant to the presentation of arguments from emotion and character as well as of those from reason, so that their position in the text is not inappropriate.

CHAPTER I.2

Let rhetoric be the power to observe the persuasiveness of which any particular matter admits. For of no other art is this the function; each of the others is instructive and persuasive about its special province, such as medicine about healthy and diseased states, geometry about the accidental properties of magnitudes, arithmetic about numbers, and so on with the other arts and sciences. By contrast, rhetoric is considered to be capable of intuition of the persuasiveness of, so to speak, the *given*. That is why we assert that its technical competence is not connected with any special, delimited kind of matter.

Now, among *proofs* some belong to the art and some do not. By those that do not I mean all that are not contrived by us but pre-exist, such as witnesses, tortures, depositions and such like. By those that do I mean all that can be established by us through the method. Of the two, we must exploit the former and invent the latter.

1356a   Of those proofs that are furnished through the speech there are three kinds. Some reside in the *character* of the speaker, some in a certain *disposition* of the audience and some in the *speech* itself,[1] through its demonstrating or seeming to demonstrate. Proofs from character are produced, whenever the speech is given in such a way as to render the speaker worthy of credence – we more readily and sooner believe reasonable men on all matters in general and absolutely on questions where precision is impossible and two views can be maintained. But this effect too must come about in the course of the speech, not through the speaker's being believed in advance to be of a certain character. Unlike some experts, we do not exclude the speaker's reasonable image from the art as contributing nothing to persuasiveness.[2] On the contrary, character contains almost the strongest proof of all, so to speak.

Proofs from the disposition of the audience are produced whenever they are induced by the speech into an emotional state. We do not give judgement in the same way when aggrieved and when pleased, in sympathy and in revulsion. (It is this aspect alone that we are claiming excites the interest of contemporary experts.) There will be a clarification of each such proof, when we discuss the emotions. Finally, proof is achieved by the speech, when we demonstrate either a real or an apparent persuasive aspect of each particular matter.

Since proofs are produced by these means, it is clear that the grasp of them belongs to whoever has mastered the *syllogism*, can scientifically consider *character and the virtues* and, thirdly, knows what, and of what kind, each of the emotions is and also from what and how they are engendered. Thus it turns out that rhetoric is, as it were, a kind of *offshoot of dialectic and of the study of ethics* and is quite properly categorized as political. Hence is it also subsumed under the schema of politics, as are those that aspire to it, whether through ignorance, humbug or other human reasons. In fact it is a fragment of, and parallel activity to, dialectic, as we said at the outset, because neither studies the circumstances of a limited field and both are kinds of capacity to furnish arguments.[3]

More or less enough has been said about the capacities of dialectic and rhetoric and their mutual relationship. Let us pass to the proofs produced by real or apparent demonstration. Just as in logic we 1356b have *induction* and the real and apparent *syllogism*, so is it with rhetoric, where *example* is *induction* and *enthymeme* syllogism, apparent enthymeme being apparent syllogism. Thus I call enthymeme the syllogism, and example the induction, of rhetoric. All exponents produce demonstrative proofs by the presentation either of examples or of enthymemes and of nothing else besides. Thus, if it is indeed absolutely necessary to demonstrate any point either by syllogism or by induction – and that is what we establish in the *Analytics*[4] – then each of these must be the same as each of the rhetorical demonstrations.

The difference between example and enthymeme was made clear in the *Topics* (where deduction and induction have previously been discussed).[5] It was that demonstration that something is so from many similar cases is in logic induction and in rhetoric example, while demonstration from the fact that, if certain conditions obtain, then something else beyond them will result because of them and through their obtaining, either in general or for the most part, is called deduction in logic and enthymeme in rhetoric. Clearly, the species of rhetoric have one or other of these resources. The situation parallels that described in the logical treatises. Some forms of rhetoric are exemplary, some enthymematic, and so too do the orators divide. However, while arguments from examples are no less persuasive, those by enthymeme make more of an impression. The reason for this, and the way in which each should be used we will give later;[6] for the moment let us get a clearer definition of them in themselves.

Persuasiveness is persuasiveness for an individual, and in some cases a proposition convinces through being itself persuasive and immediately credible and in others by the belief that it has been demonstrated from premisses that are so. No art, however, investigates particulars, medicine not considering what produces health in Socrates or Callias but in a particular type or group (this is characteristic of an art, the particular case being unconstrained and not within the cognizance of science). So rhetoric similarly will consider not the opinions of individuals, such as Socrates or Hippias, but of groups of a certain kind – as also does dialectic, the premisses of whose deductions are not random (even madmen have some opinions) but drawn from matters calling for rational discussion, while rhetoric's premisses are matters about which it is the estab-
1357a lished custom to deliberate. Its function is in fact concerned with just those things about which we deliberate but of which we have no arts, and with audiences of limited intellectual scope and limited capacity to follow an extended chain of reasoning. And deliberation is about matters that appear to admit of being one way or another;

no one consciously deliberates about things that cannot either have been different in the past or be about to be different in the future or be disposed differently in the present, as there would be no profit in it.

The *premisses* of syllogisms and conclusions can be either the conclusions of previous syllogisms or not the products of, but requiring, syllogism, through not being received opinions.[7] The former cannot be followed through with ease because of their length (on the assumption that the judge is an ordinary man), nor can the latter be persuasive through their not following from agreed premisses or received opinions. Thus both enthymeme and example must concern things that can for the most part be otherwise, example being inductive and enthymeme deductive, and arise from few facts, often fewer than with the first syllogism; for if any of them were well known, there would be no need to mention them. The hearer supplies them for himself, as for example that Dorieus won a garland in a contest. It suffices to say that he won an Olympic contest. There is no need to add that the prize is a garland, as everybody knows that.

The premisses of rhetorical deductions are seldom necessary. For most of the objects of judgement and investigation admit of being otherwise. Deliberations and investigations are about the bases of action, and all actions are of this kind, none of them being, so to speak, of necessity. And things which happen for the most part and admit of being otherwise must be deduced from similar premisses, and necessary conclusions from necessary premisses, another point that became clear in the *Analytics*.[8] So it is obvious that, while some premisses of the enthymemes will be necessary, most will be probable, and since enthymemes are in fact derived from probabilities and signs, probabilities must correspond to the probable, and signs to the necessary, premisses.

For *the probable is what happens for the most part*, not absolutely, as some define it, but in connection with things that admit of being otherwise, being so related to that in relation to which it is probable as is the general to the particular. With *signs*, on the other hand, *1357b* some are in the relation of a particular to the general and some in that of a general principle to the particular. Among them the necessary sign is evidence, while the other, which is not necessary, lacks a specific name. By necessary signs I mean possible premisses of syllogisms, and this is why that variety of signs is called evidence; for whenever speakers feel that it is impossible to refute what has been said, they reckon that this offers evidence and that the point has been conclusively demonstrated (in the early language 'evidence' and 'conclusion' are synonyms). Moreover, some signs stand as the particular to the general in the way that one might say that there is a sign that the wise are just in the fact that Socrates was wise and also just. This is indeed a sign, but a refutable one, even if what it indicates is true, since it is non-deductive. A necessary sign would be if one were to say that the patient was ill because he was feverish or that the animal had given birth because she had milk. This type of indication alone constitutes evidence, since it alone, if true, cannot be refuted. There is also that sign which stands as the general to the particular, such as if one were to say that the patient's rapid respiration is an indication of his fever. This can also be refuted, even if true, as non-feverish animals can also gasp for breath. For the present, then, we have outlined what probability, signification and evidence are and how they differ. More explicit definitions of them have been given in the *Analytics* and it has also been explained why some are, and some are not, deductive.

It has also been said that the *example* is an induction and it has been explained in connection with what. It is related neither as the part to the whole, nor as the whole to the part, nor as the whole to the whole, but as part to part, as like to like – whenever both items are subsumed under the same genus, but one is more familiar than the other, then the latter is an example. For instance, that Dionysius, in asking for a bodyguard, was plotting tyranny, is demonstrated by the earlier example of Pisistratus, who petitioned for a bodyguard for just this reason and when granted it became tyrant, and also of Theagenes in Megara, and indeed all the known cases serve as an example for that of Dionysius, of whom it is not yet known whether he is seeking it for this reason. They all fall under the same general principle, that *he who is plotting tyranny asks for a bodyguard*.[9]

1358a   We have described the premisses of the so-called demonstrative proofs. The most important variety of enthymeme, and that most neglected by almost all, is the same as that of the syllogisms in logical method. For some arguments are related to rhetoric as also to the dialectical method of syllogism, but others to various arts and capacities, some in existence, some yet to be comprehended; this is naturally missed by students, who seize on characteristic arguments[10] and leave the domain of the enthymeme. The point will become clearer when expanded. I am saying that logical and rhetorical syllogisms concern subjects about which we use *common topics*, which are common to moral, scientific and political questions and to questions of many different specific characters, such as the common topic of greater and lesser, which can be used equally well for syllogisms and enthymemes in matters of morality, science or whatever, despite their specific differences. Special topics, by contrast, arise from premises connected with each particular species and natural kind; for instance, there are scientific premises, from which it is impossible to derive ethical syllogisms or enthymemes, and vice versa, and it is the same with all studies. The common topics, furthermore, give us no competence connected with any natural kind, as their subject-matter is not so connected; on the other hand, in so far as one selects special arguments with greater skill, one will surreptitiously be developing a science different from dialectic and rhetoric, because should one attain to any first principles, one's activity will be no longer dialectic or rhetoric but that science whose principles one is using. However, the majority of enthymemes are in fact derived from special and particular topics, relatively few from common topics. Just, then, as in the *Topics*, here too we must distinguish for the enthymemes the special topics and common topics from which they are derived. I use the term *special topics* for premises peculiar to a particular kind and *common topics* for those similarly common to all. Let us, accordingly, deal first with the special topics. Even before that, however, we must understand the *genres of rhetoric*, so that, when we have discriminated how many there are, we may separately master the elements and premises of each.[11]

CHAPTER I.3. THE GENRES

Aristotle outlines the three genres of rhetoric and suggests rather artificially that their number is a logical necessity. The most junior of the three by some margin is certainly display oratory, whose inclusion here may also be an innovation for a rhetorical treatise. The activity had been steadily rising in importance during the fourth century BC largely because of the school of Isocrates. In any case, it receives far less attention in this work than do political and forensic speaking. The primary purpose of the present chapter is to bring out the characteristic subject-matter of each of the genres, which it is necessary to understand in order to be able to invent the appropriate special topics for the enthymemes to be deployed in each genre of oratory. It is this that justifies the rather over-schematic flavour of the chapter.

CHAPTER I.3

The genres of rhetoric are three in number, which is the number of the types of audience. For a speech is composed of three factors – the speaker, the subject and the listener – and it is to the last of these that its purpose is related. Now the listener must be either a spectator or a judge, and, if a judge, one either of the past or of the future. The judge, then, about the future is the assembly member, the judge about the past is the juror, and the assessor of capacity is the spectator, so that there must needs be three types of rhetorical speech: *deliberative, forensic* and *display*.

1358b

Now the kinds of deliberation are *exhortation* and *deterrence*. For, in all cases, both those who privately advise and those who address the people at large are doing one or the other of these. The kinds of forensic oratory are *prosecution* and *defence*, in one or other of which the litigants must perforce be engaged. The kinds, finally, of display speaking are *praise* and *denigration*. The time-orientations of each are: for the deliberator the *future* (for it is about what is to be that he deliberates, whether urging or dissuading), and for the litigant the *past* (for both prosecution and defence make claims about what has happened), while for the display orator the *present* is most important (for it is on the basis of how things are that all men accord praise or blame), though they also often make additional use of historical recollection or anticipatory conjecture.

Each of the types has a different *objective*,[12] and, as there are three types, so are there three objectives. The objective of the deliberative orator is *advantage* or *harm*, as to exhort is to urge as being more advantageous, to deter to dissuade as being more harmful, and other aspects, such as justice or nobility, are ancillary. That of the forensic speaker is *justice* and *injustice*, though he too will bring in other aspects as ancillaries. The objective of display oratory is *nobility* and *baseness*, to which speakers also relate the other aspects.

Here is a sign that the objective of each type is as given. Orators would on occasion not quibble with other aspects of their case – the litigant would not dispute whether an event had occurred or been harmful, but he would never concede that he was in the wrong. For in that case there would be no need of a trial. Similarly, deliberators frequently concede other aspects of their claims, but never that they are urging a disadvantageous course of action or deterring their audience from a beneficial one – on the other hand, they often do not trouble their heads at all as to the injustice of unprovoked subjugation of one's neighbours. Those, again, giving praise or blame do not consider whether their subject has acted for or against *1359a* his interests, but rather count it often to his praise that he acted nobly in contempt for his own advantage. For instance, Achilles is commended for his service to his companion Patroclus, when he knew that he would consequently die while he might otherwise live. Such a death was the nobler course for him, but his interest was to live.[13]

It is clear from what has been said that it is in the first place necessary to be in possession of premisses in regard to these matters. (Evidence, probability and signs are the premisses in rhetoric.) Deduction in general is derived from premisses and the enthymeme is a deduction consisting of the premisses just mentioned. Moreover, impossibilities can neither be about to be done nor have been done – only possibilities can; neither can things that have not happened have been done nor can those that will not happen be destined to be done. So the deliberative, forensic and display orators must all alike possess premisses of the possible and impossible and of things having happened or not and being about to happen or not. Furthermore, as all speakers, both praising and denouncing, both urging and deterring, both in prosecution and in defence, seek to demonstrate not only the points that we have mentioned but also that the advantage or disadvantage, the glory or the shame, the justice or the injury are either great or small, either describing them in themselves or comparing one with another, it is clearly also necessary to be in possession of premises connected with absolute and relative size and smallness, both in general and in particular, such as which is the greater or lesser advantage or just or unjust deed, and so too with the other aspects. It has, then, been explained from what subjects premises must be drawn, and we may pass to determining the premises special to each type, such as those with which deliberation is concerned and those with which display oratory has to do and, thirdly, those connected with litigation.

③ Does Aristotle think (status) reputation ~~is important to happeness~~ ~~part of~~ is part of happeness

④ Mention one thing Aristotle lists as "good"

2, C, TaF: A rejects slavery

(Groups: how would Aristotle respond to Rich's essay? Give quotation from A & from R for support)

Or — find something he'd agree with

SECTION THREE: DELIBERATION

CHAPTER I.4. THE PROVINCE OF DELIBERATION

Having established the tripartite generic division of oratory, within the scope of his exposition of the special topics, Aristotle passes to the treatment of the first genre, that of deliberative oratory. This is consistent with the preference expressed for deliberative as against forensic oratory in the introduction and may have been another novelty about the work. He immediately, however, encounters a difficulty which is characteristic of his treatment of the special topics and thus of demonstration as a whole. This is that he must present topics that are special to the subject-matter of deliberative oratory, which is politics, without straying into the exposition of theses in political science, which would of course be to depart from the scope of the present work. The distinction should be that a premiss of political science deals with what is necessarily the case in the political sphere, while a special topic of deliberative oratory has to do with what is likely to seem probable in connection, primarily, with political subjects. In any case, this chapter contains a list of the five main subject-areas of deliberative oratory – revenue, foreign policy, defence, trade and legislation – and these locate the activity clearly within its political context, offering support to the claim that rhetoric must be considered a political skill. It is thus in the next chapter that he begins the discussion of what is really characteristic of the special topics of deliberative oratory, namely the points that are suggestive of expediency or inexpediency.

CHAPTER I.4

First, then, we must grasp what sort of advantages or disadvantages it is that are the subject of the deliberator's *deliberation*, given that

83

they are not all things, but only *such as admit of being or not being the case*, while those that either are or will be of necessity or are incapable of either existing or coming to be are not subjects of deliberation. Nor even, indeed, are all contingencies. There are certain advantages of nature or luck among things that can either be or not, and it is no part of the task to deliberate about them. Rather, the subjects of deliberation are clearly such things as are naturally traced back to us 1359b and the cause of whose coming to be lies with us, since our consideration continues until we discover whether or not the proposed course can or cannot be carried out.

The accurate enumeration and assignment to species of the customary subjects of debate and, as far as this is possible, their precise definition we need not at the moment pursue. They do not, indeed, come within the ambit of rhetorical skill, belonging rather to a more intellectual and veridical competence.[1] In fact, we have even now assigned to rhetoric many more than its proper subjects of interest. For what we had occasion to remark above is true – that rhetoric is a compound of the science of dialectic and the deliberative study of morality and is akin both to dialectic and to sophistry. And in so far as it might be attempted to establish either of the latter not as capacities but as sciences, this would be a surreptitious obfuscation of their true nature by a slide to the foundation of the sciences of the given subjects, not merely of arguments. Nevertheless, such aspects as it is germane to our task to distinguish, leaving the residual enquiry to political science, let us now outline.

The most important subjects of deliberation, and those most often discussed by deliberative speakers, are in fact five in number. These are: *revenue, war and peace*, the *defence of the realm, imports and exports* and *legislation*.

● In the matter of revenue, the would-be orator must know the nature and extent of the city's sources of income, so that if any is deficient it may be topped up and if any is inadequate it may be augmented. He must also know all the expenses of the state, so that if any is unnecessary it may be cut and if any is too large it may be diminished – it is not only by addition to existing possessions that wealth is achieved but by the avoidance of expense. And one should not only survey these from one's own experience but become a student of what has come to light elsewhere for the purpose of deliberation on these points.

- In connection with war and peace, the speaker must know both the present and the potential strength of the city, the nature of existing forces and of such as might be added, and also what wars she has had and in what way she has been at war. The wars, moreover, not only of his home city but also of neighbouring ones, and of those with whom war is to be envisaged, must be familiar to him, so that there may be peace with those that are stronger and that the home city may enjoy the option of *1360a* war with the weaker. It must also be known whether or not the forces are comparable, since here too there can be gain and loss. Furthermore, the speaker should have made a study not only of his own city's wars but also of those of other cities and of their outcomes, as it is natural for similar circumstances to have similar effects.

- In connection with the defence of the realm, the speaker must not be unaware of how the city is defended. He must know the numbers of the guard and the character and location of the guard-posts (impossible unless he gets to know the countryside), so that if the guard is inadequate it may be bolstered and if supernumerary pruned and the concentration be more on the vital points.

- As to the food supply,[2] he must know the extent and nature of what outlay suffices the city, both on home-grown and imported goods, and what produce should be exported, what imported, so that there may be treaties and agreements with trading partners. For the people must be kept on good terms with two groups – those who are stronger than they and those who are commercially useful. *not those who are weaker*

- For national security, it is necessary to be able to consider all these matters, but no less should the orator have expertise about legislation. For in the laws lies the salvation of the state. It follows that he must know how many forms there are of constitution, what measures are advantageous to each and by what intrinsic or antagonistic factors they are prone to be overthrown.

The meaning of destruction by intrinsic factors is that, apart from the ideal constitution, all the other forms of constitution are destroyed by excessive relaxation or intensity. For instance, democracy is destroyed not only by being so weakened by relaxation as to arrive finally at oligarchy but also by great intensification – just as hooked or snub noses attain the intermediate state not only by relaxation but also by becoming so pronouncedly hooked or snub as not even to be held to be a nose.[3] Not only is it useful as regards legislation to know what constitution is advantageous, by a survey of those in the past, but also to know what other sorts of constitution suit what other sorts of people. So descriptions of travel round the world are clearly useful for legislation (for from them we can ascertain the laws of the nations) and for policy questions the researches of those who have written of affairs. (All this, however, is in the remit of politics, not of rhetoric.)

Such, then, are the most important matters on which the framer 1360b of a deliberative speech must possess knowledge. It is time to go through the bases of exhortation or deterrence connected with them, as with all other issues.

CHAPTER I.5. HAPPINESS

The exposition of the subject-matter of deliberative oratory now begins. The business of deliberation and advice is to present the advocated course of action as likely to promote some desired end, so that it is by investigating the ends of conduct, those things which men actually tend to seek out, that we will discover the sources of deliberative persuasiveness. This assumption prevails throughout the discussion of deliberation in the following four chapters. Fortunately for Aristotle, this enables him to begin his enquiry from the assumption that is central to his ethical theory, which is that the supreme goal of all human action is happiness [eudaimonia] and that all other objectives can be theoretically subsumed under the quest for this. The present chapter is accordingly devoted to a minute analysis of the constituents of happiness, which can obviously be compared with the similar, though less particular, examination in the first book of the Ethics. It must

must be said, however, that, while the connection between happiness and the special topics of deliberative oratory has been argued for and is in general plausible, it is obviously the case that many of the constituents of happiness, as defined by Aristotle or by anybody else, do not lie within the power of the subject and thus by Aristotle's very reasonable criterion fall outside the range of things which are the proper subject of deliberation.

CHAPTER I.5

There is pretty much an objective at which everybody aims, both each in private and all together, both in pursuit and in avoidance. And this, to put it in a nutshell, is *happiness* and its elements.[4] Thus, for the sake of example, let us grasp what happiness is quite in general, so to speak, and from what its elements are composed. For all exhortations and dissuasions are concerned with happiness and things conducive to it and contrary to it – one must do those things that procure happiness or one of its elements, or make it larger rather than smaller, and not do those things that destroy or hinder it or produce its opposites.

Let happiness, then, be virtuous welfare, or self-sufficiency in life or the pleasantest secure life or material and physical well-being accompanied by the capacity to safeguard or procure the same. Surely everyone would agree that one or more of these is happiness. If, then, happiness is some such thing, its elements must be:

- Gentle birth, a wide circle of friends, a virtuous circle of friends, wealth, creditable offspring, extensive offspring and a comfortable old age; also the physical virtues (e.g. health, beauty, strength, size and competitive prowess), reputation, status, good luck and virtue [or also its elements, prudence, courage, justice and moderation].[5]

For a man would enjoy the greatest *self-sufficiency* if he possessed both the *internal and the external advantages*, there being no others besides. The *internal advantages* are those connected with the soul and those with the body; the *external* are good birth, friends, cash and status, to which we deem it appropriate that positions and luck should be joined. That is how life is really secure. So let us, in the same spirit, examine what constitutes each of these elements.

● Well, good birth, for a people and state, is to be indigenous or ancient and to have distinguished founders with many descendants distinguished in matters that excite envy. For the individual, it is good descent in both the male and the female line, with legitimacy in both, and, just as with the city, the distinction of their earliest ancestors for virtue, wealth or some other of the sources of status and the eminence of many of their line, both male and female, both young and old.

1361a ● Creditable and extensive offspring are straightforward elements. For the community, they are the presence of much excellent youth, excellent in point of physical virtue, such as size, beauty, strength and competitive capacity – the virtues of soul of the young man are restraint and courage – while for the individual they are that his own children are numerous and of this kind, both female and male (the physical virtues of women being beauty and proportion, those of the female soul being restraint and dignified energy). The presence of each of these must be sought alike both in public and in private, both among men and among women. When states, like that of the Spartans, give women an absurd position, they effectively throw away half their happiness.

● The elements of wealth are abundance of money and land, the possession of estates outstanding for number, extent and beauty and also that of furniture, slaves and cattle of outstanding numbers and quality, all these being owned, secure, liberal and useful. Utility has more to do with fruitfulness, liberality with consumption (by fruitful I mean sources of income, by consumptional I mean things from which nothing of value comes apart from their use). The definition of security is present possession in such a way that the owner has the use of the goods, and that of ownership is the right of alienation, whereby gift or sale is meant. In general, being rich lies more in using than in having, as wealth is the realization and consumption of this sort of thing.

● Good repute is being generally taken to be a serious figure or to possess something that everybody wants, or the majority, or the virtuous or the prudent, and honour is a mark of a reputation for good works, and it is those who have done good works that are rightly and most particularly honoured, although a man capable of good works is also honoured. Good works pertain either to safety and the necessities of existence, or to wealth or to some one of the other good things, whose possession is not easy either in general or in that place or at that time – many men seem to attain status for seemingly slight services, but this is due to the times and places.

- The elements of honour are: sacrifices, memorials both in verse and without metre, rewards, sanctuaries, precedence, tombs, statues, public maintenance, barbarian practices, such as genuflection and standing back, and gifts, which are valued by all recipients. Indeed, a gift is a surrender of property and an indication of status, which is why it is sought by both the mercenary and the ambitious, providing as it does what they _1361b_ both seek, as the mercenary are after possessions and the ambitious are after status.

- The excellence of the body is health, and that in such a way that those using their bodies are free from disease – many men are healthy (as Herodicus is said to have been) whom none would call happy for their health, because of their abstinence from either all or most human activities. Beauty differs for each stage of life. The beauty of a young man is to have his body useful for the toils of competition and force, being yet pleasant to look on for enjoyment, which is why the pentathletes are most beautiful, being at the same time naturally suited to both speed and force. That of the man in his prime is related to military service and combines a pleasant appearance with awesomeness, and that of an old man is sufficiency against inevitable troubles and freedom from pain through lack of any of those things that plague old age. Strength is the power to manipulate another at will, which must be done by dragging, pushing, lifting, pressing or squeezing, so that the strong man is strong in either some or all of these. The virtue of size is so to exceed the majority in all three dimensions as not to render one's movements the slower for the excess. Competitive physical prowess is composed of size, strength and speed (the swift man is indeed also strong). For the man who can throw his legs in a certain way and move them swiftly and a long way is a runner; he who can exert pressure and hold a man down is a wrestler; he who can drive back with his punches is a boxer; he who can do both the last two is a pancratiast; and he who can do the lot is a pentathlete.

- A good old age is a slowness to age and freedom from pain. For a man has a good old age neither if he is quick to grow old nor if he ages slowly but with discomfort. It is a product both of the excellences of the body and of luck. For the man who is not free of disease or is weak will not be spared suffering and discomfort and none persists to old age without luck. There is, however, another capacity for longevity distinct from strength and health – many are long-lived without the bodily excellences; but precision about these matters is not required by the present discussion.

- The enjoyment of a wide and virtuous circle of friends is evident from the definition of the friend as such a man who performs for the sake of the other what he deems to be in the other's interest. The man who has many such has many friends and, if they are respectable, he has good ones.

1362a
- Good fortune is the presence or acquisition of either all or most or the most important of the good things for which chance is responsible. And chance is responsible for some things also produced by skill but also for many non-technical advantages, such as those of nature (though chance effects can also be unnatural). For it is an art that is responsible for health, and nature for beauty and size. And it is in general advantages of this kind, from good luck, that are the object of envy. Chance is also responsible for inexplicably good things, such as if all a man's brothers are ugly but he is good-looking, or if others failed to notice the treasure but one man were to find it, or when the weapon strikes a man's neighbour, not himself, or if someone who regularly made a journey were the only one not to, while others did for the first time – and were killed. All such cases are held to be strokes of fortune.

- As to virtue, given that its most appropriate place is the discussion of praise, we will give a definition when we come to talk about praise.[6]

CHAPTER I.6. THE GOOD AND THE EXPEDIENT

The connection between the present chapter and its predecessor, with which it would seem to overlap, is far from perspicuous, but a hint of justification of this arrangement can be found in the opening paragraph, where it is stressed that deliberation is primarily about means rather than ends. One does not deliberate about whether, but about how, to be happy. Thus the deliberative orator must 'possess topics' on the means to achieve happiness even more than on happiness as an end. In practice, this means that for the most part the same desirable objectives are listed here as good things, whereas before they were elements of happiness, and that in so far as there is a distinction it lies in their being here regarded more from a practical, realizable perspective. It is remarkable how little trace there is of the Platonic insistence on the difference in kind between moral and non-moral goods, the former being entirely commingled with the latter in the survey.

CHAPTER I.6

We have established the legitimate objects of *exhortation* as being imminent or present and those of *deterrence*, which are the opposites. Now, since the assigned scope of the deliberator is *expediency* (for debates are not about the end but about the means to it, which are the measures that are practically expedient, expediency being a good thing), we must grasp the fundamentals of *goodness* and *expediency* in general.

Let the good, then, be whatever is to be chosen for its own sake and that for which we choose other things, and the objects of general desire or that of all sensory or intelligent creatures, or what would be for others if they acquired mind, and such things as intuition would attribute to each individual, and what particular intuition does assign to each individual; for this is the good for the individual, in the presence of which he is well disposed and self-sufficient.

Self-sufficiency is also a good, as well as whatever produces or preserves all these things and that which they accompany, and the things preventative and destructive of their opposites. Accompaniment is of two kinds, either simultaneous or subsequent, knowledge being, for instance, subsequent to understanding, but life simultaneous with health, and production is of three kinds – one whereby being healthy produces health, another whereby food produces health and a third whereby exercise produces health, in that it *usually* produces health. These points being established, the acquisition of good things must be good, as is the rejection of bad things – the advantage of lacking a bad thing is immediate and that of having a good thing is subsequent.

- Also the acquisition of a greater in lieu of a lesser good and of a lesser rather than a greater evil; in so far as the greater exceeds the lesser, the one case is acquisition and the other rejection.

- The virtues must also be a good thing (for those that have them are also well disposed and they are productive of good things and efficient – we must still explain separately of what and what kind of good things each is productive) and so must pleasure be, which all animals naturally crave.

So both pleasant and beautiful things must be good, the former just as productive of pleasure, whereas some beautiful things are pleasant and some intrinsically eligible.

To give an itemized list, the following things must be good.

- Happiness: it is intrinsically eligible and self-sufficient and we choose many things for its sake.
- Justice, courage, restraint, magnanimity, splendour and the other similar dispositions: they are virtues of the soul.
- Also health and beauty and such like: they are bodily virtues and productive of many advantages, health, for example, being productive of pleasure and living, which is why it is held to be the best of all things, as being responsible for two of the things most valued by the majority of men, namely pleasure and life.
- Wealth: it is the virtue of possession and brings many advantages.
- Friendship and the friend: the friend is intrinsically eligible and also brings many advantages.

- Status and reputation: these are pleasant and advantageous and are, for the most part, accompanied by those things that earn them.
- Verbal and practical capacity: all such things bring advantages.
- Also native wit, memory, aptitude to learn, quick wits and so on: these capacities all have their good consequences.
- Even being alive: intrinsically eligible, even if no other advantages were to come of it.
- Also justice: a kind of communal expediency.

This pretty well concludes the list of the non-controversially good things. Where there is controversy, the deductive premisses are of the following kinds.

- That whose opposite is an evil is a good.
- That whose opposite is in one's enemies' interest; for instance, if their being cowards heavily favours their enemies, courage is patently exceedingly advantageous to the citizenry.
- In general, whatever the enemy wants or in whatever they rejoice, its opposite is an apparent good. Hence the point of

Right glad would Priam be . . .[7]

This is, however, not universal but for the most part. There is nothing to stop the same thing's being on occasion expedient for opponents. Hence the remark that evils bring men together, *1363a* whenever the same thing threatens them both.

- What is not excessive is good and what is greater than it should be bad.
- The object of much effort or expenditure: it is certainly an apparent good and the sort of thing that is adopted as an end, and that of many, and an end is a good thing. Hence:

A glorious prize for Priam . . .[8]

and:

Shameful it were for so long to remain . . .[9]

Hence too the proverb about the water-jar by the doorway.[10]

93

contestable

- What the many aspire to and what is openly contested; for what everybody craves would be a good thing, and the many seem to be like humanity as a whole.
- What is praised – none praises what is not good.
- Even what hostile or base men applaud – their judgements in fact seem to go for everyone's, even when those who have been badly treated by something, praise it, since they agree because it is obvious, just as the base are those whom their friends criticize and the good are those whom their enemies do not criticize. This is why the Corinthians assumed they had been insulted by Simonides when he wrote:

  Troy finds no blame in Corinth . . .[11]

- What a wise or good man or woman has preferred, as Athene chose Odysseus, Theseus Helen, the goddesses Paris and Homer Achilles.
- Preferred things generally, in fact; and men prefer to do the things we have mentioned and what harms their enemies, what helps their friends and what is possible (the last being double), both what might happen and what might easily happen, easily being either painlessly or in a short time, difficulty being defined either by discomfort or by delay.
- Whatever occurs as desired; and men want either no injury or one less than the advantage (which happens if the retribution is either unnoticed or trivial).
- Personal things, things that no one else has, and outstanding things – one's status is so much greater.
- Things that suit people, which are what belong to them by birth or position, and what they feel they lack, even if they are bagatelles – the desire to have them is not diminished a whit.
- Things easily accomplished. They are possible and they are easy, being what all men, or most, or equals or inferiors accomplish.
- Things that amuse friends or are detested by enemies.
- Things that those admired prefer to do. Also things men are adept at and at home with, which are thought to be more easily accomplished.

- Things that no scoundrel would want, which are the more to be praised.
- Whatever men happen to be keen on, since it seems to be not only pleasant but also the better course. And especially, for each group, whatever they are '-loving', e.g. victory for the 'victory- *1363b* loving', status for the 'status-loving', money for the 'money-loving', and so on.

These, then, are the points from which proofs are drawn in connection with the advantageous and expedient.

CHAPTER I.7. RELATIVE EXPEDIENCY

With further inconsistency, Aristotle passes from the exposition of expediency itself to that of relative expediency, which ought really to be covered by the common topic of extent. This discrepancy clearly provides some evidence for the disjointed composition of the work, but it might also be commented that Aristotle simply considered relative expediency and goodness to be subjects so vital for the deliberative orator as to require separate treatment in the context of deliberation rather than merely to be left for consideration in the context of the general topic of extent.

CHAPTER I.7

Since it is often agreed that two options are expedient and the controversy is about which is more so, the next step should be to discuss *relative advantage and expediency.*

Let the exceeding advantage, then, be so much and more and that which is exceeded be what is below it, the greater and more numerous being always relative to a lesser, and large and small and many and few being relative to majority dimensions, the excessive being the large, the deficient the small and the same going for many and few.

Since, then, we are calling good what is *intrinsically eligible* and not for the sake of something else, and what is generally aimed at, and what creatures with mind and prudence would choose, and what are productive or preservative of these or what they accompany, and since the objective is that for whose sake other steps are taken, and the good for the individual is what has these features in relation to himself, then *advantages more numerous than one or a few*, when the one or few are of the same series, must constitute the *greater good* – they are in *excess*, and the *normal* is what is exceeded. Also:

- If the greatest advantage of one kind exceeds the greatest of another or others of its own kind, and, when one kind exceeds another, then the greatest of the first exceeds that of the second, as, for example, if the greatest man is larger than the largest woman, then men in general are also larger than women in general, and if men are generally larger than women, then the largest man is also larger than the largest woman, as there is a proportion between excess between groups and that between the largest individuals in them.

- Also when *a* accompanies *b*, but not *b a*, accompanying either simultaneously or sequentially or potentially, since the use of the accompanying thing is given in that of what it accompanies. (Being alive simultaneously accompanies being healthy, but not the other way round; knowledge sequentially accompanies learning; and fraudulence potentially accompanies temple-robbing, as the temple-robber might well defraud.)

- Things that exceed by more are greater, as they must also exceed that larger by less. Also things productive of a greater advantage are greater goods, since to be productive of the greater is to be greater.

- That whose productive cause is greater, in the same way. For if the salubrious is more eligible than the pleasant and a greater good, then so is health a greater good than pleasure.

1364a
- The eligible in itself more than the not eligible in itself, as strength is greater than health, since the one is not intrinsically eligible, while the other is, which was what a good thing was shown to be.

- If one thing were to be an end and the other not, the latter being chosen for the sake of something else, the former for itself, as exercise is chosen for the well-being of the body.

- What needs less of some other thing or things, since it is more

96

self-sufficient, and this means what needs fewer or easier things.

- When one thing could not be without the other, or would not be able to come about, but the other could without it, as what lacks the need is more self-sufficient, so that it is obviously a greater good. If one thing should be a principle and the other not, or if one a cause and the other not, for the same reason; for without cause and principle it is impossible for a thing to be or originate. And of two principles, what comes from the greater principle is the greater good, and similarly with two causes. And conversely, of two principles the principle of the greater good is greater, and of two causes what comes from the greater cause is greater. So it is clear from what has been said that a thing can be shown to be greater in both ways; both if one thing is a principle and the other not, is it held to be greater, and if one is not a principle and the other is. For the end and not the principle is greater, just as Leodamas in his prosecution of Callistratus said that the adviser did a greater harm than the doer, as the deed would not have been done without an adviser, and again, against Chabrias, that the doer was more at fault than the adviser, as the act would not have occurred if there had not been someone to do it, since the purpose of conspiracy is action.[12]

- What is relatively rarer more than what is abundant, as gold than iron, although it is less useful – its possession is a greater good through its being harder to find. In another way the abundant is a greater good than the scarce, as its use is in the excess, as what occurs many times exceeds what occurs seldom, whence the saying

Water is best . . .[13]

- In general, what is harder is better than what is easier, as it is rarer. In another way, what is easier is greater than what is harder, since it is as we wish it to be.

- That whose opposite is the greater and that whose remark is more serious. Virtue is greater than non-vice and vice than non-virtue, the first in each pair being ends, the second not.

- Things whose functions are more or less noble are greater goods

97

or evils, and also of those things whose defects and virtues are more important the functions are greater, and those whose functions are nobler or baser are greater, since, as are the causes and principles, so are the effects and, as are the effects, so are the causes and principles.

- Things whose excess is more eligible or more noble, as accurate sight is more eligible than accurate smell (and indeed sight than smell in general), and companion-loving is nobler than money-loving, so that companionship is also nobler than money-mindedness.

1364b

- And conversely, the excesses of better things are better and those of nobler things nobler.

- Things the desire for which is nobler and better, since greater urges are for greater things, and the urges to better and nobler things are better and nobler for the same reason.

- Things of which the sciences are nobler or more serious and the actions are nobler and more weighty, since as is the science so is the reality, and each thing determines its own science. And the sciences of more serious and nobler things, analogously, for the same reason.

- What the wise would judge to be good or have so judged or all men or the absolute or relative majority or the most powerful, this is a greater good, either in general or as they judge in relation to their wisdom. This is also a common feature with other items, since the nature and quantity and quality are also as science and wisdom proclaim. However, we have been speaking of the case of the good, which is defined to be what the wise individual would choose in each case, since what wisdom favours is clearly a greater good.

- The properties of better men either in general or in so far as they are better, in the way that courage is better than strength.

- What the better man would choose, either in general or as a better man, for example to receive rather than to do an injustice, which is what the more just man would choose.

- The more pleasant is greater than the less pleasant, since all things pursue pleasure, and yearn to be pleased for its own sake, and it is by these that the good and the end are defined. And what is less painful is more pleasant, as is what is pleasant for a longer time.

- The nobler is a greater good than the less noble, as the noble is either the pleasant or the intrinsically eligible.
- Things of which men the more wish to be productive either for themselves or for their friends are greater goods and those to which this less applies are greater evils.
- Longer-lasting things are better than shorter-lived ones and secure things than insecure ones, as the use of the former is in the excess in time and that of the latter is in the excess in volition, since the use of secure things is more readily available whenever we should want it. Just as if one of the cognates and inflexional congeners are given, the others follow, so is it with advantages; for instance, if 'more bravely' is nobler and more eligible than 'more moderately', then so is courage than moderation and to be courageous than to be moderate.
- What all choose is greater than what not all choose, and what greater numbers than what lesser numbers choose, since the good was shown to be what all aimed at, so that the more who aim the greater the good.
- What litigants or enemies would both choose, or both those who judge or those whom they judge, either what everyone would choose, or what those in power or those with knowledge would choose. Sometimes, too, what all have a share in is the greater good, since there is disgrace in non-participation, and sometimes what none or a few share, as it is rarer.
- Things that are more praised, as they are more noble, and in the same way things for which the rewards are greater, since rewards are a kind of value.
- Things for which the punishments are greater are greater evils.
- Things greater than recognized, or obvious advantages, are greater. Being divided into their parts, things also seem greater, as their excess is more apparent. Hence Homer says that Meleager was persuaded to fight by

> All ills that come to men whose city falls;
> The people are laid waste, the streets afire,

And strangers drag the children all away . . .[14]

- By composition and construction, as in the case of Epicharmus, for the same reason as with division (as composition reveals much excess) and because it appears as the cause and principle of great advantages.[15] Since the harder and rarer is a greater good, occasions, ages, places, times and possibilities make advantages great; for if things are contrary to possibility, to age and to one's like, and if it is so, or here, or then, it will have the greatness of noble, good and just things or their opposites, whence the epigram on an Olympic victor:

> Having upon my back a hardy yoke,
> Fish out of Argos to Tegea I took . . .[16]

Likewise Iphicrates praised himself by mentioning the condition from which he rose.[17]

- The home-grown is better than the acquired, as it is harder. (Whence the bard's claim: 'Self-taught am I.')
- The greatest part of a great advantage, as Pericles in delivering the funeral speech said that the young men had been taken from the city as the spring might be taken from the year.[18]
- Things more needed are more useful, such as things needed in old age and during illnesses.
- Of two things that which is nearer to the objective, and that which is related to the chooser more than in general.
- The possible more than the impossible, the one being useful for the chooser, the other not.
- Things near the end of life, as it is things at the end, rather, that are ends.
- 1365b Things related to reality rather than to opinion, the definition of being related to opinion being what someone who did not expect these to be detected would not choose. This is why being treated well is thought to be more eligible than acting well, as one accepts the one even if it is not noticed but no one would wish to do well without being noticed.
- All things that we wish to be rather than to seem, as they are more connected with reality, which is why they say that justice

is a small thing, as it is better to seem than to be just, but not so with health.

- Things more useful for many purposes, such as things useful for living and for living well and for pleasure and for doing good deeds, which is why health and wealth are thought to be the greatest goods, as they have all these features.
- What is relatively painless and produces pleasure, which has two advantages – both pleasure and lack of pain.
- Of two things that which added to the original makes the whole greater.
- Things whose presence is noticed rather than things whose presence is not, as they pertain more to reality, which is why being rich would seem a greater good than being thought to be rich.
- What is loved, in one case on its own, in another with other things, which is why there is not the same penalty for blinding one eye of a man with both eyes and of a man with one, as something most loved is taken in the latter case.

We have pretty well covered, then, the points from which proofs are drawn in exhortation and deterrence.

CHAPTER I.8. CONSTITUTIONS

This chapter amounts to an appendix to the discussion of deliberative oratory. It reverts from strictly 'topical' material to the political science of Chapter 1.4. So important is the consideration of the constitution of the state in which the deliberator is offering his advice that the theory of constitutions must be reckoned as part of the art of oratory as well as of the science of politics. Thus Aristotle rounds off the discussion of deliberation with a brief summary of his doctrine of constitutions. Practical common sense triumphs over a pedantic obsession with order and taxonomic distinctions in a way characteristic of the work throughout.

CHAPTER I.8

However, the most important and decisive of all factors relating to the ability to persuade and counsel well is the grasp of all the *constitutions*[19] and the distinction of the customs, regulations and interests of each. For all are persuaded by what is to their advantage, and what is to their advantage is what preserves the constitution. Again the pronouncement of the dominant element is itself decisive and it is by constitutions that the dominant elements are discriminated – there are as many of them as there are constitutions. Now there are four constitutions – *democracy, oligarchy, aristocracy* and *monarchy* – so that the dominant and decisive element in judgement must be either some part or the whole of these.

- Democracy is that constitution in which offices are assigned by lot.
- Oligarchy that in which they are assigned by men of property, and aristocracy that in which they are assigned by those of upbringing – and by upbringing I mean that which is dictated by custom.
- For in an aristocracy it is those who abide by the customary practices that rule. They cannot but be thought to be the best, whence the name.
- 1366a Monarchy is, as its name suggests, the constitution in which one man is master of all; of this there are two kinds, that with a certain regularity being kingship and that without limits being tyranny.

And we must not overlook the purpose of each constitution, as it is things conducive to this purpose that are chosen.

- The purpose, then, of democracy is freedom, that of oligarchy is wealth, that of aristocracy has to do with education and customs, and that of tyranny is security.

So clearly we must distinguish the manners, customs and interests related to the purpose of each constitution, given that men make their choices by reference to that. And since proofs are produced not only by demonstrative but also by ethical argument (for the speaker convinces by seeming to be of a certain character, that is, if he should seem to be good or benevolent or both), we ought to grasp the characters of each of the types of states; for the characteristics of each state must necessarily be the most persuasive in relation to it. And characteristics can be grasped by the same means in each case; for it is in moral purpose that the characteristics become apparent, and purpose bears upon the end.

The things, then, at which one should aim as being the case or being about to be so, when we are exhorting, and from what points we should draw the proofs that involve expediency, and also through what characteristics and customs of the constitutions and in what way we will prosper, to the extent appropriate to the present occasion, have been pronounced — they will be more accurately discussed in the *Politics*.[20]

[handwritten notes]

Quiz:

1) Oligarchy vs Aristocracy
   — def
   — purpose

2) Which is better —
   what all choose or
   some choose (all)
   p99

3) better — that which is
   rare
   or
   abundant (rare)
   97

Having poi   rt of
the treatmen   that
it is the hig   tory,
which is ver   ing,
he himself   akest
material in t   el to
that used for   arly
defined as the exhibition of the nobility or baseness of the subject and then
the topics are examined by which men are to be persuaded of these.
Nobility is closely connected with virtue, which might be thought to come
more properly within the compass of forensic oratory. The connection with
nobility, however, allows Aristotle to draw material for this Section from
his ethical theory, just as he has drawn it from his political theory in the
discussion of deliberation. Praise & blame

CHAPTER I.9

Let us move on to *virtue and vice*, and *nobility and baseness*, which are
the targets of those who laud and censure. To the discussion of these
it will be incidental that we also reveal the points on the basis of
which we are supposed to be of a certain character-type, which was,
after all, our second kind of proof, since from the same considerations we will be able to make both ourselves and another credit-
worthy as regards virtue. And since it is possible to praise, both in
jest and seriously, often not only a man or a god but even inanimates
and any one at random of the other animals, in the same way we

should adopt our premises about these as well, so that whatever we say for the sake of example should go for them as well.

The noble, then, is that which is praiseworthy through being intrinsically eligible or what, being good, is also pleasant, because it is good. And if this is the noble, then virtue must be a noble thing, since, being good, it is also praiseworthy. And *virtue* is, as is generally thought, *the capacity to produce advantages and to preserve them, and also the capacity for many and signal good works, for all men in all cases.* Its elements are:

1366b

- Justice, courage, restraint, splendour, magnanimity, liberality, prudence and wisdom.[1]

And the *greatest virtues must be those most useful to others,* if virtue is indeed a capacity for beneficence, and that is why

- The just and courageous are held in especial honour, the one being useful to others in war, the other both in war and in peace.
- So also liberality; for the liberal-minded are concessive and non-contentious in money matters, on which other men are especially keen.
- Justice is the virtue through which each group of men retain their own things, in conformity with the law, injustice being the vice through which they have those of others, in defiance of the law.
- Courage is the virtue by which men are productive of noble actions amid danger, as custom ordains and while obedient to the laws, cowardice being its opposite. Restraint is the virtue by which men are so disposed towards bodily pleasures as custom decrees, and intemperance is its opposite.
- Liberality is beneficent in regard to money, illiberality the opposite.
- Magnanimity is the virtue productive of great benefactions, and pettiness is its opposite, and splendour is the virtue that produces greatness in expenditure and its opposite is meanness.
- Prudence, finally, is that virtue of the intellect by which men are able to deliberate well about the good and bad things we have mentioned, with a view to achieving happiness.

For the present circumstances, then, we have said enough about virtue and vice in general and about their elements and it is not hard to see about their other aspects. For it is obvious that things that produce virtue are *noble* (as they are related to virtue) and also things produced by virtue, and of this kind too are the signs and products of virtue. And since the signs of virtue and such things as are the products or undergoings of a good man are noble, then anything that is the product or sign of courage or is courageously done must be noble, and similarly just products and justly done acts (but not undergoings; for in this alone of the virtues a just undergoing is not always noble – as in the case of punishment, it is nobler when suffered unjustly than justly), and so on with the other virtues. *Noble* too are:

- The things that win rewards and status, especially those that bring honour rather than money.
- Any of the eligible deeds that someone does not do for himself, and deeds that are good *simpliciter*, and whatever a man might do for his country overlooking his own interest, and deeds good in nature, and deeds good, but not for the doer, as such deeds are done for their own sake.
- Things that can pertain to a dead man rather than one alive, as things belonging to one alive have a greater element of interest.
- All tasks done for others, as they are less self-interested. And all good deeds that concern others and not the doer, and good deeds for those who have been beneficent, as that is justice. And benefactions, as they are not self-directed.
- The opposites of the things that bring disgrace. For we are ashamed of saying, doing or intending mean things, as Sappho remarked in her poem indeed. Alcaeus had written:

1367a

> I fain would speak, but back am held
> By shame . . .[2]

And she replied:

> Hadst thou desired in good and noble wise
> And did your tongue to evil speech not cling,

> Then would no shame possess your eyes,
> And gladly of the right wouldst sing . . .[3]

- And things about which men <u>contest</u> without fear; for they undergo this in connection with advantages pertaining to reputation.
- The virtues and works of those who are naturally more serious are nobler, such as th<u>ose of a man than those of a woman.</u>
- Things that bring enjoyment to others rather than to the doers – which is why justice and righteousness are noble.
- The punishment of enemies without appeasement, since <u>fair returns</u> are just and justice is noble and it belongs to the courageous man not to be defeated.
- <u>Victory and status</u> are among the noble things, as they are eligible though fruitless, and reveal a superiority of virtue.
- <u>Memorable things,</u> the more so the more memorable. And things whose consequences lie after death, and things that bring status, and outstanding things and things belonging to one man only are nobler, as they are better remembered.
- <u>Unproductive possessions,</u> as they are more liberal.
- Things peculiarly noble for each group, and such things as are signs of the things praised among each group, growing one's hair being, for instance, noble among the <u>Spartans</u>, as a sign of a free man, since it is not easy for a long-haired man to perform any manual task.
- The pursuance of <u>no banausic occupation</u>, as it is the mark of a free man not to live in dependence on another.

(We must also accept things very <u>close to the norm</u> as being the <u>same for praise and criticism</u> – the cautious man is cold and deliberate, the stupid man is honest or the imperturbable man mild – and we must describe each according to the best of the things that are close to him, as that the irritable or unbalanced man is open and the haughty man magnificent and proud, and those in the excess are *1367b* described as those in virtue, as that the rash man is courageous and the spendthrift liberal; for that is what the many will believe and it can also be reasoned, fallaciously, from the motive. For if someone takes risks when there is no need, all the more will he do so when it is noble, and if someone is generous to people at random, all the more will he be so to his friends – for it is an excess of virtue to do well to all. It must also be borne in mind among whom the praise is being given. For just as Socrates said, it is not hard to praise the Athenians among the Athenians. We should also proclaim the presence of the object of honour among each group – among Scythians, say, or among Spartans or philosophers. And in general we should move from the honoured to the noble, since they are indeed thought to border on each other). Also:

- Everything in accordance with propriety, such as things worthy of one's ancestors or former achievements; for this brings happiness and there is nobility in the further acquisition of status.
- If something is against propriety, but towards the better and nobler side, such as if one is restrained in good fortune and magnanimous in bad, or, in becoming greater, one is better and more easily reconciled. This is the point of Iphicrates' remark – 'from what rags to what riches'[4] – and the line on the Olympic victor:

> Bearing a hardy basket on my shoulders . . .[5]

and the line of Simonides:

> Her father, husband, brothers – rulers all . . .[6]

Now since praise comes from *actions*, and *purposive action* is peculiar to the *serious man*, we must try to exhibit a *purposefully active man*, and it is useful that he should often seem so to have acted. Accordingly, attendant circumstances and chance events must be treated as purposed; for if many similar cases are brought forward, they will seem to be an indication of virtue and purpose.

A laudation is a speech indicative of greatness of virtue. So we must show the subject's actions to have been of the appropriate kind. The encomium, on the other hand, treats of attendant circumstances as proofs, such as good birth and education, since it is likely that good sons will come from good fathers and that the appropriately raised man will be of the appropriate sort, which is why we make encomia on those who have accomplished achievements. Achievements are indications of disposition, since we would praise even someone who had not accomplished any, if we were confident that he was of the right kind. Deeming blessed or happy are the same as each other but different from laudation and encomium and, as happiness includes virtue, so does deeming happy include laudation and encomium.

Praise and deliberations have a common form. For the things that one might put forward in giving advice would become encomia by a change in the expression. Since, then, we understand what we 1368a should do and of what sort we should be, we must take these things said as suggestions and change and adapt their expression; for instance, that we should pride ourselves on the effects not of chance but of ourselves is the way to make the point as a suggestion, and the way to make it as praise is as follows: 'He is proud not of the effects of fortune but of himself.' So, whenever you wish to praise, see what suggestion you would make, and whenever you wish to make a suggestion, consider how you would praise. (And the expressions will have to be the converse, whenever a prohibition is being changed into a recommendation.)

We must also use many of the *amplificatory factors*, such as:

- If the subject is the only one or first or among few or has performed the action most significantly; for all these aspects are noble.
- Arguments from times and occasions, in so far as the norm is exceeded.
- If the subject has often succeeded in the same task; for that would seem to be a great thing and not a product of fortune but of himself.
- If institutions that exhort and honour are invented and established because of the subject; also if he is the first on whom the encomium is being made, as with that to Hippolochus, or the erection of a statue in the Agora, for Harmodius and Aristogeiton (on the other hand, similarly with the opposites).[7]

And if you do not find these in the subject himself, you must compare him with others, as Isocrates did through his unfamiliarity with forensic oratory. But he must be compared with well-known people; for that is amplificatory and noble, if he is better than serious men. Amplification comes naturally under praise, since it lies in the excess, and excess is among the noble things. So even if we should compare him not to men of standing, we should to the rest, since the excess is held to indicate virtue. In general, in common forms of speech augment is most expedient in epideictic speaking (for the audience take the actions as agreed, so that it only remains to add greatness and nobility to them), examples in deliberative oratory (for we give judgement by predicting future events from past ones), and enthymemes in forensic oratory (for the past is particularly amenable to the demonstration of cause and responsibility through its obscurity).

Such, then, are the points from which more or less all speeches of praise or censure are made, and those which we should have in mind in praising or censuring, and the things from which encomia and invective are produced. When we have grasped these, their opposites are obvious, censure being based on the opposite points.

SECTION FIVE: LITIGATION

CHAPTER I.10. INJUSTICE

Once again, the discussion begins with a clear statement of the subject-matter. In the case of litigation this is injustice (adikia), *a wide concept in Greek that covers crime, tort and breach of contract. To understand what exactly injustice is, it is necessary to grasp the concept of law, of which a crisp exposition is given. It is evidently also necessary to grasp the forces which drive men to break the law, and these can be divided into the universal search for the expedient and the specific search for pleasure. Expediency has been treated in the discussion of deliberation, and Aristotle announces the discussion of pleasure at the end of the chapter.*

CHAPTER I.10

Our next task is to discuss *prosecution and defence* and say from how 1368b many elements and of what sort the deductions are to be made. Three areas must be understood: the first, from what and how many motives men commit injustice; the second, in what disposition of themselves; the third, to what type of people and in what condition. So let us define injustice and proceed in order. *Let injustice¹ be voluntary illegal harm.* Now *law* is either particular or general. By particular law I mean that written down in a constitution, and by general I mean those unwritten laws which are held to be agreed by all men. *Voluntary actions* are those done with knowledge and not under duress. Of actions done with knowledge not all are purposed, but of those purposed all are done with knowledge, as none is unacquainted with the thing he purposes. The motives from which men choose to harm and do base deeds against the law are vice and lack of self-control. For if a group of men have either one or several vices, in connection with that in which they are vicious they will also be unjust: the illiberal man, for instance, in matters of money; the intemperate man in those of the bodily pleasures; the soft man in tolerance; the coward in connection with dangers (he abandons his associates in danger through fear); the ambitious man because of status; the sharp-tempered man through anger; the victory-lover through victory; the sour man through revenge; the stupid man through being illuded about justice and injustice; the shameless man out of contempt for reputation; and similarly all the others in connection with each of the areas. The situation with these matters, then, is clear, both from what has been said in connection with the virtues and from what will be said in connection with the emotions. It remains to discuss the motives for crime, the state of mind and the victims.

Let us, then, first distinguish what men are *aiming at* and what sort of thing they are *avoiding* when they set out to do wrong. For it is obviously necessary for the prosecutor to consider how many of these and of what sort are available to his adversary and for the defendant to know which and how many of these are not present. All men, then, perform all actions either of themselves or not of themselves. Of the things not performed of themselves, they do some through chance and some from necessity, and of those done from necessity some are by force and some by nature, so that everything that they do not do of themselves is done either by chance or by nature or by force. And of the actions they do of themselves, and for which they are themselves responsible, some are done through habit, some through desire, and of these some through rational and some through irrational desire. Wishing is the desire for a good thing (none wishes something unless he thinks that it is a good thing) and the irrational desires are anger and appetite. Thus everything that men do must be done through seven causes:

- Through chance, through nature, through compulsion, through habit, through calculation, through anger or through appetite.

It would be superfluous to make further distinctions by age, condition or the character of the acts of the subject; even if it is a property of the young to be hot-tempered or appetitive, <u>they do not do this sort of action because of their youth</u> but through hot temper or appetite. Nor do men act because of wealth and poverty – rather it is a property of the poor to have an appetite for money because of their lack of it and of the wealthy, because of their riches, to have an appetite for unnecessary pleasures. They too, however, act not because of wealth and poverty but through their appetite. Similarly, too, the just and unjust and the other groups said to act from their dispositions act from these motives, either through calculation or through emotion (but some act from honest habits and emotions and some from the opposites). It is, however, a property of such dispositions that such consequences follow, and the opposites from the opposites. For immediately, perhaps, to the temperate man, because of his temperance, honest opinions and desires attach in regard of pleasures, and to the intemperate man the opposites on these very matters. Thus we must leave such distinctions aside and consider what actions usually accompany what types. If a man is white or black or large or small, none of these things is ordained to accompany him, but if he is young or old, or just or unjust, it makes a difference. In general, whatever properties cause the manners of men to differ, such as seeming to himself to be rich or poor, will make a difference, as also good fortune or bad. We will discuss these points later; for the moment let us consider the remaining matters first.

The *things arising from chance* are of the kind of which the cause is indefinite, not arising for the sake of anything nor in all cases nor for the most part nor in an ordered manner (it is clear about these points from the definition of chance). The *things arising from nature* 1369b are of the kind of which the cause is both within them and ordered, as they turn out in the same way either in all cases or for the most part. With unnatural events it is not at all necessary to be precise as to whether they arise by some natural factor or some other cause, though chance might also be thought to be the cause of such events. *Actions arising by force* are such as occur against appetite and the calculations of the agents themselves. *Actions produced by habit* are those that men do through having often done them before, and those done by calculation are those of the aforementioned advantages thought to be in their interest by the agents, either done as an end-purpose or conducive thereto, whenever action is taken out of expediency. (For even the unrestrained perform some expedient actions, though not for the expediency but for pleasure.) Actions taken through anger or rage are those of revenge. Revenge and punishment, however, are different: punishment is for the sake of the person punished, revenge for that of the avenger, so that he may be satisfied. (What anger is, accordingly, will be explained in the discussion of the emotions.) Actions taken from appetite are all those that seem to be pleasant. Among pleasant things there are the customary and the acquired; for many things are not pleasant by nature, but are done with pleasure after habituation – so that we may say in general that all actions that men perform of their own accord are either advantageous or apparently so, or either pleasant or apparently so. And since all actions taken of the agent's own accord are done willingly, and all those not so taken unwillingly, then all things that men do willingly would be either advantageous or apparently so, either pleasant or apparently so. For I also include the avoidance of real or apparent evils and the exchange of greater ills for lesser among good things (for they are in a way purposed), and either the avoidance of the really or apparently unpleasant or the exchange of greater for lesser similarly among the pleasant things. So we must grasp the number and character of expedient and pleasant things. Well, expedient things we have earlier given in the discussion of political oratory. So let us now discuss the pleasant. And we must think our definitions sufficient, if they are in each case neither unclear nor pedantic.

CHAPTER I.II. PLEASURE

Pleasure is a subject that uniquely combined Aristotle's interest in biology and in morals and it receives many illuminating discussions in the corpus. The present chapter again strays some way from what might be thought essential for the forensic orator seeking to show that a particular crime was motivated by the search for pleasure. However, here as much as anywhere, we see Aristotle's determination that the evidently important and powerful skill of rhetoric should be brought within the purview of science by being given a sound philosophical and psychological grounding.

CHAPTER I.II

*Let us then suppose pleasure to be a certain process of the soul and specifically an instantaneous sensory resolution to the natural state, and pain the opposite.*² Now if pleasure is of this kind, obviously the pleasant is also whatever produces the said disposition, while what 1370a destroys it or produces the opposite resolution is the painful. The pleasant, then, must be both a tendency towards the natural state for the most part – and especially when the things that happen by the state have lost their own nature – and habits (indeed the habitual becomes like what is in fact natural, as habit is a thing similar to nature, since frequent is close to universal occurrence, and nature is connected with universal, habit with frequent, occurrence), and also what is not enforced (for violence is unnatural, and so what is enforced is unpleasant, and it has been well said that 'all action forced is naturally cruel'),³ but worries and serious moods and concentrations are unpleasant, as these are forced and violent, unless they have been habituated – but, if so, habit makes things pleasant. The opposites of the last are pleasant: accordingly, unbuttonedness, leisure, lack of worry, games, relaxation and sleep are among the pleasant things, as none of them comes by coercion. Also every object of an appetite is pleasant, as appetite is the desire for the pleasant.

Now some *appetites* are *irrational* and some *accompanied by reason*. I call *irrational* all those based on a supposition (these are of the kind that are said to be natural, such as those present to us from the body, such as – with nourishment, thirst and hunger – there being a particular species of appetite for each species of nourishment, and those connected with objects of taste, sexual desire and touch in general, as well as smell, hearing and sight), while those *accompanied by reason* are those which we have from being persuaded, since men have an appetite to see and possess many things from hearing and being convinced. And since being pleased consists in perceiving a certain affection, and imagination is a kind of weak perception, then in recollection and expectation there should always be present a certain imagination of what is recalled or expected. And if this is so, then obviously there are also pleasures of recollection and expectancy, since they also involve perception. So all *pleasant* things must be either in the perception of things present or in the recollection of things past or in the expectation of things to come, as we perceive things present, remember things past and expect things to come.

1370b • The objects of memory, therefore, are pleasant not only in so far as they were so as present things, when they were present, but in some cases even when they were not pleasant, if their subsequent consequences are noble and good. Hence the remark:

> Sweet for survivors to recall their toils . . .[4]

and:

> Even of pains a man has later joy,
> Recalling all he suffered, all he wrought . . .[5]

(The reason for this is that it is also pleasant not to be enduring an ill.)

• The objects of expectation are also pleasant, the ones whose presence seems to bring great joy or great advantage and to bring advantage without pain.

• In general, all things whose presence gives pleasure, also for the most part please us in recollection or expectation. Hence even to be angry is pleasant, as Homer wrote on the subject of anger:

> Which sweeter far is than the ooze of honey . . .[6]

(For no one is angry with someone whom it seems impossible to avenge, and with those far in excess of themselves in power they are either not angry or much less so.)

• Also most appetites are accompanied by a certain pleasure, as either in remembering how they succeeded or in hoping how they might, men are gladdened by a certain pleasure, as those beset by thirst in fevers are glad both to remember how they drank and to look forward to drinking, and lovers are always given pleasure by discussing or writing or doing something about the loved one. For in all these cases, as they remember, they think that they are beholding the beloved. This, indeed, is for all men the beginning of love, when not only are they charmed by the beloved's presence but, recalling him in his absence, are visited by a certain pain at his not being present, and similarly a certain pleasure supervenes on grief and lamentation. The pain comes from something's not being there, the pleasure from recollection and from, in a way, seeing the person and what he did and what he was like. This is also why it was quite reasonable to say:

> So spake he, and in all the longing moved
> For weeping . . .[7]

- Being revenged is also pleasant. For it is pleasant to achieve anything in which it is painful to fail, and those who are angry are insuperably pained by the failing of revenge, though they are delighted by the expectation of it.
- Winning is also pleasant, not just for the victory-loving but for all. For it produces the imagination of superiority, for which all have an appetite either more or less strongly. But since winning 1371a is pleasant, competitive and emulous games must also be pleasant (for in them winning often comes about), as well as 'knuckle-bones', ball games, dice-playing and backgammon. It is also the same with the sports that are taken seriously. Some become pleasant if one is accustomed to them, some are immediately so, such as hunting and all sports of the chase. For where there is competition, there is also victory. Hence is forensic and disputational activity pleasant for those habituated and skilled in it.
- Also status and reputation are among the most pleasant things, as to each enjoyer of them there occurs the imagination that he is of a kind with the serious man, and especially when those speak well of them whom they think to be telling the truth. And of this kind are those near at hand rather than at a distance and associates and fellow-citizens rather than those from abroad, those now alive rather than posterity, the wise rather than the

foolish, the many rather than the few. For the groups mentioned are more likely to be right than their opposites. For of the things for which one has a sovereign contempt, such as children or animals, the admiration or good opinion is of no weight for its own sake but, if at all, for some other reason.

- The friend too is among pleasant things; for friendship is pleasant (no one is a lover of wine to whom wine is not pleasant) and being befriended is also pleasant. For in this case too there is the imagination that one has the property of being a good man, for which all who behold it have an appetite; and to be befriended is to be loved for one's own sake.

- Being admired is also pleasant for the same reason as being honoured.

- Also flattery and the flatterer are pleasant things; for the flatterer is an apparent admirer and an apparent friend.

- It is also pleasant to do the same things many times (since the customary has been agreed to be pleasant). But also changing is pleasant, as changing occurs in the natural direction. For always the same thing produces an excess of the established disposition. Hence:

Sweet is the change of all things . . .[8]

- For this reason intermittence is pleasant, both in men and in matters. For change is variation from the present, and the intermittent is also rare.

- Also learning and admiring are for the most part pleasant. For admiration contains the appetite for learning, so that the object of admiration is an object of appetite, and in learning a resolution to the natural condition occurs.

- Also to treat well and to be well treated are among the pleasant things. To be well treated is to receive what one desires, and to 1371b treat well is both to possess and to do so in large measure, of which both are desirable. And because good works are pleasant, propping up one's neighbours is pleasant for men, as is making good their lacks.

- And since learning and admiration are pleasant, the following must also be:

Both what is imitative, such as drawing, sculpture and poetry, and everything that should happen to have been well imitated, even if the object of imitation is not pleasant itself. For the pleasure is not in that, but there is rather a deduction that this is that, so that some learning results.[9]

Also dramatic reversals and narrow escapes from danger, since all these evoke amazement.

- Also, since the natural is pleasant, and related things are natural to each other, all cognates and similars are pleasant for the most part, such as man to man, horse to horse, youth to youth, whence the proverbs: 'Each age delights its age'; 'Always the like'; 'Beast knows beast'; 'Crow with crow'; and all the rest.

- And since everything that is cognate and similar is pleasant, and each man is especially this to himself, all men must be more or less self-loving, as all these things are particularly present in relation to the self.

- And since all men are self-loving, their attributes must also be pleasant to all, such as their works and their words. Hence are men for the most part lovers of flatterers and lovers of their like and their children, their children being their own products.

- It is also pleasant to make good lacks, as the things then become one's own achievements.

- And since to rule is extremely sweet, to be thought to be wise is also pleasant. For being prudent is ruler-like, and contemplative wisdom is the science of many things that evoke amazement.

- Again, since men are for the most part status-loving, criticizing one's neighbours and ruling them must be pleasant, and spending time in what one thinks oneself to be best at, as indeed the poet insists,

> Using the greatest part of every day,
> In tasks in which he even outdoes himself . . .[10]

- Similarly, since sport and all relaxation are among pleasant things, so must laughter and ridiculous things be pleasant, whether men, words or actions. (A definition is given of the ridiculous in the *Poetics*.)[11]

Let this, then, suffice on the subject of pleasant things, unpleasant things being obvious from their opposites.

CHAPTER I.12. THE CRIMINAL MIND

Aristotle might well have felt that his exhaustive discussion of what men find pleasant might suffice on the subject of the causation of crime, but this is far from the case. To become convinced that an individual has committed an illegal act one needs to believe not only that he would derive some pleasure from the deed but also both that he himself was in an appropriate state of mind and that his victim or victims were of a suitable kind. Here, as so frequently in the Ethics, *Aristotle displays his genius for the scrutiny of the mechanics of human behaviour, of the precise combination of separately identifiable factors that must occur for a given action to take place.*

CHAPTER I.12

These, then, are the *motives* for injustice. Let us now speak of the *unjust state of mind* and of the *victims*. Men do injustice when:

- They think that the crime is capable of being accomplished and capable for themselves, and also if they think they would get away with doing it or on being caught would not be punished, or that they would be punished but that the penalty would be less than the gain to them or to those for whom they are concerned. The sort of things that seem possible and the sort that seem impossible will be given below (for these are common to all arguments). Those who most think that they can do injustice without being punished are those who are able to make a speech – men of affairs and those with experience of many trials.
- Also if they have many friends and if they are rich. Especially, then, if they are in the groups mentioned do they think that they can do it, and if not, even if they have friends of this kind,

or supporters or associates. For it is for these reasons that they both act and are undetected and avoid punishment.

- Also if they should be friends of the victims or the judges. For friends are off their guard against injury and tend to settle before prosecution, while judges favour those who are their friends and let them off altogether or with slight penalties.

Things that go undetected are:

- Characters unsuited to the accusations, such as a weakling accused of assault or a poor or ugly man of adultery, and crimes that are too much in the open and before men's eyes. No precautions are taken against them; after all, who would imagine that they could be attempted?
- Also crimes so enormous and outrageous that none would commit them – against such no precautions are taken. For all men guard against the usual things, both with diseases and with crimes, and nobody is on his guard against a disease that nobody has yet caught.
- Also men who have no enemies or many, since the former think that they will not be noticed as they will not be suspected, and the latter escape notice through its not being supposed that they would try anything against those on their guard and from having it as their defence that they would never have tried.
- Also those with the ability to conceal the crime either by their behaviour or by some hiding-place, or who have friendly dispositions.
- Also those who, if they are caught, have a means of avoiding justice either by temporal deferment or by corrupting the juries.
- And those who, if a punishment is awarded, have a means of avoiding execution or of causing a temporal delay. Or if through poverty the criminal has nothing to lose. Also those for whom the advantages are obvious, great or close and the punishments small, unclear or remote.
- Also crimes for which the punishment could not be as great as *1372b* the advantage, as is considered to be the case with a *coup d'état*.
- And situations in which the crimes are gains and the punishments

mere rebukes. And, by contrast, those in which the crimes
lead to a certain praise, such as if in doing them a man happened at the same time to avenge his father or mother, as with
Zeno, and the punishments are merely related to money, exile
or some such thing. For men do injustice for both reasons and
in both conditions, though not the same types but those opposite
in character.

- Also those who have often not been detected or not punished,
  and those who have often failed (for there are also some in
  these groups, just as in warfare, who wish to fight again).

- And those for whom the pleasantness would be immediate and
  the pain later, or the gain immediate and the punishment later.
  For the lawless are of this kind, and lawlessness is connected
  with all objects of desire.

- And also, by contrast, those for whom the pain or the punishment would be more immediate and the pleasure or advantage
  later or more long-lasting, as the temperate and prudent pursue
  such things.

- And those who have the possibility to seem to have acted from
  chance or from necessity or nature or habit and in general to
  have committed an error not a crime.

- And those who have the possibility of receiving indulgence.

- Also those who are deficient. There are two kinds of deficiency:
  it is either of a necessity, as with the poor, or with a superfluity,
  as with the rich.

- Also those with an excellent reputation or a very bad one, the
  former in being thought unlikely to do it, the latter in getting
  no worse a reputation.

These, then, are the *conditions* in which men attempt to commit
crimes, and they commit them against the following *sorts of men* and
do the following things:

- Those that have what they lack either in respect of necessities or
  of excess or of enjoyment, both the remote and the near. For
  their seizure is swift and the vengeance of their victims is slow,
  as with men despoiling Carthage.[12]

- Also men not on their guard or suspicious but trusting, as it is easier to avoid their general notice.
- Also the easy-going, as they would be vexed by a prosecution.
- Also the demure, as they are not combative about money.
- Also those who have been wronged by many and have not prosecuted, as being, according to the proverb, 'Mysian plunder'.[13]
- Also those who have yet to be wronged and those many times wronged. For both are off their guard, the former as never wronged, the latter as not likely to be again.
- Also those who have been slandered or are easy to slander; for such men would neither choose to prosecute, from fear of the judges, nor be able to persuade them, as being hated and envied.
- And those against whom the criminal has the excuse that either *1373a* their ancestors or themselves or their friends either have done ill or are so intending either to himself or to his ancestors or to those dear to him. For, as the proverb goes, only wickedness needs an excuse.
- Also both enemies and friends; the latter are wronged more easily, the former more agreeably.
- Also those without friends and those not clever in speech or action; for either they will not attempt to prosecute or they will reach a settlement or they will achieve nothing.
- And those for whom it is not profitable to spend time awaiting the verdict or execution, such as foreigners and craftsmen; they will be fobbed off with little and will soon stop.
- Also those who have committed many injustices or the same kind of injustice. For it seems to be similar to not committing a crime when some crime is committed such as the victim himself is accustomed to commit – I mean if one were to do violence to someone accustomed to assault others.
- And those who either have done one ill, or have wished to, or do wish to, or who intend to do so; for this has both pleasure and nobility, and seems close to not doing wrong.
- Those by wronging whom one pleases, either friends or admirers or lovers or masters, or in general those in deference to whom they live their lives.

- And those from whom one can expect indulgent treatment.
- And those whom one has previously prosecuted or been at issue with, as Callippus did in the case of Dion;[14] for these things seem close to not committing injustice.
- Also those likely to be wronged by others if not by the criminal himself, so that there is no possibility of deliberation, in the way that Aenesidemus is said to have sent Gelon the *cottabus* prize[15] when he enslaved a city – because the latter did first what he was himself intending.
- Also those after wronging whom one will be able to perform many just acts to them, as being easily healed, in the way that Jason of Thessaly said that one should commit some crimes in order also to be able to do many just deeds.
- Also crimes which all or many habitually commit; as they think they will receive pardon.
- Also things that are easy to conceal, and such are:

  > Things that are quickly consumed, such as foodstuffs, or things easily changed in shape or colour or mixtures, or what it is easy to hide in many places; and such are things easily lifted and hidden in small places.

  > Things of which there are many indistinguishably similar in the property of the criminal.

  > Things that those wronged would be embarrassed to mention, such as assaults on women of the household or themselves or their children.

  > Things about which the prosecutor would seem to be being litigious; such being minor things and those about which there is forgiveness.

The conditions, then, in which men do injustices, and what sort of crimes and against what sort of victim and why, are more or less the ones given.

CHAPTER I.13. CRIME AND PUNISHMENT

In this chapter, after the analysis of what an unjust act is – namely the breaking of a general or particular law – and after the explanation of the circumstances in which such things occur, Aristotle passes to the subjects of punishment and mitigation. He introduces the important notion of equity, by which a defendant might appeal to be given the benefit of the doubt. He does not discuss the purpose of punishment but outlines the grounds on which the orator might plead for its suspension or intensification.

CHAPTER I.13

Now let us distinguish all *crimes and punishments*, starting first from 1373*b* the following point. Just and unjust acts are defined in relation to two kinds of law and in relation to persons in two ways.

By law I mean on the one hand particular law and on the other general law, special being that defined by each group in relation to itself, this being either unwritten or written down, and the general law being that of nature. For there is something of which we all have an inkling, being a naturally universal right and wrong, even if there should be no community between the two parties nor contract, to which Sophocles' Antigone seems to be referring, in saying that it is just, though forbidden, to bury Polynices, as this is naturally right:

> For not from yesterday, not just today,
> Lives this command, but always. Whence it came
> None knows . . .[16]

And as Empedocles says about not killing animate beings: this is not right for some and wrong for others,

> But as a law for all through the broad earth
> Mightily stretches and the boundless air . . .[17]

And, as Alcidamas says in his Messenian oration, 'God sent all men forth free; none has nature created a slave.'[18] Furthermore, justice in relation to the person is defined in two ways. For it is defined either in relation to the community or to one of its members what one should or should not do. Accordingly, it is possible to perform just and unjust acts in two ways, either towards a defined individual or towards the community. The adulterer and mugger wrongs one of the individuals, the draft-dodger the community.

Now that all *kinds of crime* have been distinguished, some being *against the community*, some *against another individual* or *group of individuals*, let us resume our discussion of what it is to be wronged. *To be wronged is to suffer unjust treatment from a voluntary agent* (for doing wrong has previously been defined to be a voluntary thing). Since it is necessary that the injured party be damaged, and damaged as an act of will, the kinds of damage are clear from what has been said above, as good and bad things were earlier given in themselves, and voluntary acts were said to be the sort that we do with knowledge. So all crimes must be against either the community or the individual and must be either of an ignorant and unwilling agent or of a knowing and willing one, and of these some through purposive action and some through emotion. We will deal with anger in the discussion of the emotions, while it has been explained above what sort of things men purpose and in what condition. And defendants 1374a often agree that they have done the deed, but do not agree either with the description of the charge or with what the charge is of, claiming, for example, that they took and did not steal and struck first but did not assault and had recourse to a woman but did not commit adultery, or stole but not sacrilegiously (the object did not belong to the god) or trespassed but not on public ground or had communications with the enemy but had not been treasonable. We must accordingly draw definitions about the nature of *theft*, *assault* and *adultery*, so that if we wish to show that they have or have not occurred, we will be able to make the judicial status of the case evident. All these things have to do with the question of the defendant's being unjust and base or not a criminal. For it is in *purpose* that baseness and criminality lie, and the names for such things indicate their purposiveness, such as violence and theft. For not all cases of striking are an assault, but only if for a reason, such as to insult the victim or for one's own pleasure. Nor are all cases of secret taking theft, but only if to the detriment of him from whom the property is taken and for the betterment of oneself. And it is the same with the other actions as with these.

Now since there were shown to be *two species* of just and unjust act (some being *written*, some *unwritten*), we have given *those on which the laws pronounce*. Of the unwritten ones there are two kinds: the first comes from an *excess of virtue and vice*, in connection with which are blame, praise and disgrace and marks of honour and rewards (such as to be grateful to the one who has treated us well and the repayment of a good turn for its doer, and supporting one's friends and all other such), and the other variety is an *omission of the special and written law*. For the *equitable* is held to be *right*, and *equity is right going beyond the written law*. This arises sometimes at the wish, sometimes not at the wish, of the lawgivers – the latter when they overlook it, and the former when they cannot give a universal definition, but while it is necessary for them to give a general rule they cannot do so but only give one that holds for the most part, and in such cases as are not easy to define through their unfamiliarity, such as the question of wounding what kind of victim and with what length of sword there must be punishment. For time would run out if they counted this up. If, then, the matter should be undefined, but there should be a need for legislation, it is necessary to speak generally, so that if a man wearing a ring should raise his hand or actually strike another, then he is guilty under the written law and commits a crime, but in reality commits no crime – a case of equity.[19] Now if *equity* is what we have said, it is clear what sort of things are *equitable* and what not, and what sort of men are *inequitable*:

- The things to which one should accord forgiveness are equitable and it is equitable not to consider errors and crimes on the same basis, nor misfortunes. For misfortunes are the kind of thing that are unexpected and not produced by wickedness, and errors are not unexpected but not from wickedness, while crimes are both not unexpected and from wickedness; for things done out of desire are from wickedness.
- It is also equitable to forgive human failings.
- And also to have regard not to the law but to the lawgiver and to look not at the words but at the intention of the lawgiver, and not to the action but to the purpose, and not to the part but to the whole, and not how someone now is but how he has always been or for the most part.
- Also the recollection rather of good than of bad treatment and of the good treatment that one has received rather than of the good deeds one has done. And enduring being wronged.

- And to wish judgement to be given rather by word than by deed, and to be willing to go to arbitration rather than to trial. For the arbitrator sees equity, the juror the law; indeed that is why an arbitrator is found – that equity might prevail.

CHAPTER I.14. RELATIVELY SERIOUS CRIMES

Just as the discussion of deliberation contained an examination of relative expediency and inexpediency, so does that of forensic oratory contain an examination of greater or lesser criminality. This chapter is, however, much shorter than the corresponding one on deliberation, no doubt because much of the potential material for it has already been covered in the discussion of equity.

CHAPTER I.14

A crime is *greater*:

- In so far as it should spring from greater injustice. Hence are the smallest things very serious, as that of which Callistratus[20] accused Melanopus, that he had peculated three half-obols from the temple-builders. For in mere justice this is not very serious. This comes about from the presence of a potential in the crime – a man who has stolen three sacred half-obols might commit any crime.
- Sometimes, then, a crime is held to be more serious in this way, sometimes when it is judged from the damage.
- Also a crime for which there is no equal recompense, but all punishment is lesser.
- And one for which there is no cure; for they are hard to remedy.
- Also things for which the victim cannot get justice because they are incurable, as justice is both punishment and remedy.
- And if the victim and injured party should have inflicted great punishment on himself, even more is it right for the criminal to be punished, as Sophocles said on behalf of Euctemon, since he killed himself after an assault, that he would demand no less a price than the victim himself had paid.[21]

1375a

- Also what someone is the only one to do, or the first, or with few others.
- Also to commit the same crime many times.
- And anything through which precautions and punishments should have been sought and found, as in Argos a man because of whom a law is ordained is punished and also those for whom the prison was built.[22]
- And a more brutal crime is greater, also what is more from forethought.
- And what the audience fear rather than pity.

And the relevant *rhetorical devices* are of the following kind:

- That the defendant has destroyed much or greatly exceeded, such as in oaths, pledges, proofs and wedding vows; for in many crimes there is an excess.
- And the crime occurs where criminals are being punished, as with false witnesses – for where would they not commit a crime, if they would do so in the very court? Also crimes to which especial shame attaches.
- And if the victim has done the offender a good turn; for the injustice is greater in that he treats him badly and not well.
- Also crimes against the unwritten rights, as it belongs to the better man to be good not from compulsion. For the written laws are compulsory, the unwritten ones not. In another way, if it is against the written laws. For the man who commits fearful crimes and punishable ones would also commit unpunishable ones.

Let such be our discussion of greater and lesser crimes.

CHAPTER I.15. NON–TECHNICAL PROOFS

This chapter forms an appendix to the discussion of forensic oratory which in some ways balances that on constitutions in the discussion of deliberation. The distinction between technical and non-technical proofs was drawn in Chapter 1.2, shortly after the definition of rhetoric, but it is only now that Aristotle turns to the latter. This seems wholly reasonable in so far as they pertain in his view only to forensic oratory and as they require less skill to exploit than do the technical proofs to invent. However, it is noteworthy that in earlier rhetorical theory non-technical proofs undoubtedly had pride of place over arguments from probability and it was part of the achievement of fourth-century rhetoric in general and of Aristotle in particular to reverse this order of priority.

CHAPTER I.15

Our next task is to add the so-called *non-technical proofs*[23] to those discussed, as they are a peculiarity of forensic oratory. They are five in number:

● Laws, witnesses, contracts, tortures and oaths.

Let us then first speak of *laws* and say how they should be used both in exhortation and in deterrence, both in prosecution and in defence. For it is obvious that:

● If the written law is contrary to our position, we must use the general law and the principles of greater equity and justice, and claim that this is the meaning of the 'to the best judgement' principle, that the juror should not always follow the written laws, that equity is permanently valid and never changes, nor does the general law (for it is natural), whereas the written laws often do, the point of the lines from Sophocles' *Antigone*.[24] Antigone defends the burial as against the law of Creon but not against the unwritten law,

1375b

> For not from yesterday, not just today,
> Lives this command . . .
> This would I not, obeying any man . . .

And we must claim that justice is the real and the expedient, but not what seems to be it, so that that is not the written law; for it does not perform the function of the law.

● We also claim that the judge is like a silver-weigher, ordained to distinguish false justice from true, and that it belongs to a better man to abide by and follow the unwritten rather than the written laws; we should also consider whether perhaps the law is opposed to an accepted law or to itself, as when sometimes one law ordains that whatever has been contracted should be decisive, while the other forbids contracts against the law, and whether the law is ambiguous, so that it can be turned round and we can see under which interpretation either justice or expediency fits it, and then one must use that.

● And if the matters for which the law was ordained no longer obtain, whereas the law does, we must try to make this clear and fight in this way against the law.

● But if the written law should be favourable to our position, then we must say that 'to the best judgement' means that giving judgement is not for the sake of what is against the law, but rather that, if he does not know what the law means, the juror should not commit perjury, also that none chooses the good in general, but relative to himself, and that it makes no difference whether the law is not given or not used.

● And that, among other skills, it is not profitable to outwit the doctor; for the error of the doctor does not do as much harm as the habituation to disobey authority, and that seeking to be wiser than the laws is what is forbidden by the most reputable legal systems.

Let these be our definitions in relation to laws.

As for *witnesses*, there are two kinds of witness, some *ancient*, some *modern*, and of the latter some sharing the danger, some free of it. By ancient witnesses I mean the *poets* and all those other *famous men* whose judgements are well known, as the Athenians took Homer as a witness about Salamis,[25] the Tenedians took Periander of Corinth against the Sigeans,[26] and Cleophon against Critias used the elegies of Solon, to the effect that his family had long been debauched. For Solon would not otherwise have written,

> Tell gold-haired Critias to obey his father . . .[27]

So such witnesses are about past events, and about future ones also prophets, as Themistocles urged putting to sea by citing the 'wooden 1376a walls' prophecy.[28] *Proverbs* too, as has been said, are a kind of evidence. For instance, if one were advising someone not to befriend an old man, this is attested by the proverb:

> Never do an old man a good turn . . .[29]

and that one should kill the sons of fathers one kills:

> Foolish to kill the father, spare the sons . . .[30]

The *modern witnesses* are *notables* who have given some judgement; for these judgements are useful for those in controversy over the same points. For instance:

- Eubulus used in his court case against Chares what Plato said against Archibius, that there had been a growth in the city of openly confessing one's baseness.[31]
- Also those sharing in the danger, if they should seem to be lying.[32]
- But such people are witnesses only of whether or not the events happened, or whether or not they are happening, but are not witnesses about the character of the events, such as whether they are just or unjust, advantageous or disadvantageous.
- Those that are remote are more convincing about these aspects, and most of all the ancients; for they cannot be corrupted.

Confirmation of witnesses is, for the man who does not have witnesses, that judgement must be from probability and this is 'to the best judgement',[33] and because it is not possible to make probability deceive with silver and probabilities are not caught in perjury, and also, for the man who has witness against the one who does not, that probabilities are not answerable to the court, and that there would be no need of witnesses, if it was sufficient to consider the matter from the speeches.

Some *testimonies* are about ourselves, some about the adversary, some about the facts, some about their character, so that it is obviously never possible to be at a loss for useful testimony. For if they are not available about the facts either in agreement with one's own position or contrary to the adversary's, yet they will be about the character either of the speaker, suggesting reasonableness, or of the adversary, suggesting baseness. The other questions about the witness

– whether he is a friend or enemy or neutral, whether he has a good, bad or indifferent reputation, and all other such differences – should be drawn from the same points from which we draw the enthymemes.

In connection with *contracts*, the use of arguments has the scope of increasing them or rejecting them, of making them convincing or unconvincing – if they are one's own, binding and authoritative, if *1376b* of one's adversary, the reverse. For making them convincing or not there is no difference from the procedure with witnesses. The contracts will be correspondingly trustworthy as are those who write them or guard them.

- If the contract is agreed to exist, then, if it is one's own, it must be augmented. For a contract is a private and particular law, and contracts do not make the law binding, but the laws do make legal contracts so, and in general the law itself is a kind of contract, so whoever weakens or removes contracts weakens or removes the laws.

- Again, most mutual matters and voluntary exchanges are done under contract, so that when they cease to be binding, men's custom with each other is destroyed. And the other points that fit this can be easily seen.

- But if they are contrary and on the side of the adversary, then first, as though one were contesting a contrary law, one must use the following points; for it is absurd if we think we ought not to obey the laws, if they are not well established but those setting them up were in error, but that it is necessary to obey contracts.

- Again, that the judge is an umpire of justice; so he should not consider the contract but what is more just.

- Also that justice is not to be deflected by deceit or compulsion (for it is natural), while contracts arise both when men are deceived and when they are compelled.

- Furthermore, we should consider whether the contract is against any of the written or universal laws, and of the written ones either the domestic or the foreign, and then if it is contrary to any other contracts either earlier or later; for if the later are valid, then the earlier are not, and if the earlier are right, the later mistaken – this can be used either way.

- We must also consider the expedient, if perhaps the contract is in any way against the judges, and all other such things; for these are similarly easy to observe.

Tortures[34] are a kind of evidence, and they are thought to carry conviction, since a certain compulsion is present. So it is not hard to say what obtains also about them, and by what arguments:

- If they are on our side, they are to be increased, on the grounds that these are the only true testimonies, and if they are against us and with the adversary, one might refute them by telling the truth about the whole genus of tortures. For no less under compulsion do men tell lies rather than the truth, either enduring rather than telling the truth or easily making false accusations so that the torture may stop sooner.
- And we should be able to refer to such past examples as the judges know.
- And we must say that tortures are not true; in that many men are thick-brained and stone-skinned and those stony in their souls are able nobly to endure coercion, and some, cowardly and cautious, before seeing the instruments, pep themselves up, so that there is nothing convincing about tortures.

We must draw four distinctions about *oaths*.[35] Either one gives and takes or neither, or one but not the other, and of the last one either gives but does not take or takes but does not give. Additionally, one may consider whether one is already sworn by oneself or by the other.

- One withholds oaths, on the grounds that men are easily forsworn, and because the adversary having sworn does not pay back, while one thinks that they will convict him if he does not swear, and this danger – that of bearing it among the jurors – is better, for one will trust them but not him.
- One refuses an oath, on the grounds that the oath is for money, and that if one were base one would have sworn; for it would be better being base for something than for nothing. That

having sworn, one will have it, and that not having done so one will not, and that it is then done through virtue and not through perjury. The remark of Xenophanes comes in here, that 'this challenge is not fair, being of an impious man against a pious one',[36] rather as it is the same as if a strong man should challenge a weak one to strike or be struck.

- If one takes the oath, it is because one has confidence in oneself but not in the other, and, turning round Xenophanes' remark, one may say that it is only fair if the unholy man should give the oath and the holy man should swear, and that it is very bad if one does not wish to oneself, on matters on which one thinks that the jurors should swear before giving judgement.

- If one gives an oath, it is because it is pious to wish to entrust things to the gods and because the other should have no need of other judges (for one entrusts judgement to him), and because it would be absurd not to be ready to swear on matters on which he requires the jurors to swear.

- Since it is in each case clear how we should speak, it is also clear how we should speak with a joint oath. For example: if the speaker wishes to take but not to give, and if he gives but does not wish to take, and if he wishes both to take and to give or neither. For it must be composed from what has been said, so *1377b* that the arguments are also composed from the foregoing.

- But if an oath should have been taken by the speaker and be against the present oath, one must say that it is not a perjury. For to do injustice is voluntary, perjury is an injustice and things done under force or error are involuntary. Here we should conclude that perjury is done with the intellect and not with the tongue. If the oath sworn should be contrary to the adversary, we may say that he destroys everything by not abiding by his oaths; for this is also why jurors apply the laws under oath. And: 'They expect you to abide by the oaths by which you swore to judge, but they themselves do not abide by theirs.' And anything else that one might say by way of expansion.

Let that much suffice on the subject of the non-technical proofs.

PART TWO: EMOTION AND CHARACTER

quiz: commonsense, (intelligence), good will,
virtue   or-status
(which does A not mention as a
cause of a speaker's [writer's]
being (persuasive)

SECTION SIX: EMOTION

CHAPTER 2.1. THE ROLE OF EMOTION AND CHARACTER

In the opening remarks to the whole work, Aristotle appeared as a staunch supporter of the prevailing Academic consensus, inherited directly from Plato, that the contemporary practice of oratory, with its shameless emotionalism and attempts at psychological manipulation of the audience, was not worthy to be classed as so rational a thing as an art. There is, to be sure, an art of rhetoric, distinct from the dialectical branch of logic though with an affinity to it, but its scope is narrowly defined. Its business is exclusively the study of those kinds of demonstration whose persuasiveness rests on probability rather than complete logical cogency. It therefore concentrates on the two methods of rhetorical persuasion: the enthymeme, the rhetorical equivalent of the dialectical syllogism, and the example, the equivalent of induction. In fact, in the first part of the work, Aristotle concentrates entirely on the former, explaining how the genres of oratory arise from the variety of propositions that can form the premises of enthymematic arguments.

On the other hand, there had also been hints of equivocation in the admittance of two species of proof — that by character and that by emotion — that cannot be classed as demonstrative. Aristotle is, by a dexterous feat of legerdemain, both having his cake and eating it. By classing the use of emotion and character as species of proof, he is able to bring these two undeniable features of rhetorical practice within the scope of a theory of rhetoric whose formal definition is that it is the study of proof and nothing more. The feeling that a double standard is being used in the castigation of his predecessors and in his own practice is reinforced by the discussion of emotion and character, especially the former, that we find in the second Part of the work. With what might well be called Macchiavellian cynicism, he demonstrates the means whereby the chosen emotion can be brought into being in the minds of the audience, with no direct connection to the specific substance of the plea. This no doubt contributes to making the overall standpoint of the work rather less Olympian than we at first feel, but it has the advantage both of giving us a clearer insight into the thinking of practising orators of the age and of allowing Aristotle to show here as elsewhere in the work his perceptiveness in the study of the mechanics of human behaviour. For his approach to the problem of creating emotion, especially, recognizes with admirable sophistication that men are in any given emotional state as a result of three factors: their underlying psychological condition, the events that provoke the emotion and the intentional objects of the emotion. This subtle schema leads to a stimulating survey of a variety of emotions, which is characteristically rich in insights and which, as Schofield has pointed out, is conspicuous for its clear appreciation of the rationality of emotion.

CHAPTER 2.1

The elements, then, from which one should both exhort and deter, both praise and disparage, both accuse and defend, and the kind of opinions and premises that are useful for the proof of these, are those that have been given. For the enthymemes have to do with these and arise from them, as befitting each particular genre of speech.

But since the objective of rhetoric is judgement (for men *give* judgement on political issues and a court case *is* a judgement), we must have regard not only to the speech's being demonstrative and persuasive, but also to *establishing the speaker himself as of a certain type* and *bringing the giver of judgement into a certain condition*. For this makes a great difference as regards proof, especially in deliberative oratory, but also in court cases – this appearance of the speaker to be of a certain kind and his making the audience suppose that he is disposed in a certain way towards them, and in addition the condition that they are themselves disposed in a certain way to him.[1] Now the appearance of the speaker to have a certain character is more useful for political oratory, and the given disposition of the audience for the courts. For things do not seem the same to those who love and those who hate, nor to those who are angry and those who are calm, but either altogether different or different in magnitude. For to the friend the man about whom he is giving 1378a judgement seems either to have committed no offence or a minor one, while for the enemy it is the opposite. And to the man who is enthusiastic and optimistic, if what is to come should be pleasant, it seems to be both likely to come about and likely to be good, while to the indifferent or depressed man it seems the opposite.

There are three causes of the speakers' themselves being persuasive; for that is the number of the sources of proof other than demonstration. They are *common sense, virtue* and *goodwill.* For men lie about what they are urging or claiming through either all or some of the following: they either have the wrong opinions through stupidity, or, while having the correct opinions, through perversity they fail to say what they think; or they have common sense and integrity but are not well-disposed, whence they might not give the best advice, though they know it; and there are no other causes besides. So it must be that the man who is thought to have all of our first list is persuasive to the audience. Now the means of appearing to have common sense and integrity can be drawn from the distinctions we have given in connection with the virtues. For from the same points one might make both oneself and another seem to be of this kind. But about goodwill and friendship we must speak in the discussion of the emotions.

Emotions are those things by the alteration of which men differ with regard to those judgements which pain and pleasure accompany, such as anger, pity, fear and all other such and their opposites. One must in each case divide the discussion into three parts. Take the case of anger. We must say *what state* men are in when they are angry, with *what people* they are accustomed to be angry and in *what circumstances.*[2] For if we have one or two, but not all, of these, it would be impossible to engender anger. And it is the same with the others. So just as, in the earlier discussion, we went through the premisses, so let us do about this here as well, drawing our distinctions in the way mentioned.

CHAPTER 2.2. ANGER

Anger is the first of ten specific emotions to be studied. Of these, four (calm, friendship, favour and pity) are positive and six (anger, fear, shame, indignation, envy and jealousy) are negative. Although the length and detail of treatment varies considerably, the tripartite schema of explanation (by psychological state, description of the provoking events and character of the human objects) is followed throughout. It is also quite apparent that Aristotle is more motivated in this Section by the general fascination that human nature had for him than by a concern to cover all aspects of rhetorical practice. He never forgets, however, the avowedly practical character of the discussion. We can also see in the treatment of each emotion a clear example of the definitional approach, in which first the emotion itself is analysed into its constituents and then these are further analysed into their own. When a level of explanation has been reached at which further analysis would be either impossible or unproductive, the elements of the explanation are then copiously illustrated.

CHAPTER 2.2

Let anger, then, be desire, accompanied by pain, for revenge for an obvious belittlement of oneself or one of one's dependants, the belittlement being uncalled for.

If, then, this is anger, then the angry man must always be angry with a *particular person* (e.g. with Cleon, but not with mankind), and because that man has done or is about to do something to the *1378b* angry man himself or one of his dependants, and with all anger there must be an attendant *pleasure*, that from the *prospect of revenge*. For it is pleasant to think that one will achieve what one seeks, and nobody seeks those things that are obviously impossible for him, so that the angry man too aims at something that is possible for him. Thus the following is a fair comment about wrath:

> Which sweeter far is than ooze of honey
> And grows in human hearts . . .[3]

For a certain pleasure accompanies it for this reason and because men dwell on their revenge in their thoughts. Thus the imagination arising on these occasions produces a pleasure like that of dreams.

Since, moreover, *belittlement is a realization of an opinion about what seems to be of no value* (for we think that both good and bad things are worth taking seriously and things tending to that condition; while whatever is of little or no importance, we suppose to be worth no consideration), there are three forms of belittlement: *contempt, spite and insult.* For to be *contemptuous* is to belittle (for it is of the things that they think of no importance that men are contemptuous and it is also such things that they belittle), and the *spiteful* man also seems to belittle. For *spite is the blocking of another's wishes not for some advantage to oneself but as a mere disadvantage to him.* Thus, in that it is not for one's own advantage, it is a belittlement. For it clearly supposes that the other will do no harm, since otherwise one would be afraid of him and not belittle him, nor be capable of performing any service worthy of mention, as one would then have the intention to be friendly. And *insult* is also belittlement. For an *insult consists of doing or saying such things as involve shame for the victim, not for some advantage to oneself other than that these have been done, but for the fun of it;* for those returning an injury are not insulting but taking revenge. The cause of pleasure for those insulting is that they think that by treating others badly they are themselves the superior (that is why the young and the rich tend to insult; for in their insults they feel they are superior); and there is a dishonouring in an insult, and to dishonour is to belittle. For what is of no worth has no honour, either good or bad. Hence the remark of the angry Achilles:

> He showed me no respect – he has my prize . . .[4]

and:

> As though I were some worthless vagabond . . .[5]

These being the reasons for his anger. For men think it right that they should be revered by those inferior to them by birth, by power and by virtue and in general by whatever it is in which they much excel; for instance, with money, the rich have this attitude to the poor, and in speaking the rhetorician has it to the men who cannot speak, and the ruler to the ruled, and the man fit to rule to the man fit to be ruled. Hence:

1379a

> Great wrath there is in god-protected kings . . .[6]

and:

> But yet a lingering grudge he bears . . .[7]

For they are vexed because of their superiority. Also with those by whom one thinks one should be well treated. These are those whom one has treated well or is treating well, either oneself or one of one's dependants, or wishes to or has wished to.

It is already clear, then, from these points in what *condition* of themselves men are angry and with whom and for what sort of things. *Their personal condition is when they are in pain*; for those in pain always aim at something.

- If, then, someone opposes whatever this is directly, such as drinking for the thirsty man, or even if not, he yet seems to be doing the same thing.
- And if one were to act against the man or not co-operate or in any other way obstruct him in this condition, with all these he will be angry. So when men are sick, or poor, or in love, or thirsty or in general in a state of unrequited desire, they are hot-tempered and easily provoked, especially towards those who belittle their current predicament, as the sick man is angry with those who attach little importance to his illness, the poor man with those who do this to his poverty, the man at war with those who do it about the war, the lover with those who do it about love, and so also with the other cases; for each man is guided towards his peculiar anger by his present suffering.
- Also if he should have been expecting the opposite. For what is greatly unexpected is the more painful, as the great unexpectedness is also more pleasant if what is wished happens. From these considerations it should be clear what seasons, times, dispositions and ages are easily moved to anger and where and when – when men are the more in these circumstances, they are the more easily moved.

In these personal states, then, men are easily moved to anger.
Now, they are angry with:

- Those that laugh at them and jeer and scoff at them (this is insulting), and those who harm them in such ways as are suggestive of insult. And these actions must be of such a kind as are neither in return for anything nor beneficial to those who do them; for it is then that they seem to be done by way of insult.

- Those who speak ill of or despise the things about which they are especially serious, as for instance those ambitious in philosophy are angry with anyone who speaks ill of philosophy, those who are proud of their beauty with anyone who speaks ill of beauty, and so also with the other cases. But all the more so, if they suspect that they do not have these things, either not at all or not securely, or are not thought to have them; for whenever they think that they are comfortably superior in the *1379b* respects in which they are mocked, they take no notice. And they are more angry with friends than with non-friends; for they think that they should rather be well-treated by them than not.

- Those who are accustomed to respect them and show them consideration, if they do not on another occasion so address them. For they think that they are being despised by them, as they would otherwise be doing the same as before. *reciprocity*

- Those who do not do good back in return for a good deed.

- Those in opposition to them, if they are inferior. For all those of this kind seem contemptuous, some as inferiors, others as those acting for inferiors.

- Those who are of no account – if these belittle them somehow, they are the more angry; for anger at belittlement was assumed to be directed against those who should not belittle, and it is appropriate for inferiors not to belittle their betters.

- Friends, if they do not speak or act well, and even more if they do the opposite, and if they do not perceive their needs, as Antiphon's Plexippus with Meleager; for non-perception of such things is a sign of disregard, as we notice what we take seriously.

- Those who rejoice and generally show delight in our misfortunes, as this is a sign either of enmity or of disregard.

- Those who do not notice if they cause pain, which is also why men are angry with those who bring bad news.

145

- Those who either hear or see shameful things connected with themselves, as they are the same as despisers and enemies. For friends are sympathetic, and the observation of our own short-comings makes us all sad.
- Those belittling them in front of five groups: those of whom they are emulous; those whom they admire; those by whom they want to be admired; those whom they respect; or those who respect them. If before one of these groups one should show them disregard, they are the more angry.
- Those who disregard those whom it is disgraceful for them not to defend, such as parents, children, womenfolk and dependants.
- Those who are ungrateful, as the disregard is against what is proper.
- Those who are ironic when they are serious, since irony is con-temptuous.
- Those who do well by others but not by themselves. For it is indeed contemptuous not to esteem someone as everybody else. Forgetfulness is also productive of anger, such as that of names, trivial as it is. For forgetfulness too is thought to be an indication of disregard. For the forgetfulness arises through lack of con-cern, and lack of concern is a species of disregard.

1380a We have jointly said with what sort of people men are angry, in what condition and for what reasons; it would obviously be neces-sary in the speech to make the audience such as to be disposed to anger, and the opponents to be such as are those with whom men are angry and guilty of the things about which they are angry.

CHAPTER 2.3. CALM

Aristotle is notoriously overfond of contrast, but it is found much less in the present discussion of the emotions than, for instance, in the discussion of the virtues in the Nicomachean Ethics. *In fact, there are only three pairs of clearly contrasting emotions in the whole discussion — anger and calm, friendship and enmity and fear and confidence — and these are all naturally at home in a discussion of the oratorical production of emotion. Given that in any rhetorical contrast a speaker has to undo the emotion-producing work of his adversary, it is perhaps strange that the discussion of the emotions is not arranged with still more emphasis on contrast. However, Aristotle points out in the other cases that the way to undo an emotion is merely the mirror opposite of the way to produce it.*

CHAPTER 2.3

Now since being angry is the opposite of *being calm*, and anger the opposite of *calmness*, we must grasp in what condition men are calm and towards whom they comport themselves calmly and by what means they are calmed down. *Let calming, then, be a suspension and placation of anger.*[8]

- If, then, men are angry with those who disregard them, and disregard is a voluntary thing, it is obvious that with those indeed who do none of these things or who do them unwillingly or seem to be of these kinds men are calm.
- And also with those who wished for the opposite of what they did.
- And with all those who behave in the same way towards themselves; for it is thought that nobody disregards himself.
- Also with those that confess and repent – because they have retribution, as it were, in the pain felt by the wrong-doers for their deeds, they cease from anger. There is an indication of this in the punishment of slaves; for those who contradict and deny we punish the more, but before those who admit that they are justly punished we cease being angry. The reason is that there is disrespect in denying what is obvious, and shamelessness is both disregard and contempt – before those whom we much despise we are not respectful.
- Also with those who humble themselves before them and do not contradict; for they appear to be agreeing that they are inferior – the inferior are afraid and nobody who fears disregards others. That anger ceases before the humble, dogs even show by not biting those who are sitting down.
- Also with those who are serious when they are serious, as these

are thought to be taking them seriously and not despising them.

- Also with those who have done them more than compensating favours.

- Also with those who beg and beseech, as they show relative humility.

- Also with those who are not insulting or mocking, nor disregardful of anyone or not of good men nor of such as themselves. (In general calming factors should be observed from their opposites.)

- Also with those before whom they feel fear or respect: as long as they feel so, men are not angry. It is impossible, after all, to be angry and afraid at the same time.

- And with those who have acted through anger they are either not angry or less angry, as they do not seem to have acted from disregard, since anger never generates disregard. Disregard is a painless thing, while anger is accompanied by pain.

1380b
- Also with those who respect them.

Obviously, when in the opposite *condition* to that of being angry, men are calm, for instance:

- When in play, in laughter, at a feast, when having a good time, in prosperity, in fulfilment and in general when free from pain and possessed of pleasure without insult and respectable good cheer.

- Also when time has passed and they are not under the immediate goad of anger. For time stills anger. And a greater anger with one man is also stopped by the previous taking of revenge on another. Hence the wisdom of Philocrates, who, when the people were enraged and someone asked, 'Why do you not give a defence?', replied, 'Not yet.' 'When then?' came the rejoinder, and his answer was, 'Whenever I shall see another man accused.' For men become calm when they have spent their wrath on another, as happened in the case of Ergophilus. For although the people were more angry with him than with Callisthenes, they let him off because they had sentenced Callisthenes to death on the previous day.[9]

148

- Also if they have gained a conviction.
- And if the offender should have suffered a greater harm than they would have inflicted out of anger – they think that they have, as it were, had their revenge.
- And if they think that they are doing wrong themselves and are justly suffering, as anger does not arise against justice. For they also do not think that they are suffering beyond what is right, and this was what anger was defined to be. And so one should first punish in speech; for even slaves are less vexed after this punishment.
- Also if they think that the offender will not perceive that the punishment is from them nor the reason for their suffering. For anger is directed towards the individual, as is clear from its definition. So the poet was right to sing:

> Say that it was Odysseus, city-sacker . . .[10]

Because Odysseus would not have taken vengeance if Polyphemus had not known both by whom and why he was injured. So neither are we angry with others who are not aware, nor with those who are already dead, as they have suffered the ultimate and will neither feel pain nor perceive anything, which is the aim of those who are angry. So the poet was right to say of Hector, when he wished to stop Achilles' anger with him after his death,

> The unfeeling earth in anger he insults . . .[11]

It is obvious, then, that those who wish to calm the audience down should speak from these premises, bringing the audience into the appropriate condition and making out those with whom they are angry to be either fearsome or worthy of respect or having done favours or acting involuntarily or being excessively pained at their deeds.

CHAPTER 2.4. FRIENDSHIP AND ENMITY

Let us now state whom it is that men *like and dislike*, and why, first defining *love* and *friendship*.

Let friendship,[12] *then, be wishing for someone what one thinks to be good things, for his sake and not for oneself, and being productive of these* 1381a *up to one's capacity.* And the friend is the man who befriends and is befriended in return, and those who think that they are in this rapport with one another think that they are friends. On these suppositions, *friends* must necessarily be:

- Those who share one's pleasure in good things and one's pain in painful ones for no other reason than for the sake of their friend. For all men are happy when what they want occurs, and are sad when the reverse happens, so that pains and pleasures are an indication of wishing.

- Those for whom the same things are good and bad are also friends, and those for whom the same people are friends and those for whom the same men are enemies. For these men must want the same things, and so by wishing for the same thing for himself and another, a man seems to be a friend of the other.

- Men also befriend those who have done well by them, either by themselves or by those whom they cherish, whether to a great extent or with good will, or in the appropriate circumstances and for their own sakes, or those whom they think would wish to do them good.

- Also the friends of friends and those whom their friends befriend, and those befriended by those whom they have befriended. And those hostile to their enemies and hating those whom they themselves hate, and those hated by those they hate. For there seem to be the same advantages for all these as for oneself, so that they are wishing good things for oneself, which was the mark of the friend.

- Also benefactors with regard to money and protection. This is why men like the liberal and the brave and the just. And they assume to be of this kind those who do not live off others. And such are those who live from their toil, and of these those who live from farming and of the others the self-employed especially.

- Also the restrained, as they are not unjust.

- Also the uninquisitive, for the same reason.
- And those of whom we wish to be friends, if they obviously also wish it. And of this kind are those who are good in respect of virtue and those with good repute either among all men or among the best or among those admired by them or among those who admire them.
- Also those with whom it is pleasant to spend time and pass the day; and of this kind are the easy-tempered and those not critical of our faults and not keen for a quarrel or implacable in discord (for all such are prone to strife, and people at strife seem to wish for opposite things), and those skilled both in cracking a joke and in taking one. In both ways they seek the same as their neighbour, being able to be mocked and mocking with grace.
- Also those who praise one's good features, and of these features especially those that one fears are not present.
- And those pure in appearance and clothing and the whole of 1381b life.
- And those critical about neither one's failings nor one's good deeds; for there can be critics of both.
- And those who do not bear grudges, nor store up wrongs against them, but are easily appeased. For as one sees them to be towards others, so does one think that they will be towards oneself.
- And those who do not speak badly and know the evils neither of their neighbours nor of themselves, but the good things; for these things are what the good man does.
- And those who do not oppose those who are angry or serious, as such men are prone to fight.
- And those who are in some way seriously disposed towards them, for instance admiring them or supposing them to be serious and being pleased with them, experiencing this especially in connection with the things about which they themselves most wish to be admired or thought to be serious or pleasant.
- And those who are like them and have the same practices, if they do not get in each other's way and their living is not derived from the same source. Hence the expression 'Potter to potter.'[13]

- Also those who are keen for the same things, in which they can jointly participate – if not, the same problem arises here too.
- And those to whom they so stand as not to be ashamed in things touching their reputation, though not despising them.
- And those before whom they are ashamed of true blemishes.
- And those before whom they are ambitious, or by whom they wish to be admired and not envied – these they either befriend or wish to be friends.
- And those with whom they would co-operate to advantage, if there should not be likely to be some greater disadvantage to themselves.
- And those who equally love the present and the absent friend; which is why all men love those who are of this kind in relation to the dead.
- And in general those who are markedly fond of friends and do not desert them; for of good men it is those good at friendship that are most liked.
- And those who do not put on a pretence with them; and of this kind are those who tell even bad things about them – for it has been said that before friends we are not ashamed of the things pertaining to reputation. So if the man ashamed is not a friend, the man who is not ashamed is probably a friend.
- Also those who are not fearsome, and those who encourage us; for no one is a friend of the man he fears.

The species of friendship are companionship, intimacy, consanguinity and so on, and the factors productive of it are the favour and acting without being asked and not revealing that one has acted. For thus the action seems to be for the friend's sake and for no other reason.

1382a Clearly we must consider *hostility and hatred* on the basis of their opposites. The things *productive of hostility* are *anger, insult, slander.* Anger arises from things related to the subject, but hostility can also arise without personal involvement. For if we suppose a man to be of a certain kind, we hate him. And anger always has to do with individuals, such as Callias or Socrates, while hatred can also be directed at types. For everyone hates a thief and an informer. And anger is curable by time, but hatred not. The former is a pursuit of pain, the latter of evil; for the angry man wants to witness the punishment, but for the hater it makes no difference, since painful things are all perceptible, while those which are particularly bad (injustice and stupidity) are least perceptible. For the presence of wickedness causes no pain. And anger is attended by pain, the other not; for the angry man is in pain, but not the hater. And an angry man might feel pity in many circumstances, but the other in none; for the one wants the man with whom he is angry to suffer in return, while the hater wants his enemy not to exist.

It is clear from this that it is possible both to demonstrate existing enmities and friendships and to create ones that do not exist and dissolve those that are claimed, and through anger and hatred to lead our adversaries in whichever direction one would prefer.

CHAPTER 2.5. FEAR AND CONFIDENCE

The discussion of fear is also combined with that of its opposite, confidence. The same subjects are covered from a more biological perspective in the De Anima (*III. 13–14*).

CHAPTER 2.5

It will next be made clear what sort of things and whom men fear and in what condition. *Let fear, then, be a kind of pain or disturbance resulting from the imagination of impending danger, either destructive or painful*; for not all evils are feared, such as that someone should become unjust or slow, but such as can produce great pain or destruction, and these if they are not remote but near, so as to seem impending. For things at a great remove are not feared. All men, for instance, know that they will die, but because it is not near, they think nothing of it. If, then, fear is this, then such things must be fearsome as seem to have great capacity to destroy or to do damage which conduces to great pain. Hence are the indications of such things also fearsome, as the fearsome thing seems near at hand. For that is what *danger* is – *the proximity of the frightening.*

Such indications are:

● The hostility and anger of those capable of taking some action (for it is clear that they wish to and that they are able to, so that they are close to doing it), and also injustice backed by power; for it is in his purposes that the unjust man is unjust.

1382b • Also insulted virtue with power (for virtuous men would obviously choose to do harm after being insulted in all cases, and are able to do so in the present one), and the fear of those who can take action; for such a man must also needs be in readiness to act. And since the generality of men tend to the bad and are not above profiteering and are cowardly in dangers, it is fearsome for the most part to be in the power of another, so that those who know that someone has done something serious show their fear either by exposing or by abandoning him.

• Also those able to do wrong to those able to be wronged; for men, for the most part, do commit crimes when they can.

• Also those who have been wronged or think that they are being wronged; for they are always looking for an opportunity.

• Those too who have done wrong are, if they have power, fearsome, from fear of suffering in return; for such a thing we supposed to be fearsome.

• Also rivals for advantages that both parties cannot simultaneously enjoy; for there is permanent contention with such people.

• Also those who are fearsome for one's superiors; for they would be the more able to harm us, if they could harm even them.

• Also those whom one's superiors in fact fear, for the same reason.

• Also those who have overcome one's superiors and those who attack their inferiors; for they are fearsome either currently or after their aggrandizement.

• And of the injured and hostile or antipathetic not those of sharp spirit and ready speech, but those who are mild and ironic and mischievous; for it is unclear when they are near to action, so that it is never obvious that they are remote from it.

• And all fearsome things are the more fearsome in so far as one's errors cannot be rectified, but are either completely unsusceptible of being put right or not in one's own power but in that of one's enemies.

• And those things in which one has no assistance or none that is easy. And to speak generally, all things are fearsome which, happening to others or likely to, are pitiable.

These then are, so to speak, more or less the most serious of fearsome things or things that are actually feared. Let us now say in what *condition* men are when they are afraid. If, then, fear is attended by a certain expectation of undergoing some destructive experience, it is clear that none of those who thought that they were going to suffer nothing would fear either such things as they would not think that they would suffer or those by whom they would not think that they were going to be harmed, nor at times when they would not so think. So it must be those who think that they will suffer something that are afraid that they will be harmed in certain ways by certain people at a certain time.

● Now those in great prosperity or seeming to be would not expect *1383a* to suffer (hence their arrogance, disregard and brazenness, the product of wealth, strength, good connections or power), nor those who reckon they have already suffered everything terrible and are numbed as regards the future, such as those who are actually being crucified; there must be some hope left of survival from their predicament. The evidence is that fear makes men deliberative, yet none deliberates about hopeless cases. So one must put the audience into the state, whenever it is for the best that they should be afraid, of thinking that they are in a position to suffer by pointing out that others, greater than them, have in fact suffered, and must show similar men suffering or having suffered, and from such quarters as they did not expect, and unexpected damages at unexpected times.

Since we have become clear to some extent about fear and fearsome things, and the condition of men in each case of fear, it is clear from this discussion what *confidence* is and about what things men are confident and in what condition they are confident. For confidence is the opposite of fear and the confidence-inspiring of the fearsome, so that the hope of safety is accompanied by the imagination of its proximity and of the non-existence or remoteness of fearsome things. Confidence is inspired by:

- The remoteness of fearsome things and the proximity of salutary ones, and also if there are many supports and assistances or great ones or both, and if one has neither done nor suffered wrong, and if either one has no opponents at all or they have no power, or, having power, are friendly or have done or received a good turn, or if one's interests coincide with those of the majority or with the stronger or with both.

It is in the following personal *conditions* that men have confidence:

- If they think that many things have come off and that they have not suffered, or if they have frequently got into danger and escaped it. For men become free from suffering in two ways: either by not having been put to the test or by having protections, as, with the dangers at sea, those unfamiliar with storms are confident for the future and those who have protection because of their experience.
- And when a thing should not be fearsome to one's equals, nor to one's inferiors nor to those to whom one believes one is superior; and one thinks this about those one has bettered – either themselves or those more powerful than them or equal to them.
- Also if one thinks that one has more and better assets, by the excess of which one is fearsome; these things are abundance of money, bodily strength, the strength of one's friends and land and equipments for war, either all or the most important.
- Also if one should have done none wrong or not many or not the sort of whom one is afraid, and in general if one's relations with the gods are on a good footing, especially from signs and oracles; anger, after all, is a source of confidence, and not to have wronged but to have been wronged is productive of anger, and divinity is supposed to support the wronged.
- Also when, in undertaking an enterprise, one thinks that one will either suffer nothing (immediately or later) or will succeed.

So much, then, for the sources of fear and confidence.

1383b

CHAPTER 2.6. SHAME

With shame the opposite, presumably pride, is given only the most cursory acknowledgement. Shame, however, is connected with honour, respect and status and these concepts require relatively extended examination in their own right. It is notable how skilfully Aristotle prevents an overlap in this chapter with the discussion of happiness in the treatment of demonstration (Chapter 1.5).

CHAPTER 2.6

Those things for which men do or do not feel *shame*, and before whom and in what condition, will next be made clear. *Let shame, then, be a kind of pain or disturbance in connection with those evils that appear to pertain to disrepute, whether present, past or future, and shamelessness be a kind of disregard and apathy in connection with the same things.* If, then, shame is as defined, then men must be ashamed at such evils as appear to be shameful either for themselves or for the objects of their concern; and of this kind are:

- All works of viciousness, such as throwing away one's shield or running away, as they are products of cowardice.
- Also to withhold a deposit – a product of injustice.
- Also sleeping with women with whom one should not or where one should not or when one should not, which are products of a lack of restraint.
- Also to profit from small, shameful things or from helpless people, such as beggars or dead men (whence the proverb about taking from the dead), as these are signs of shameful money-grubbing and illiberality.
- Also not giving financial assistance when one can or giving too little.
- Also being assisted by those less well off, and borrowing when the other is himself likely to ask, and asking for a loan when one is being asked back, and the converse, and to praise so as to seem to be asking and persisting in one's demands even after rebuttal; for all these things are signs of illiberality, and the

praise of those who are present also is a mark of flattery, as also excessive praise of good points and omission of bad ones and excessive distress at the distress of one present and all other such things, which are signs of flattery.

1384a
- Also failure to endure hardships borne by the old or the delicate or those of greater estate or in general those less able, which are all signs of softness.

- Also being benefited by another, and especially frequently, and to criticize the good deed; for all these are signs of small-mindedness and pettiness.

- Also constantly talking about oneself and making claims and representing other men's achievements as one's own – all signs of braggartry.

- And similarly with other moral failings, their products and signs and similarities; for they are base and shameless.

- And in addition not to have a share in goods in which all men share, or all similar men or the majority – by similars I mean compatriots, fellow-citizens, contemporaries, relatives and in general those on a par – for it is indeed shameful not to have a share of, say, education to the appropriate extent and similarly with the others.

- And all these things the more if it seems to be one's own fault; for they are thus the more out of vice, if one should oneself be responsible for those faults that have been or those that there are or will be.

- And men are ashamed at having undergone or undergoing or being about to undergo such things as pertain to dishonour and blame; and such are things pertaining to debasements either of the body or in base deeds, of which perversion is one.

- Also those things that pertain to incontinence, both voluntary and involuntary (those that pertain to force are involuntary); for to endure without defence is a sign of unmanliness or cowardice.

The things, then, of which men are ashamed are these and such like. And since shame is an imagination connected with disrepute, and felt for its own sake and not for its consequences, and none considers reputation except through those who confer it, one must needs feel shame before those whom one *holds in regard*; and one has *regard* for:

- Those who admire one and those one admires and for those by whom one wishes to be admired and those against whom one is ambitious and those whose opinion one does not despise. Men wish, then, to be admired by these men and admire those who have some good thing of those held in honour, or those from whom they happen to have great need of something within their control, as with lovers; they are ambitious against one another.
- And men have regard for prudent people as truth-tellers, and such are those who are older and educated.
- Also things more before men's eyes and in the open (whence the proverb about shame dwelling in the eyes);[14] for this reason men feel more shame before those who will always be present and those who pay heed to them, as both these groups have *1384b* been in their sight.
- Also before those not guilty of the things alleged; for it is clear that they have opposite outlooks.
- Also those who are not tolerant of those that seem to err; for what someone has done himself, this he is said not to criticize in his neighbours, so that it is evident that he criticizes the things that he does not himself do.
- Also those who pass on gossip to many people – for not to disapprove and not to gossip come to the same; and it is those that have been wronged that gossip, from their being on their guard, and also the malicious – for if they slander even those who have not erred, they will slander those that do so all the more.
- Also those whose time is spent on the errors of their neighbours, such as satirists and comedians; for they are in a way malicious tell-tales.
- Also those among whom one has had no lack of success, as they are almost in the position of admirers. Thus men are ashamed before those who first ask for something as they have not yet

lost their reputation among them; and of this kind are those who have lately wished to be their friends (for their best points have been observed; whence the aptness of Euripides' reply to the Syracusans),[15] and those known for some time and those that are not aware of one's misdeeds.

- And men are shamed not only at the shameful things mentioned but also at the signs of them, for instance not only at making love but also at the signs of it, and not only when doing base things but even when mentioning them. Similarly they are not only embarrassed by the groups mentioned but also by those who will inform them, such as servants and their friends.

- And in general they are not ashamed before those whose opinion of the truth they greatly despise (for none feels shame before children and animals), nor of the same things before those who are acquaintances and those who are not, but with acquaintances about things pertaining to real shame and with those who are not about those pertaining to conventional shame.

Shame occurs in the following personal *conditions*:

- First of all if they should happen to have connected with them some of those we have mentioned. And these are those who are admired or admire, or those by whom they wish to be admired, or those of whom they have some need which they would not fill if in disgrace. And these are either those seeing (as in Cydias' public address about the settlement on Samos – for he invited the Athenians to suppose that the Greeks were standing round them in a circle, so as not merely to hear but also to see what they might decree),[16] or those near by or those likely to find out; that is why in misfortune men never want to be seen by their rivals – for our rivals are our admirers.

1385a - Also when they have deeds or words to be ashamed of, either of themselves or of their ancestors or of others with whom they have a certain affinity. And in general those whom they themselves respect; and these are the groups mentioned and those connected with them, or those of whom they have been teachers or advisers, or if there should be other similar ones before whom they are ambitious. For out of shame before these they both do and do not do many things.

• And when likely to be seen and caught in the open, with those who know they are the more ashamed; hence indeed the poet Antiphon, about to be knouted by Dionysius, asked, when he saw those to die with him veiled as they went through the gates, 'Why do you veil yourselves? Unless tomorrow any of these people is going to see you.'[17]

So much about shame; with the case of shamelessness we will clearly make adequate progress from the opposites.

CHAPTER 2.7. FAVOUR

The Greek word kharis *is at least as wide in meaning as* philia. *It covers both favour and gratitude, as well, indeed, as charm (derived from its cognate* kharisma), *grace and general agreeability. The discussion of it here is the shortest of the treatments of the emotions, no doubt mainly because most of the possible material has already been used in the discussion of friendship. There is also no real opposite – a feature, too, of the remaining items in the list, with the interesting exception of pity.*

CHAPTER 2.7

To what people men show *favour* and in what circumstances and what personal conditions will become clear after we have defined favour. *Let favour, then, be that by which he that has it is said to do a good turn – a service to the asker in return for nothing else – to the advantage not of the server himself but of the beneficiary.* It is a great favour if the petition is urgent, or the service is of great and difficult things, or on the appropriate occasions, or when he acts alone or first or conspicuously. And the requests are the desires, and of these especially those whose non-requital brings pain. And of these kinds are the appetites, such as sex, and those occurring in the discomforts of the body or in dangers; for both the man in danger and the man

in pain have appetites. Hence those helping someone in poverty
or exile, even if the service should be slight, gain favour through
the greatness of the need and the situation, such as the man who
gave the mat in the Lyceum.[18] The service should especially have
to do with the same degree, and if not with an equal or greater
one. Thus, since it is clear both to whom and in what circumstances gratitude occurs and for men in what condition, it is clear
that it must be established from these points, one side showing
either to be or to have been in the appropriate pain and need and
the other to have performed in this need the appropriate service
or to be performing it. It is also clear whence the element of
1385b favour can be removed and men made ungrateful; one must show
that the service either was done or is being done for the doer's
sake (this would not be a favour), or that it was done by chance
or compulsion, or that it was a return and not a gift, either with
or without knowledge; in either case, there is an element of repayment, so that in these circumstances it would also not be a favour.
We must also consider it under all the categories; for favour is
either a particular thing or an amount or a kind or a time or
place. And an indication of lack of favour occurs if they should
not perform even a lesser service, and if they did the same or
equal or more for one's enemies; for it is clear that these things
are also not for one's own sake. Or if a negligible favour was
done by those who knew it to be so; for none agrees that he
needs trivia.

CHAPTER 2.8. PITY

*With the discussion of pity, Aristotle reaches one of the most central
interests of his predecessors and a subject almost exclusively appropriate to
forensic oratory. His treatment of it here is relatively summary by contrast
with its traditional importance, but this is no doubt partly because considerations of the arousing of pity occur with peculiar frequency in the discussion
of style. This is also one of the clearest points of contact between the
Rhetoric and the Poetics, where pity, of course, plays a key role in the
famous definition of tragedy.*

CHAPTER 2.8

We have spoken of giving and withholding favour. Let us now say what things are *pitiable* and what men people *pity* and in what personal condition.[19] *Let pity then, be a certain pain occasioned by an apparently destructive evil or pain's occurring to one who does not deserve it, which the pitier might expect to suffer himself or that one of his own would, and this whenever it should seem near at hand.* For it is clear that the man who is to have pity must think that he is such as to suffer something bad either in himself or in one of his friends, and an evil of such a kind as given in the definition or similar or equivalent.

- Hence those who are wholly destroyed do not pity (for they would no longer expect to suffer anything, as they have already suffered everything), nor those thinking themselves to be in excessive happiness, who are rather arrogant; for if they think that they have all good things, they will obviously think that they also have the impossibility of suffering any harm, which is also among the good things.

- And those who are of the kind who might think they would suffer, who have already suffered and escaped, and those who are maturer both in prudence and in experience, and the weak and those who are relatively cowardly and the educated, as they calculate easily.

- Also those who have parents or children or wives; for these are theirs and they have the possibility of suffering the things mentioned.

- And those not under the influence of bravery, such as in anger or confidence (for these emotions take little account of what is to come), nor those of an arrogant disposition (for they also pay little heed to future suffering), but those who are intermediate to these.

- Nor again those in great fear; for terrified men do not feel pity, because of its being supplementary to their proper emotion.

- Also if they should think that there are some reasonable men; for he who thinks none to be such will think that all men are worthy of evil.

1386a ● And in general whenever they should be in a state to remember such things having happened either to themselves or to one of their friends or to expect these to happen.

We have said in what personal condition men feel pity, and what they pity is clear from the definition; for all painful and bitter things that are destructive are pitiable, and those that are annihilatory, and those great evils for which chance is responsible. The painful and destructive things are death, bodily tortures and injuries, old age, disease and shortage of food, and the evils for which chance is responsible are having few or no friends (hence is it also pitiable to be torn from friends and comrades), ugliness, weakness, deformity and the occurrence of an ill from a source from which a good thing was expected, and this frequently happening, and some good having come only after suffering, as when the gifts of the king were sent to Diopeithes after his death,[20] and either nothing good's occurring or, when it does, there being no enjoyment of it.

These and the like are the *things* about which men feel pity. The *men* they pity are:

● Acquaintances, if they are not very close to them in kinship (with the latter their attitude is as for their future selves; hence indeed Amasius did not weep when his son was taken off to be executed, as they say, but did when his friend was begging him[21] – for the latter was pitiable, the former terrible; and what is terrible is different from the pitiable and drives out pity and is often useful for the opposite feeling, as men no longer pity when what is terrifying is near them), and men also pity their equals and contemporaries, by character, by habit, by esteem and by birth; for in all these cases it seems more likely that it could also happen to them – in general we should note here too that whatever men fear for themselves they pity when they happen to others.

● But since it is when they are near to hand that sufferings appear to be pitiable, while things that either have happened or will happen over ten thousand years and which they neither expect nor recall they either do not pity at all or not to the same extent, it is necessary that those who co-operate with it by gestures free of vice and clothes and general histrionics, should be more pitiable (for they make the evil seem more near, putting it before their eyes as it has happened or will happen – also things that have recently happened or will soon do so are *1386b* the more pitiable), both for this reason and because of the signs, such as the clothing of those who have suffered and so forth, and also the deeds and words and all the other things of those who are in suffering, such as those who are actually dying.

● And it is especially pitiable that serious men are in such predicaments; for all these things make the situation more pitiable through its appearing near, and because the suffering is undeserved and occurring before our eyes.

CHAPTER 2.9. INDIGNATION

Indignation is interestingly introduced as the opposite of pity, though it is admitted that it is so only after a fashion. Pity is grief at undeserved misfortune and indignation is grief at undeserved success. We might naturally classify the latter as envy, but, although Aristotle does not specifically distinguish between them in the text, he would surely do so on the grounds that indignation, unlike envy, cannot be removed by the subject's enjoying the same degree of success as the object. This certainly seems to reflect an intuitive difference between the emotions.

CHAPTER 2.9

The opposite of pity is particularly what men call *indignation*; for to grief over undeserved misfortune the counterpart is in a way of the same kind – grief over undeserved good fortune. Both experiences belong to a good character; for one should sympathize and feel pity for those who are unjustly faring badly and indignation at those undeservedly doing well; for the unjust is what occurs against merit – which is why we also ascribe indignation to the gods.[22]

Now it might seem that *envy* is in the same way the opposite of pity, as being itself close to, or identical with, indignation, but it is different; for envy too is a disturbing pain occasioned by prosperity,

165

though not of the unworthy man but rather of the equal and similar. And not the expectation that something different will happen to oneself, but disturbance on account of one's neighbour, should be the same for both groups; for the emotion will not be on the one hand envy and on the other indignation, but fear, if pain and disturbance are present, because of the fact that there will be some bad consequence for oneself from the other's prosperity.

And it is clear that the opposite emotions will also accompany these; for the man who is grieved by those who undeservedly fare badly will be delighted or be made to feel free from grief by those who fare badly in the opposite way, just as for parricides and murderers, when they are punished, no good man would be saddened; for one should be happy about such things, as also with those who deservedly fare well; for both things are just and make the reasonable man happy; for he must think that what has happened to his like might also happen to him. And all these traits belong to the same character, and the opposites to the opposite one; for the 1387a same man delights in malice and in envy; for things whose happening makes him sad, must make such a man glad by their removal and destruction. Thus all these feelings prevent pity (but they differ for the reasons given), so that they are all equally useful for making things not seem pitiable.

Let us, then, speak first of *indignation*, saying at what men feel it and in what circumstances and personal conditions, and then subsequently let us discuss the other emotions. The position is clear from what has been said; for if *indignation is grieving over undeserved good fortune*, it is first of all clear that we cannot be indignant at all good things; for if a man is just or brave or acquires a virtue, he will not be the object of indignation for this (nor do men pity their opposites), but men do feel indignation about wealth and power and such things as, in a word, the good are worthy of and those who have good features by nature, such as good birth and beauty and so forth.

- And since what is primordial seems to be something close to nature, it must be good that those that have the same advantage, if they should happen lately to have acquired it and for this reason their success, are more the objects of indignation; for the newly rich give more offence than those rich for many years and from their family. Similarly those who rule and have power and have many friends and good children and so forth. And if through these some other good thing should come to them, in the same way; for in this case too the newly rich give more offence in rule through their wealth than those of established money. And similarly also with the other cases. The reason is that one group seem to possess their own property, the others not; for what always seems to be of a certain kind is thought to have truth, so that the others seem not to have their own things.

- And since each good thing is not appropriate to a contingent holder, but there is a certain analogy and harmony, as the beauty of arms is suited not to the just but to the brave man, and splendid matches not to the newly rich but to the well-born, so if a man that is good does not achieve what suits him, indignation is called for.

- Also quarrels between an inferior and a superior, particularly with those in the same activity, whence indeed the remark:

> Battle he shunned with Ajax, son of Telamon,
> For wroth would Zeus be if he sought to fight
> With one far better . . .[23]

And if not, then the inferior with a superior in any respect, as *1387b* if a musician quarrelled with a just man, as justice is a better thing than music.

From these remarks it is clear with whom and on what grounds men are indignant; they are the ones mentioned and their like. They are in themselves *prone to indignation*:

- If they happen to be worthy of the greatest advantages and have obtained them; for those not similar to them cannot justly be thought worthy of similar advantages.

- And secondly, if they happen to be good and serious men; for they judge well and hate injustice.

- Also if they are ambitious and eager for certain offices, and especially if they are ambitious for the very things of which others are unworthy incumbents.

- And in general those who think themselves worthy of the things of which others are unworthy are indignant at those people for those things. Hence also the slavish and worthless and unambitious are not disposed to indignation; for there is nothing of which they think themselves to be worthy.

It is also clear from this in the misfortunes and discomfitures of what sort of men one should be glad or free from grief; for from what has been said the opposites are apparent, so that if the speech puts the jury into the appropriate state and shows that those asking to be pitied and the grounds of their request are not worthy to obtain it, but worthy not to obtain it, it will be impossible to pity them.

CHAPTER 2.10. ENVY

The discussion of envy is relatively brief because, no doubt, of its affinity to indignation, which has been treated at some length. The negative effect of envy on pity is stressed at the end, in a way which perhaps blurs slightly the contrast between envy and indignation.

CHAPTER 2.10

It is also clear whom men *envy*, on what grounds and in what conditions, given that *envy is a certain pain occasioned by apparent prosperity in the good things mentioned in the case of those like us, not for the acquisition of something, but because of those who have it.* For the men who will envy are:

- Those who have or seem to have some equals; and I mean equals by birth, by affinity, by age, by condition, by reputation and by possessions.
- And those who are not far off having everything (hence those who do great things and the fortunate are envious); for they think that all men are coveting their achievements.
- And those who are exceptionally honoured in some respect and especially for wisdom and happiness.

- And the ambitious are more envious than the unambitious. Also the seeming-wise; for they are ambitious for wisdom. And in general those who want a reputation for something are envious about it.
- Also the small-minded; for all things seem great to them.
- And some of the objects of envy have been mentioned; for the exploits or possessions about which men want reputation and *1388a* are ambitious and yearn for reputation, and all strokes of good fortune, about more or less all these there is envy, and especially for things that men desire themselves or think that they should have, or in the possession of which they are slightly in excess or slightly deficient.

It is also clear whom they envy; for it has already been said; for they envy those near them in time and place and age and reputation. Hence:

> Relationship knows also how to envy . . .[24]

- Also those before whom they are in rivalry; and they are in rivalry before the groups mentioned; but before those of ten thousand years ago or who have still to exist or are dead none is in rivalry, nor with those by the Gates of Heracles. Nor with those than whom they are thought by themselves or by many to be greatly inferior, nor with those whom they are thought greatly to excel, and one envies these similarly and about the same things.
- And since men are ambitious before competitors and rivals and in general before those who aim for the same things, these must be especially envied, whence the remark:

> Potter to potter . . .[25]

- And those whose success would be a blame for them (these are both near and similar); for it is clear that with these they will not achieve the good, so that this makes the envy painful.
- Also with those who either have or have acquired the sort of things that suit themselves or that they themselves once had; whence the old envy the young and those who have spent much those who have spent little on the same thing. And those who fail or achieve slowly envy those who achieve fast.

- It is also obvious what makes such men happy and in what circumstances and conditions; for the opposites of the condition that makes them unhappy will make them happy. So that if judges should themselves be put into this latter condition, while those who are asking for pity or to gain some advantage are in the condition we have described, it is obvious that they will not get pity from those in charge.

CHAPTER 2.11. JEALOUSY

The contrast between jealousy and envy is, of course, a notorious philosophical chestnut. Aristotle seems to draw the distinction primarily in terms of the idea of rivalry. Thus envy is an emotion primarily felt towards one's betters and jealousy one felt primarily towards one's equals. In any case, the present context does not require precise delineation of the conceptual boundaries here, so much as presentation of the ammunition available to the orator. It is noteworthy that at the end of the treatment of emotion Aristotle stresses the importance no less of removing than of creating the various feelings, though his account has been framed very much in terms of production rather than removal.

CHAPTER 2.11

In what conditions men are *jealous* and in what circumstances and for what, will next be revealed; for if *jealousy is a certain pain at the apparent presence of valued goods which one might have oneself in the case of those naturally similar to us, not because they are the other's but because they are not one's own* (hence jealousy is both reasonable and belongs to reasonable men, while envy is base and belongs to the base; for the one makes himself get good things by jealousy, while the other does not allow his neighbour to have them through envy), then:

1388b   • Those who think themselves worthy of advantages that they do not have must be jealous, if it is possible for them to get them; for none asks for things that seem impossible (hence the young and the magnanimous are of this kind).
- And jealous of those who have such good things as are worthy of

men held in respect – and these are wealth, many friends, political office and so forth; since they should have the goods that those good by nature should have, they are jealous of such goods.

- Also of those whom others think worthy of such goods.
- Also those whose ancestors or relatives or household or race or city is renowned are jealous about these advantages; for they think that these are proper to them and that they are worthy of them.
- And if respected goods are objects of jealousy, then the virtues must be of this kind, and things that are helpful and beneficial to others (for men honour benefactors and good men), and good things of which one's neighbours have the enjoyment, such as wealth and beauty rather than health.

It is also clear what men are the objects of jealousy:

- For those who have acquired the same or same sort of things as those mentioned are objects of jealousy (and these things are the ones mentioned, such as courage, wisdom and rule – for rulers can do well by many people), and also generals, orators and all who are capable of such things.
- And those whom many wish to be like, or many wish to know or to be friends with, or whom many admire, or whom they themselves admire.
- And those of whom laudations and encomia are spoken either by poets or by speech-writers. For men despise the opposites; for contempt is the opposite of jealousy, and despising to being jealous.
- And those who are in such a condition as to be jealous of some or to be the objects of jealousy must be contemptuous of these and of those who have the faults opposite to the good things that are the objects of jealousy. And so often they despise those in good fortune, because fortune has come to them without the good things that are respected.

The things, then, by which the emotions are engendered and dissolved, from which come the related proofs, have been given.

SECTION SEVEN: CHARACTER

CHAPTER 2.12. YOUTH

After consideration of the factors productive of emotion comes that of those by which men are given at least the appearance of being of a certain character. The third species of proof was laid down at the start to be that by character, but this seemed to mean that there was a form of persuasiveness inherent in the speaker's himself appearing to be of a certain kind. In the discussion in this Section, however, the emphasis seems rather to be on the presumable characteristics of the audience, which it will be useful for the speaker to grasp. Once again these are subjected to analysis, the determinants of character being pronounced to be emotion, psychological condition, age and fortune. Since the first two of these have been dealt with in the preceding Section (psychological condition being treated as a subsidiary aspect of emotion), it remains for this Section to study the effects on character of age and fortune, both of which, in Aristotle's view, lie outside our control. After a brief introductory paragraph, he passes immediately to the treatment of the three ages and their effects on character. The treatment is colourful and crisp, but here more than anywhere else in the work we see the shadow of the doctrine of the mean in the Ethics. The characteristics of youth and age are symmetrically opposed and between them stands the middle position of the prime of life. The whole Section also bears an obvious affinity with the Characters of Aristotle's friend and colleague Theophrastus.

CHAPTER 2.12

Let us after this go through the *characters* of men in regard to their emotions, habits, ages and fortunes. *By emotions I mean anger and desire and the sort of things about which we have spoken, under habits the virtues and vices, and we have also discussed these above, and also the preferences of each group and their products.*[1] The *ages* are *youth, prime* and *old age.*[2] By *fortune* I mean good birth, wealth *1389a* and capacities and their opposites and in general good fortune and misfortune.

Now the *young* are by character appetitive and of a kind to do whatever they should desire.

● And of the bodily appetites they are especially attentive to that connected with sex and have no control over it, and they are easily changed and sated in their desires, and also desire intensely but promptly cease (for their wishes are sharp and not great, like the thirsts and hungers of the ill), and they are irate and hot-tempered and of a kind to harken to anger. And they are inferior to their passions; for through their ambition they do not tolerate disregard but are vexed if they think they are being wronged.

● And they are ambitious, but even more keen to win (for youth craves excess and victory is a kind of excess), and they are both of these things rather than money-loving (they are least money-loving of all through their never yet having experienced shortage, as remarked in Pittacus' apophthegm on Amphiaraus,[3] and they are not sour-natured but sweet-natured through their not having yet observed much wickedness, and credulous through their not yet having been many times deceived, and optimistic – for, like drunken men, the young are warm by nature – also because they have not frequently met with failure.

● And for the most part they live in hope; for hope is of the future and remembrance of the past, and for the young the future is long and the past short; for on one's first day one can remember nothing but hope for everything. And they are easily deceived for the reason given (that they easily hope), and they are relatively courageous (for they are spirited and optimistic, whose effects are the one absence of fear and the other confidence; for in anger none is afraid and to hope for some good thing is a source of confidence), and they are bashful (for they do not yet assume certain things to be fine, but have merely been given a traditional education),[4] and they are magnanimous (for they have not yet been humiliated by life, but have no experience of necessities, and magnanimity is to deem oneself worthy of great things; and this belongs to the optimist).

- And they prefer doing what is noble to what is in their interest; for they live rather by character than by calculation, and calculation is connected with interest but virtue with nobility. And they love their friends and comrades more than the other ages through their pleasure in being together and never yet having made judgements in terms of interest, so as not even to have done so of their friends.

1389b

- And in all things they err rather towards the excessively great or intense, against the remark of Chilon[5] (for they do everything in excess: they love and hate excessively and do all other things in the same way), and they think they know everything and are obstinate (this is also the reason for their doing everything in excess), and they commit their crimes from arrogance rather than mischievousness. And they are prone to pity through their supposing all men to be honest and of the better sort (for by their own freedom from malice they measure their neighbours, so that they think that these are suffering undeservedly) and they love laughter, whence also their love of wit; for wit is educated arrogance.

CHAPTER 2.13. OLD AGE

Here, as in the treatment of youth, we are reminded that interest in human character-types had grown greatly on the post-Euripidean Attic stage, with an inevitable effect on the sister art of oratory. The present discussion should serve to remind us that the relegation of character to a secondary role to plot in the analysis of tragedy in the Poetics *should not be taken to indicate any lack of interest on Aristotle's part in the art of characterization for its own sake.*

CHAPTER 2.13

This, then is the character of the young. The *old*, those past their prime, have for the most part their characteristics from the opposites to these:

- For from having lived for many years and been frequently deceived or in error, and from most of their affairs having been bad, they do not have confidence in anything and are less vigorous in all things than they should be.

- They have many opinions but no knowledge, and in their deliberations they always add 'perhaps' and 'maybe', and say everything like that and nothing without reservations.

- And they are sour-tempered; for sour temper consists in taking everything for the worse. They also nourish suspicions through their lack of credulity, and are incredulous through their experience.

- And for these reasons neither their loves nor their hatreds are strong, but, as in the advice of Bias, they both love as being likely to hate and hate as being likely to love.

- And they are small-minded from their humiliations in life; for they desire nothing great or exceptional but the necessities of life. And they are illiberal; for money is one of the necessities, and also they know from experience that acquisition is hard and throwing away is easy. And they are cowards and fear everything in advance; for their disposition is the opposite of that of the young.

- For they are chilled, where the young are warm, so that the way of old age is prepared by cowardice; for fear is indeed a kind of chilling. They are also life-loving, and more so on their last day from desire for what is absent, and it is what men lack that they most desire.

- And they are more self-loving than is right; for this too is a kind of small-mindedness. And they live for their interests and not for nobility, more than is right, through their being self-loving. For one's own interest is a relative good, nobility a good absolutely. And they are shameless rather than shame- *1390a* prone; for through their not considering nobility and interest on the same footing they disregard the impression they make.

- And they are pessimistic because of their experience (for most of the things that happen are bad; for most things turn out for the worse), and also from cowardice. And they live in memory rather than in hope; for the rest of their life is short and what has passed is long, and hope is of the future, memory of past things; which is also the reason for their garrulity; for they are always talking about the past, since they take pleasure in recollection.

- And their spirits are both sharp and weak and some of their appetites are lacking, the others feeble, so that they are neither desirous nor active in accordance with their desires, but in accordance with profit. Hence people of this age seem to be moderate; for their passions have withered and they are slaves to profit.

- And they live by calculation rather than by character; for calculation has to do with advantage and character with virtue. And their crimes they commit for mischief not for arrogance.

- But old men are also prone to pity, though not for the same reasons as young men; for the latter are so from philanthropy, the former through weakness; for they think that all these things are near for themselves to suffer, and this was what produced pity. Hence their proneness to lamentation and their being neither witty nor laughter-loving; for morosity is the opposite of the love of laughter.

The characters, then, of the young and older generations are of this kind. So that since all men accept speeches directed at their own age and their kind, it is not hard to see by what employment of arguements men and speeches will appear to be of the appropriate kind.

CHAPTER 2.14. PRIME

The evident admiration that Aristotle here displays for middle age over the other periods of life is, of course, very much in keeping with his whole outlook. One notable feature of his account is a clear distinction between the period of physical prime (between thirty and thirty-five) and that of mental prime (around forty-nine), unusual in treatments of the subject at this date.

CHAPTER 2.14

Now it is obvious that those in their *prime* are mid-way in character between each of the two groups, avoiding the excess, and neither greatly confident (for that would be rashness) nor excessively fearful, but being well set towards either extreme, neither trusting all men, nor trusting none, but rather judging according to the truth, and neither living for nobility alone nor for self-interest but for both, *1390b* and neither tending to extravagance nor to meanness but seeking a balance, and similarly in point of temper and desire, and showing moderation with courage and courage with moderation. For these things are separated in the young and the old; the young are courageous and immoderate, the old moderate and cowardly. And to speak in general, in respect of the useful points wherein age and youth are distinguished, those in their prime have both of these, and in respect of those in which they are excessive or deficient, of these they seek the moderate and balanced. The body is in its prime from the ages of thirty to thirty-five, and the soul around the age of forty-nine.

Let this much suffice on the subject of youth, age and prime and on the characters which each have.

CHAPTER 2.15. BIRTH

Aristotle now passes to the effects of fortune on character. He considers birth, wealth and power, all of which he believes to lie equally outside our control. The treatment of all three is conspicuous for its brevity and unremarkable in its conclusions. It is sustained in the same neutral tone as the entire discussion of emotion and character.

CHAPTER 2.15

Concerning the advantages that come from *chance*,[6] those through which the characters of men also take their qualities, let us speak next.

● The character of good birth is for the man who has it to be relatively ambitious; for all men, when they have something, are wont to accumulate it, and good birth is the reputation of one's ancestors.

● And the character of the descendants is contemptuous even of the equals of their ancestors, because the same things in being remote rather than near are more easily boasted of. The well-born is by the virtue of the stock, and nobility by keeping within nature; hence it does not normally happen to the well-born, who are for the most part silly; for there is a certain harvest in the generations of men as in those things that grow in the land, and sometimes if the race should be good, there occur over a certain time exceptional men, and then it again relapses. Gifted families mutate towards more unbalanced characters, as with the descendants of Alcibiades and those of Dionysius I, but static ones mutate rather to foolishness and dullness, such as the descendants of Cimon,[7] Pericles and Socrates.

CHAPTER 2.16. WEALTH

● The characteristics attendant on wealth are open for all to see; for men become arrogant and haughty, being affected in a certain way by the possession of wealth (their disposition reflects their having all good things; for wealth is a kind of value of the worth of other goods, so that all things seem to be purchased by it), and also luxurious and snobbish, luxurious through their maintenance and the display of their happiness, snobbish and cavalier from the fact that all men are accustomed to spend time in the pursuit of what is valued and admired and from the assumption that all men have the same ends as themselves.

● And it is also reasonable that they be affected in this way (for there are many people who want what they have; whence the remark of Simonides about rich and wise men to the wife to Hiero. She had asked him whether it is better to be rich than to be wise: 'Rich,' said he, because he saw the wise sitting at the doorways of the rich), and they also think that they are worthy to rule; for they think that they have the things that make men fit to rule. And in sum, the character of the rich man is that of the mindlessly happy one.

1391a

● But the characters differ between those who have recently acquired wealth and those who have long had it, in that the newly rich have all the disadvantages in a much worse way (for to be newly rich is to be uneducated, as it were, in wealth). And the crimes they commit are not mischievous, but some out of arrogance and some from incontinence, whence their tendency towards assault and adultery.

CHAPTER 2.17. POWER

● Similarly most of the characteristics connected with power are apparent. For power has some similar features to wealth and some better; for those in power are more ambitious and manly in character than the rich, through their attempting exploits which they have the chance to carry off through their power, and they are more serious through their having public concerns, being forced to consider things connected with their power, and they are rather solemn than heavy; for their rank makes them more conspicuous, through which they are moderate, and their solemnity is a chastened and apt heaviness; and if they commit crimes then these are not small but great.

Good fortune both has the characteristics of the things mentioned in its subdivisions (for the good fortunes that are thought to be most important tend towards these three), and also good children, and possesses unusual success in regard to the advantages of the body. Men are excessively haughty and excessively unthinking through their good fortune, but one excellent characteristic is attend- *1391b* ant on good fortune, that men love the gods and stand in a certain relation to them, believing in them through what has come to them by fortune.

We have dealt, then, with the characteristics due to age and fortune; for the opposites of the ones discussed will be obvious from the opposite situations, such as the character of poor, unfortunate and powerless men.

PART THREE: UNIVERSAL ASPECTS

SECTION EIGHT: COMMON TOPICS

CHAPTER 2.18. THE ROLE OF COMMON TOPICS

Aristotle announces that the discussion of the subject-matter specific to the demonstrative proofs of the various genres has now been covered, as well as the factors that can be exploited to induce emotional states and which shape the character of the listeners. It remains, then, only to discuss those aspects that are common to all species of proof. The aspects of oratory that apply to any speech, on whatever subject, in whatever genre, before whatever kind of audience and with whatever emotional content, are the common topics, the style and the composition. Many critics have had difficulty with this arrangement of the material. There are two main objections: first, that the subject of the common topics really belongs with the discussion of demonstration, from which it is unnaturally separated by the Sections on emotion and character; and second, that the discussion of style and composition, belonging as it does to the traditional contents of rhetorical treatises repudiated by Aristotle, has no real place in his original design. These points have been taken, along with other evidence, to indicate that the work as we have it must have been composed at various different periods of time. This thesis may be correct, but, without prejudice to it, it seems possible to defend the extant arrangement. The use of common topics is something that can enhance not just any of the demonstrative proofs but any form of proof at all, demonstrative, emotional or ethical, and clearly the same can be said for style and composition. It is thus perfectly reasonable that, after dealing with the specific forms of proof and their various subdivisions, Aristotle should now pass on to conclude with a survey of those features of rhetoric that can improve the effectiveness of any or all of them.

However, even if the overall arrangement of the work can be defended, there remain serious difficulties about the planning of this Section itself. Essentially it deals with two important types of common topic, those of possibility and those of degree, separated by an excursus on the general forms of rhetorical argument, the example and enthymeme, to which is added the maxim as a sort of intermediate case, with a comprehensive survey of the premises of general demonstrative enthymemes and a distinction between the real and the apparent enthymeme. It is difficult to defend this ordering, except to say that the topics of possibility are conveniently got out of the way at the start and those of degree naturally lead on to the treatment of style, while it was reasonable enough for Aristotle to feel that a presentation of the most common premises of general demonstrative enthymemes should be preceded by an elaboration, lacking so far, of the differences between the characteristic forms of persuasive argument outlined at the start of the work.

CHAPTER 2.18

Now the use of persuasive arguments is directed towards judgement (for there is no further need of argument about matters about which we know and have decided), and it occurs either if one exhorts or dissuades by using arguments on an individual, as do those ticking off or persuading (for the individual is no less a judge; for the one to be persuaded is in general, so to speak, the judge), or before litigants, or if one were to be speaking against a supposition; this last is the same situation (for we must use argument and refute the opposition, against whom, as against litigants, the speech is made), and similarly in epideictic speeches (as the speech is composed before the spectator as before a judge; although there is only the judge, simply speaking, in the one who judges things sought in public contests; for he enquires how the things contested are, and the things about which there is deliberation). About the characteristics of constitutions we have already dealt in the treatment of political oratory – so that we should now distinguish how and by what points speeches are to be given character.

Now since with each kind of speech the end was different, but with them all opinions and premises are drawn from the things by which they bring proof both in political debate and in display and in legal controversy, and we have also given definitions about those things by which one can give a speech character, it remains for us to go through the *common topics*.[1] For all speakers must use in their speeches the commonplace about the *possible and impossible*, and try to show in some cases that something will happen and in others that it has. Again the commonplace about *extent* is common to all speeches; for all men use diminution and increase both in political oratory and in giving praise or blame and in prosecuting or defending. When we have made these definitions, let us try to speak about 1392a the enthymemes in general, if we can, and about examples, so that by adding what still remains we may fulfil our original undertaking. Now of the commonplaces that of *amplification* is most proper to epideictic oratory, as has been said, that of *what has happened* to forensic (for it is about past things that the judgement is), and that of the *possible and future* to deliberative oratory.

CHAPTER 2.19. THE TOPICS OF POSSIBILITY

The topics of possibility form, as remarked earlier, a relatively self-contained subject and provide a good introduction to what is characteristic about the common topics in general. They are forms of argument which can be filled with more or less any content and their presentation is necessarily somewhat arid. The whole treatment has a natural affinity to the Topics *itself, though Aristotle is at pains not to lapse into the presentation of dialectical, rather than rhetorical, material.*

CHAPTER 2.19

First, then, let us speak of the *possible and impossible*:[2]

- If one opposite should be capable of either being or coming to be, then the other opposite should also be thought to be possible; for instance, if it is possible that a man be cured, then it is possible that he should be ill; for there is the same possibility for opposites in so far as they are opposites.
- And if one like thing is possible, then so is the other; and if the harder of a pair is possible, then so is the easier. If a thing can

become serious and noble, then it can come about absolutely. For it is harder for a beautiful house to come into being than for a house. And of that whose beginning can come to be, so can the end; for none of the impossibles either comes to be or begins to come to be. For instance, that the diagonal should be commensurate could neither come to be nor begin to come to be.

- And of that whose end is possible, so is the beginning; for all things come about from their beginning.

- And if what is later in essence or origin can come about, then so can what is prior; for instance, if a man can come about, then so can a child (for that comes first), and if a child, then also a man (for the child is the beginning).

- And those things for which there is natural desire or appetite can come to be; for none has desire or appetite for the most part for the impossible. Also things for which there are sciences and skills, it is possible that they can both be and come about.

- And those things the principle of whose origin is in things that we could force or persuade; and these are the things to which one is superior or friendly or responsible.

- And the whole of things whose parts are possible is possible, and the parts are possible for the most part of things whose whole is possible; for if a front, leather upper and toe-cap can be made, then so can sandals, and if sandals then also a front, cap and upper.

- And if the whole genus is among the things that can be done, then so is the species, and if the species, then the genus. For example, if a boat can come to be, then so can a trireme, and if a trireme, then a boat.

- And if one of a naturally related pair can be done, then the other also; for instance, if a double, then also a half, and if a half, then a double.

- And if a thing can come about without skill and preparation, then it is all the more possible through skill and elaboration. Hence the remark to Agathon:

> Some things indeed we do by skill, and some
> Come by necessity or chance to us . . . [3]

1392b

186

- And if it is possible for worse, inferior and less thoughtful men, then it is also more so for the opposites, just as Isocrates also said that it would be strange if Euthynus understood and he himself could not find the answer.[4]

It is obvious that the situation with the impossible will arise from the opposites of what has been said.

Whether something *has happened* should be considered from the following:

- First of all, if that which is less constituted to come about has occurred, then what is the more so is likely to have occurred.
- And if what was accustomed to happen later has occurred, then the prior has happened. For instance, if a man has forgotten, then he has previously learned.
- And if a man could and wished to, then he has done it; for all men, when, being able, they wish to, act; for there is nothing to stop them.
- Also if he wished and there was nothing external stopping him, and if he could and was angry, or could and had an appetite. For thus for the most part men do what they wish if they can, the base through weakness of the will and honest men from their appetite for honest things.
- And if a man intended to do something, then he also did it; for it is likely that the intender also actually acted.
- And if what was naturally antecedent or ancillary to something has occurred, then it has also; for instance, if there was thunder, then there was also lightning, and if a man did something, then he also tried.
- And if what naturally occurs later has happened and that for the sake of which something happens, and the prior and that for the sake of it happened, such as if it thundered, then there was lightning, and if he did it, then he tried.

Of all these things, some are of necessity and some hold for the most part so. And about *non-occurrence* it will be clear from the opposites of what has been said.

From the same things it will also be clear about *what is to be:* 1393a

187

- For what is within wish and capacity will be, and things involved in desire, anger and calculation accompanied by capacity, these will either be in the urge to action or in intention; for the most part it is imminent rather than non-imminent things that happen.
- And if something is preceded by what naturally happens before; for instance, if it clouds over, then it is likely to rain.
- And if what is for something's sake has occurred, then it is likely that this too will occur; for instance, if there is a foundation, then there is likely to be a house.

And the position with *size and smallness* of affairs and about the *greater and lesser* and in general about *large and small* is clear to us from what has already been said. For in the treatment of deliberative oratory there was a discussion of the greatness of good things and about the larger and smaller in general, so that since for each speech the ordained end is the good (for instance, the advantageous, the noble and the just), it is obvious that in all cases the amplifications must be drawn from them. Beyond this, further enquiry about size and excess in general would be empty words; for particular points are more influential for practical need than general ones.

So about the possible and impossible, and whether something happened or did not or will happen or will not, let this suffice, and also about the greatness or smallness of the matters.

CHAPTER 2.20. EXAMPLE

We now embark on a survey not of the common topics but of the forms of rhetorical argument, though this turns out to be preliminary to a lengthy presentation of general demonstrative topics, which requires an understanding of the enthymeme. The introduction had suggested that the characteristic forms of rhetorical argument were two in number, example and enthymeme, but to these a third, the maxim, is now added. Aristotle evidently finds example relatively less interesting, and soon passes to the related subjects of parables and story-telling.

CHAPTER 2.20

It remains to speak of the *proofs common to all*, since we have spoken of the special ones. Now the common proofs are two in number: *example* and *enthymeme*. For the maxim is a division of the enthymeme. Let us, then, speak first of the example; for the example is similar to induction, and induction is the beginning.

There are two species of *example*: one species of example is the *narration* of preceding events, the other *inventing* them oneself. Of these latter one is comparison, the other fables, like those of Aesop and the Libyan fables.[5]

Mention of facts is of the kind as:

- When someone says that one should be prepared against the king and not allow Egypt to be defeated, given that previously Darius did not cross into Greece before he had taken Egypt, but *1393b* when he had taken her he did cross over, and again Xerxes did not make his attempt before he had taken her, but when he had taken her he crossed over, so that if the present king were to conquer her he would cross over, so that this should not be permitted to him.[6]

Comparison is like:

- The sayings of Socrates. For instance, if one were to say that magistrates should not be chosen by lot on the grounds that this would be the same as if one chose athletes by lot – not those who could compete, but those to whose lot it fell – or should choose by lot which of the sailors should steer, as though it ought to be the one to whose lot it fell and not the one with understanding.

An example of a *fable* would be that of Stesichorus about Phalaris and that of Aesop in support of the demagogue:

- When the Himeraeans elected Phalaris as plenipotentiary general and were intending to give him a bodyguard, Stesichorus discussed the other aspects and then told them a story of a horse who had a meadow to himself. Then a stag came and damaged the pasture and the horse wished to take revenge on the stag.

So he asked a man if he could help him punish the stag, and the man said that he would if the horse would take a bit and he could get on top of him with his spears. The horse agreed, but when the man mounted him, instead of taking revenge on the stag he made the horse his slave. 'In the same way,' said Stesichorus, 'take care that you do not, from the wish to punish your enemies, suffer the same fate as the horse. You have the bit already, by electing him plenipotentiary general. If you give him a guard and allow him to mount you, you will immediately be slaves to Phalaris.'[7]

- Aesop was giving a public speech on Samos for a demagogue under trial for his life. He told how a fox once crossed a river and fell into a ditch. Not being able to get out, she lay there for a long time in a bad way and had many fleas on her, when a hedgehog came wandering along. When he saw the vixen he took pity on her and asked if he should drive away the fleas, but she would not let him. When he asked why, she said, 'Because they are already full of me and are drawing little blood, but if you drive them away, then other thirsty ones will come and drink the rest of my blood.' 'Now you too, men of Samos, will no longer be harmed by this man (for he is rich), but if you kill him, then other poorer ones will come, who will deprive you by theft of the rest of your property.'[8]

1394a

They are also populist arguments, and they have the advantage that it is hard to find similar events that have happened, but it is easier to invent stories. For one must make them up, just as with parables, if one can see the similarity, which is easier after a philosophical education. So the things told by stories are easier to provide, but points from facts are more useful for deliberation, since for the most part future things are similar to those that have happened.

One must use examples when one does not have enthymemes for demonstrative proof (for conviction is produced through these) and when one does have enthymemes, as with witnesses, using them as a supplement to the enthymemes. For when deployed at the start they resemble induction, and induction is not suited to rhetoric except in a few cases, but as supplements they are like witnesses, and a witness is always persuasive; so too if one puts example first, one must give many, but as a supplement one example would suffice; for even one good witness is useful.

We have, then, given the number of species of example and how and when they should be used.

CHAPTER 2.21. MAXIM

The maxim is of interest as being the isolated conclusion of an enthymeme in something like the way in which the topic is an isolated premiss. This characterization of the maxim makes it clear that Aristotle does not mean by the enthymeme merely an argument with one or more suppressed premisses, as some have supposed. Rather the hallmark of the enthymeme is the probability rather than necessity of its premisses – the topics. There is an interesting discussion of the psychological effect of the maxim, with which the proverb is associated.

CHAPTER 2.21

About the use of *maxims,* when we have said what the maxim is, it would be easier to say of what sort of things and when we use them and whom the use of maxims suits in speeches. *The maxim, then, is a declaration, but not indeed about particulars,* such as what sort of a man Iphicrates is, but general, nor about all cases, as that the straight is opposite to the curved, but of things in connection with which actions are done, and things that are to be chosen or avoided for action, so that since the enthymeme is the syllogism about such things, maxims are, more or less, the conclusions of the syllogisms and the premisses, when the reasoning has been removed. For example,

> The man of cunning and of natural wit
> Should never raise his children over-wise . . .[9]

This, then, is a maxim; when one adds the why and the wherefore the whole is an enthymeme, such as:

> For added to their branded idleness
> They earn malicious envy from the people . . .[10]

1394b and:

> A man cannot be happy in all things . . .[11]

and:

> There is no mortal that is truly free . . .[12]

which is a maxim, but with its continuation an enthymeme,

> For he is either slave of wealth or chance . . .[13]

Now if the maxim is what has been said, there must be four species of maxim; they will be either with or without supplement. Those that need demonstration will be those that say something paradoxical or controversial; those that say nothing paradoxical will be without sequel. And of these some must have no need of a sequel from their being known in advance, such as:

> 'Tis best for man, as I think, to be healthy . . .[14]

(For so it seems to most men.) And some maxims on being spoken must be immediately clear to those who reflect, such as:

> He is no lover that not always loves . . .[15]

And of those with sequel some are parts of an enthymeme, such as:

> The man of cunning . . .[16]

and some are enthymematic, but not part of an enthymeme; these indeed are the especially esteemed ones. These are the ones in which the reason for what is said shines through, as in:

> Do not, thou mortal, harbour deathless anger . . .

for to say, 'Do not harbour . . .' would be a maxim, but the addition of being a 'mortal' gives the reason. And it is the same with:

> Mortal should mortal thoughts be, not immortal . . .[17]

It is clear, then, from what has been said how many species of maxim there are, and in what connection each is appropriate. Those without supplement do not fit with controversial or paradoxical contents, but if one adds the sequel it should either be in such a way as to use the maxim as a conclusion (as if one were to say, 'I say that, since one should neither be envied nor idle, the child should not be educated'), or in saying this first then add what precedes it; but if one adds the reason for things that are not paradoxical but unclear, then this should be as succinct as possible. In such cases Laconic apophthegms are also appropriate, and riddles, such as using what Stesichorus said at Locri, that they should not be arrogant, so *1395a* that the cicadas should not sing from the ground.[18]

The use of maxims suits the older age, and in connection with things of which one has experience, so that it is improper for one of the wrong age to use maxims, as also with story-telling, and if they are about things of which one is inexperienced, then the effect is foolish and uneducated. And there is a sufficient proof in that peasants are particularly maxim-prone and readily cite them.

To speak generally of what is not general is most appropriate in complaint and exaggeration, and in these either when beginning or having made one's demonstration. But one should use even the tritest and most banal commonplaces, if they should be useful; for from their being banal, as all men agree with them, they are thought to be right; for instance, for one summoning men who have not sacrificed to danger:

> One sign is best – to struggle for one's country . . .[19]

and before those who are numerically inferior:

> Common is Ares . . .[20]

and for suggesting the destruction of the children of enemies although they have done no wrong:

> Foolish to kill the father, spare the children . . .[21]

Some of the proverbs are also maxims, such as the proverb 'An Attic neighbour'. One should also use maxims in contradiction of remarks that have great popularity (by very popular ones I mean such as 'Know thyself' and 'Nought in excess'), when they are either likely to make one's character appear better or are spoken emotively. An emotive example would be if one should in anger say that it was false that one should know oneself; for if this man knew himself, he would never have claimed the generalship. But one's character is better presented by one's saying that one should not, as they say, love as being destined to hate, but rather hate as being destined to love. And one should reveal one's moral purpose in one's language, and, if not, give the reason. For instance, one might say, 'One should love not as they say, but as being destined always to love; the alternative is for the traitor', or, 'What has been said does not please me; for the true friend should love as though he would always love', and, 'I also dislike "nothing in excess", for one should excessively hate the wicked.'

1395b   Maxims give great assistance to speeches, for one thing, through the stupidity of the listeners; for they are delighted if someone in generalizing should arrive at opinions that they hold in the particular case. The following will clarify what I am saying, and also how one should hunt for maxims. The maxim, as has been said, is a general assertion, and the listeners are delighted when a point is generalized which they happen to presuppose in the particular case. For instance, if someone should happen to have bad neighbours or children, he would accept someone's saying that there is nothing worse than neighbourhood or that there is nothing more foolish than child-raising. So one should guess at the sort of opinions that the audience happen already to have presupposed, and then speak in general about them. So the use of maxims certainly has this advantage for one reason, but the other is more important; for it gives the speeches character. Those speeches have character in which the moral purpose is clear; and all maxims have this effect through the fact that their user makes a general assertion of his purposes, so that, if the maxims are good, they also make the speaker seem of good character.

Let this much suffice about what the maxim is, how many species of it there are, how one should use it and what utility it has.

CHAPTER 2.22. ENTHYMEME

It is here that Aristotle gives his official account of the enthymeme, which is in so many ways the core of his system. The concept of the enthymeme as a syllogism of probability is elaborated and it is subdivided into the two forms of the assertorical and the refutational enthymeme, showing that it is as much a destructive as a constructive device. Above all, the close connection between the enthymeme and the topic is spelt out, which prepares the way for the extensive list of common topics that is to follow.

CHAPTER 2.22

Of *enthymemes* let us say in general in what way we should seek them out, and then let us go through the topics; for each of these two things is a different species. It has already been said that the enthymeme is a syllogism and in what way it is a syllogism, and in what way it differs from dialectical syllogisms; for one must draw its conclusion from not too remote premises and not from all ones. Obscurity is produced, first of all, from the length of reasoning, and, secondly, it is a waste of time as one is stating the obvious. This is also the reason for the uneducated person's being more persuasive than the educated one before mobs, just as the poets say that the uneducated 'speak more musically before the people'. For the educated speak common and general things, while the uneducated speak from what they know, and things nearer to the mass mind. So we should not take all received opinions as our premises but a limited group, such as are accepted either by the judges or by those of whom they approve, and this because the opinion thus seems to 1396a be clear to all or the majority. And one's conclusions should not only be from necessary premises but also from those holding for the most part.

One must first, then, understand that of that about which one should speak and reason, either in a political syllogism or whatever, one must first grasp the elements, either all or some of them. For if you had grasped none of them, you would not be able to draw conclusions from anything. I mean such things as:

- How we should be able to advise the Athenians either to fight or not to fight a war, if we do not know what their capacity is, whether naval or of infantry or both, and how great it is, and what are their incomes and friends and enemies, and also what wars they have fought and how, and the other such things; or how could we give them praise, if we did not know about the sea battle of Salamis or the battle of Marathon or the achievements of the children of Heracles or some other such things. For on fine records that they have or are thought to have praise is always given.

- And similarly criticism is drawn from the opposites by considering what properties of the appropriate kind the subjects have or are thought to have, such as that the Athenians enslaved the Greeks, and that they enslaved those who had fought against the barbarians and done great deeds, the Aeginetans and Potidaeans, and all other such things, and any other such error that they might have to their account.[22]

- And similarly those prosecuting and defending make their prosecutions or defences from a consideration of their subject's properties.

It makes no difference whether the subject is the Athenians or the Spartans, a man or a god, about following this same course. If indeed one was advising Achilles, or praising or criticizing him, or prosecuting or defending him, we have to grasp his real or apparent properties, so that we can speak from them, praising or blaming if he has anything noble or shameful to his account, accusing or defending if he has anything just or unjust, and advising if there is anything advantageous or injurious. It is the same as for these about any subject-matter whatever; for instance about justice, as to whether or not it is a good thing, we must discuss this from the properties of justice and of the good. Thus since all men indeed obviously demonstrate in this way, whether they reason more rigor-
1396b ously or more loosely (they do not draw their premisses from all matters but from the things pertaining to each particular and it is obvious to reason that it is impossible to demonstrate in any other way), it is clearly necessary, as we said in the *Topics*, first to have the premisses selected for each particular subject concerning what is possible and most suitable. About things arising on the spur, one must look for topics in the same way, looking not to the indefinite but to the properties relevant to the speech, and sketching the most important and relevant aspects of the affair. For the more properties that one grasps, the more easy is it to demonstrate, and the more relevant they are, the more particular and less general is their

effect. By common aspects I mean praising Achilles because he is a man and because he is one of the demi-gods and because he went on the expedition to Troy. For these properties he also shared with many others, so that such a speech would be no more a praise of Achilles than of Diomedes. Special features are those that pertain to nobody except Achilles, such as the killing of Hector, the best of the Trojans, or Cycnus,[23] who being invulnerable prevented them all from disembarking, and that he was the youngest and that he went on the expedition though not under oath, and all other such things.

This then is one manner of selection – the first, that by topics. Let us now set forth the *elements of the enthymemes*. By an element of an enthymeme and a topic I mean the same thing. But let us start by discussing some points that we must make first. There are two species of enthymemes. One *demonstrates* that something is or is not the case, and the other is *refutational*, and the difference between them is like that between refutation and syllogism in dialectic. Now the demonstrative syllogism is that which concludes from un-controversial premises, and the refutational that which arrives at controversial conclusions.

The topics more or less concern each of the species of useful and necessary things. For the premises are selected about each particular, so that the topics from which should be drawn enthymemes about good and bad, or noble and shameful, or just and unjust, or about characters and emotions and habits in the same way, these topics are already selected for us. But in another way we must also grasp them *1397a* in general relevance to all things, and let us in our discussion mark off the refutational and demonstrative topics, and those of the apparent enthymemes, which are not really so, since they are not indeed even syllogisms. When these things have been made clear, we must give definitions about solutions and objections, and we must specify from what sources one should deploy solutions and objections to the enthymemes.

CHAPTER 2.23. DEMONSTRATIVE COMMON TOPICS

There now follows an impressively long list of common topics, designed to equip even the most desperate orator with an abundance of ammunition.

Indeed it is perhaps here that we see most clearly the practical character of the work. One might compare the section almost to a kind of rhetorical phrase-book. It is, however, important that, as remarked above, Aristotle never loses sight of the contrast between specifically rhetorical and more generally dialectic topics. The whole passage is a paradigm of the activity of invention in which especially the classical orator was expected to show prowess.

CHAPTER 2.23

One of the *demonstrative topics* is

● That from contraries; for it must be considered whether one opposite is a property of the other, as a destructive point if it is not, and as a constructive one if it is, such as that being moderate is a good thing, in that behaving immoderately is harmful. Or as in the Messeniacus: 'If war is responsible for the present evils, then we should right them by peace.'[24]

> For if it is not right even with those
> Who have done wrong to us freely to fall
> To anger, neither then if one should do
> Good under duress should we give him thanks . . .[25]

> But if convincing lies 'mongst mortal men
> Are widespread, then the converse also holds,
> That many truths go unbelieved of men . . .[26]

● Another is that from the similar cases; for the property should apply or not in a similar way, for instance the argument that justice is not always good; for then to do something justly would be good, but it is not in fact preferable to be justly put to death.

● Another is that from things in mutual interrelation. If it is a property of the one to have acted nobly or justly, then it is one of the other to have suffered so. As the tax-collector Diomedon said of tax-rights, 'If it is not shameful for you to sell them, then it is not so for us to buy.'[27] And if justice and nobility also characterize the undergoing of the action, then they do as well the carrying of it out. But one can also derive a fallacy from this. For if something is justly done to someone, it may yet not have been so when done by you; so one must consider separately whether the sufferer deserved to suffer and whether the agent was right to act, and then it is suitable to use the topic in either 1397b way. For sometimes such a difference emerges and yet nothing prevents the use of the topic, as in the case of the Alcmaeon of Theodectes, who to Alphesiboea's question 'No mortal man did then your mother hate?' replied, 'With a distinction must we answer that.' And when she asked him how, he replied, 'They deemed that she should die, but not by me.'[28] Also that from the trial of Demosthenes and those who killed Nicanor; for since they were judged justly to have killed him, it was thought that he had been justly put to death.[29] Also about the man murdered at Thebes, about whom the topic bids the judges decide whether he deserved to die, on the grounds that it is not unjust to kill one who justly dies.[30]

● Another is from greater and less. For example, 'If not even the gods know everything, hardly will men do so.' For this is as much as to say: 'If a property is lacking in one more likely to have it, then it will obviously also be lacking in one who is less so.' Also the proof that a man assaults his neighbours from the fact that he even assaults his father derives from the principle: 'If the rarer applies, then the more common does too.' For men strike their fathers less commonly than their neighbours. Either then can the topic be used in this way or in circumstances in which what tends to have a property lacks it, or tends less to have a property has it, and one must use whichever of the two conclusions is required, and then that the property applies or not. Also if there is neither less nor more. Hence:

> Your father pity earns, who loved his children;
> Does Oeneus not, who lost a famous son? . . .[31]

And the claim that, if Theseus did no wrong, then neither did Paris, or if the Tyndarids did no wrong, then neither did Paris, and if Hector rightly killed Patroclus, then Paris rightly killed Achilles.[32] And that if other skilled men are not base, then neither are philosophers. And if generals are not worthless just because they are often put to death, then neither are sophists. And the argument: 'If an individual should care for your reputation, citizens, then should you all care for that of the Greeks.'

- Another is from the consideration of timing, for instance as Iphicrates said in his speech against Harmodius, 'If I had asked for the reward of a statue before I did the deed, you would have granted it me. Will you not grant it now that I have done it? Do not, then, make a promise for the future and cancel it when the service is in the past.' And again the argument to the Thebans that Philip should be allowed through them to Attica, in that if he had asked them before he helped them against the Phocians, they would have promised.[33] So it would be absurd if they did not let him through because he let the opportunity go before and trusted them.

- Another is from the things said by the adversary against the speaker, as in the *Teucer*.[34] But this is different from the way that it is used by Iphicrates against Aristophon, asking if he would betray the ships for money. When he denied it, he then said, 'If you, Aristophon, would not betray them, then would I, Iphicrates, do so?'[35] But it must be the case that the adversary is thought more likely to commit a crime. If not, the effect would be laughable. If, for example, against a prosecution of Aristeides[36] someone else were to use this, it would conduce to the prosecutor's not being believed. For in general the accuser wishes to be better than the accused. So there is a need to refute this. And in general it is absurd, whenever someone criticizes in others what he does himself or would do, or if he urges them to do what he himself neither does nor would do.

- Another is that from definition, such as that of what the *daimonium* is. 'Is it not a god or the product of a god? Yet whoever thinks that the product of a god exists must also think that there are gods.'[37] Also Iphicrates' definition that the noblest is the best on the grounds that even Harmodius and Aristogeiton had no noble aspects before they did a noble deed, and that he is more closely similar to them than his adversary, in that, 'My actions, indeed, are more closely related to those of Harmodius

1398a

and Aristogeiton than yours.'[38] Also the remark in the *Alexander* that all men would agree that the unorderly are not content with the enjoyment of a single body.[39] And the reason that Socrates gave for not paying a call on Archelaus; for he said that it was arrogance to be unable to retaliate equally when treated well as when treated badly. For all these topics by defining and fastening the what-it-is lead to deductions about the subject of discourse.

- Another is that from differences of meaning, as is discussed in the *Topics* in connection with the right usage.

- Another is that from division, such as that all men commit crimes for three reasons (either for one thing or the other or a third), and for two of them it is in the present case impossible, while not even the accused would claim that it was due to the third.

- Another is that from induction. As the argument in the case of the woman of Peparethus, that women always discern the truth 1398b about parentage; the truth was also given by the mother to the orator Mantias, who was in controversy with their son.[40] At Thebes, too, when Ismenias and Stilbon were in controversy over a son, Dodonis declared that he was the son of Ismenias, and for this reason it was accepted that Thettaliscus was the son of Ismenias.[41] And again from the *Law* of Theodectes, 'If to those who have looked after other men's horses badly men do not entrust their own, nor their ships to those who have sunk other men's, surely, if the same goes for all cases, to those who have badly guarded the safety of others it is not advisable to entrust one's own.'[42] And Alcidamas' argument that all men respect the wise: 'The Parians indeed honoured Archilochus although he slandered them, and the Chians honoured Homer although he was not a citizen, and the Mytilenaeans honoured Sappho although she was a woman, and the Spartans honoured Chilon and put him in their senate although they were the least intellectual of men, and the Italian Greeks honoured Pythagoras, and the Lampsacenes publicly buried Anaxagoras although he was a foreigner and still honour him now, and the Athenians were happy when they had the laws of Solon and the Spartans when they had those of Lycurgus, and at Thebes when the guardians became philosophers the state was happy.'[43]

- Another is from an earlier judgement about the same or a similar or an opposite matter, especially if all men give this verdict and at all times, and if not, at least the majority, or the wise, either all or most, or the good, or the judges themselves, or those whose views they accept, or those to whom it is impossible to judge to the contrary, such as those in office, or those to whom it is not noble to judge the opposite, such as gods or a father or teachers; as with what Autocles said against Mixidemides,[44] that it would be a fine thing for the Areopagus to pass judgement on the Solemn Goddesses but not on Mixidemides. Or Sappho's argument that death is an evil, as the gods have decided so or otherwise they would die. Or like the argument of Aristippus against what he thought was one of Plato's more orotund remarks, saying, 'But our companion would have had none of this', meaning Socrates. And the question that Hegesipolis, having first consulted the oracle at Olympia, put to the god in Delphi, whether he thought the same as his father, as it would be shameful to say the opposite.[45] And what Isocrates wrote, to the effect that Helen was a serious woman, if that was indeed what Theseus thought, and that Paris was, given that the goddesses so judged, and that Euagoras was serious because, as Isocrates puts it, 'When Conon was in trouble he abandoned all others and betook himself to Euagoras.'[46]

- Another is that from listing parts, as in the argument in the *Topics* about what process the soul is, being either one or the other.[47] And there is an example from the *Socrates* of Theodectes: 'Against what holy place has he blasphemed? What gods has he not honoured that the city honours?'

- Another is that, since with most events it happens that the results are both good and ill for the same person, we should urge or dissuade from the consequence, and prosecute or defend, and praise or blame. For instance, 'The bad consequence of education is that one is envied, but the good consequence is that one is wise. One should not then be educated, as one should not be envied; yet one should be educated, as one ought to be wise.' This topic is the art of Callippus, if to it is added the possible and the others that have been given.[48]

● Another is that, whenever one has either to urge or dissuade about two things that are opposites, one can use the previously mentioned method on them both. But the difference is that in the earlier case any sort of thing is opposed, but in this one opposites. For example, the priestess who did not let her son give a public address: 'If,' she said, 'your words are just, men will hate you, and if they are unjust, then the gods will. Yet also one should make a political speech; for if your words are just, the gods will love you, and if they are unjust, then men will.' This is the same as the remark about buying bilge in buying salt.[49] And retortion is when, given that there is a good and bad consequence to each of two opposites, each of the two consequences is the opposite of each of the other two.

● Another: since men do not praise the same thing openly and secretly, but in public praise especially just and noble things, but privately wish rather for what is to their advantage, is to try to conclude the one from the other of these (this is the most important of the paradoxical topics).

● Another is from predicting the result of the present case by analogy, such as the words of Iphicrates, when his son, being too young in age, was being coerced because of his size to perform public service, saying that if they thought the largest of boys were men, then they should vote that the shortest men were boys. Similarly the point of Theodectes in the *Law*: 'You 1399b make mercenaries, such as Strabax and Charidemus, citizens because of their reasonable character; will you not make exiles of those of them who have conducted themselves disastrously?'[50]

● Another is from the fact that if what happened was the same, then the causes of its happening would be too. For example, Xenophanes[51] said that the same blasphemy is committed by those who say that the gods are born and by those who say that they die; for in either case the result is that there is a time when the gods do not exist. And in general to take what results from each thing always to be the same: 'You are about to judge not about Isocrates but about education, about whether one should engage in the practice of philosophy.' And that to give earth and water is to be enslaved, and that participation in the common peace is the obeying of an order. And we must take up whichever of the two alternatives should be useful.

- Another is from the same things' not being always preferred before and after, but in reverse order, like this enthymeme: 'Given that in exile we were fighting to return, are we, now that we have been restored, to flee so that we need not fight?' For on one occasion they chose to stand at the price of fighting and on the other not to fight at the price of staying put.[52]

- Another is with a thing for the sake of which something is likely to be or happen, to claim that this is the reason for its being or happening, as if someone were to give someone something, just so that in removing it he should upset him. Hence also the remark:

> To many men the god through no goodwill
> Has given blessings great, but so that they
> May the more clearly know catastrophe . . .[53]

And the lines from Antiphon's *Meleager*:

> Not just to kill the beast, but that through Greece
> To Meleager's prowess they bear witness . . .[54]

And the point from the *Aias* of Theodectes, that Diomedes chose Odysseus not out of honour, but that his companion should be the lesser man; for he might well have done it for this reason.[55]

- Another is common to both litigants and political orators: to consider incentives and disincentives, and the reasons both why men act and why they run away. For these are the factors, which, if they be present, we must act on and, if not, not act on, such as if a thing is possible or easy or useful either to oneself or to one's friends or harmful to one's enemies, and, if it should be subject to punishment, if the punishment is less than the advantage, and speakers both urge from these points and dissuade from the opposites. And from these same points they *1400a* both prosecute and defend; from the dissuasive points they defend, and from the suasive ones they prosecute. This topic is the whole skill of Pamphilus and Callippus.[56]

● Another is from things that are thought to happen but are incredible, because they would not be expected, if it was not the case or nearly the case that they happen. And that they all the same occurred; for men assume either familiar or likely things to happen. If, then, the thing is incredible and not likely, it must be true; for it is not because of its probability and persuasiveness that it is thought so, as with what Androcles, the Pitthian, said against the law. Since they were heckling him as he said, 'The laws need a law to put them right', he went on that fish need salt, yet it is neither likely nor persuasive that those brought up in sea-water should need salt, and, similarly, pressed olives need oil, although it is incredible that the things from which oil comes should need oil.[57]

● Another is the refutational topic: that of considering things that are not agreed, if something unagreed occurs in the places, times, actions and arguments, separately with reference to the adversary, such as, 'He says that he loves you, but he conspired with the thirty', and separately for oneself, 'He says that I am litigious, but he cannot show that I have brought a single case', and separately for oneself and the adversary, 'He has never lent anything, while I have bailed out many of you.'

● Another is with previously slandered men or cases, or ones thought to be, to give the reason for the bad repute. For there is some reason for which it seems to be the case. For instance, when a woman embraced her own son, so that it was thought to be because she enjoyed intercourse with the young man, when the reason was given the imputation was removed. Another example is when, in Theodectes' *Aias*, Odysseus tells Aias why he is braver than he but not thought to be so.[58]

● Another is from the cause: if there is a cause, then the result is the case, and if there is not, it is not the case. For the cause accompanies what it is a cause of, and nothing occurs without a cause, as Leodamas said in his defence. When Thrasybulus accused him of having his name on the column on the Acropolis, but of having erased it under the thirty, he replied that it was not possible; for the thirty would rather have trusted him if his hatred for the people was written in stone.[59]

- Another is if something could have been better done another way, or could now be, than in that which the other is either advising or doing or has done; for it is obvious that, if it is not *1400b* so, the defendant has done no crime; for none willingly and knowingly chooses bad things. But this is sometimes false; for it often later becomes clear how it was better to act, having previously been unclear.

- Another is, when something opposite is about to be done to what has been done, to consider both at the same time. For example, when the people of Elea asked Xenophanes if they should sacrifice to Leucothea and sing funeral hymns to her or not, he advised that if they thought she was a goddess they should not sing to her and if they thought she was human they should not sacrifice.[60]

- Another topic is that of prosecuting or defending from errors. For example, in the case of Carcinus' Medea, some accuse her of killing her children, for they did at least not appear (for Medea made a mistake in the sending away of her children), and she gives as her defence that she would not have killed her children, but Jason. For she would have been mistaken not to have done this, if she had also done the other thing. This topic and species of the enthymeme is the whole earlier art of Theodorus.[61]

- Another is that of the name. As Sophocles said,

> Clearly of iron you are, and bear the name . . .[62]

And as men are accustomed to speak in the praises of the gods, and in the way that Conon called Thrasybulus 'thrasybulus' (bold counsellor), and Herodicus said of Thrasymachus, 'You are always thrasymachus' (bold in battle), and of Polus, 'You are always polus' (the colt), and said of the lawgiver Dracon that his laws are not of a man (for they are harsh) but of a dragon; and in the way that Euripides' Hecabe says of Aphrodite, 'Rightly the goddess's name begins with mindlessness', and as Chaeremon said that Pentheus was named from his coming disaster.[63]

Refutational enthymemes, however, are better known than demonstrative ones, because the refutational enthymeme is a single conclusion from opposite premises in a short space, and next to each other their opposition is more apparent to the listener. And of all syllogisms, both refutational and demonstrative, the ones that cause most stir are those which in the beginning, though they are not superficial, men anticipate (for the audience take pleasure in themselves for anticipating the point), and those which they are only so much behind as to recognize the point just as they are being spoken.

CHAPTER 2.24. ILLUSORY TOPICS

In addition to the real common topics, which it is the business of the orator to invent, there also exist illusory enthymemes, to which he may have to resort himself, but which he will in the normal way be more concerned to expose in his adversary. Thus the discussion of the apparent enthymeme forms a natural bridge across to the subject of the refutational enthymeme which is to follow.

CHAPTER 2.24

Now since it is possible for some syllogisms to be *real* and for others to be *not real but apparent*, there must be on the one hand the real and on the other the apparent enthymeme, since the enthymeme is a kind of syllogism.

● Now one of the topics of the apparent enthymemes is that *1401a* drawn from diction. Of this, one element, as in dialectic, is to give the final statement as a conclusion without having completed a syllogism: 'Not this and this, so necessarily that or that.' In the case of rhetorical syllogisms, to speak concisely and antithetically has the air of an enthymeme (for diction of this kind is the province of the enthymeme); and this seems to come about from the form of the diction. Now for speaking in syllogistic style it is useful to give headings of many syllogisms – that the subject saved some, punished others and liberated the Hellenes. For each of these is shown from other premisses, but when they are put together an extra point seems to arise from them too.

● Another form of false enthymeme is that by homonymy, such as saying that a mouse is a major animal, as from it comes the most respected of rites. For the mysteries are the most respected of all rites. Or if in the praise of dogs one were to include that in the sky, or Pan, in that Pindar said:

> O holy, whom the Olympians call
>   The mighty goddess' many-formed hound . . .[64]

Or that to be nobody is to be a dog without honour, so that it is obvious that the dog is respected. And to say that Hermes is the most social of the gods, as he alone is called 'common' Hermes. And that reason is the most serious of things in that good men are worthy not of money but of esteem; for 'worthy of reason' is not said in a single way.

● Another is to speak by composition of the divided or division of the composite; for since what is not the same often seems to be the same, we must take up whichever of the two possibilities is more useful. This is the argument of Euthydemus, such as that one knows that there is a trireme in the Piraeus, since he knows each subdivision.[65] Also that a man knowing the letters also knows the word, since the word is the same as the letters. And that since twice as much is unhealthy, not even the single amount is healthy; for it would be absurd if two of something were bad but one good. In this way, then, it is refutational, but in the following way demonstrative: two wrongs don't make a right. But the whole topic is fallacious. Again the remark of Polycrates on Thrasybulus, that he destroyed thirty tyrannies, this by combination.[66] Or the fallacy in the *Orestes* of Theodectes, which comes from division:

> Just is't that she who should her husband kill . . .[67]

... should die, and the argument that it is just for a son to avenge his father; and these things have in fact happened – but perhaps when they are combined, it is no longer just. And it *1401b* could also be the fallacy by ellipse, by excluding the killer from the statement.

● Another topic is to establish or reject by exaggeration. This occurs whenever, without having shown that he did it nor that he did not do it, one exaggerates the deed. For this makes it appear either that he did not do it, when the one who faces the charge amplifies it, or that he did do it, when the prosecutor does so. But this is not an enthymeme; for the listener is tricked into thinking that he did or did not do it, when this has not been demonstrated.

● Another is that from indication. This one is also extremely specious. For example, if someone said, 'Lovers are beneficial to cities; for the love of Harmodius and Aristogeiton removed the tyrant Hipparchus', or if one were to say that Dionysius was a thief, because he was wicked. This is obviously highly non-deductive, since not every wicked man is a thief (but every thief is wicked).[68]

● Another is that from accidental property, like what Polycrates said of the mice, that they helped by biting through the bow-strings.[69] Or if one were to say that to be invited to dinner is the most honourable thing, since from his not being invited Achilles was in a rage with the Achaeans on Tenedos. But the reason for his anger was an insult, and this was simply occasioned through his non-invitation.[70]

● Another is that from the attendant circumstance, as in the *Alexander*[71] the argument that Paris is magnanimous, in that despising association with the masses he spent his time alone on Ida; for since that is what the magnanimous are like, he could be thought to be magnanimous. And that since someone is a narcissist and wanders by night he is an adulterer, since they are of this kind. Similar too is the argument that the poor both sing and dance in temples, and that exiles can live wherever they please; for since these seem to be properties of those who are fortunate, those who have them would also be thought fortunate, but it makes a difference in what way; hence this also falls under ellipse.

- Another is by giving the non-cause as cause, such as something's occurring at the same time or after the action; for men take its occurring *after* as its occurring *because*, and especially those in political life, as Demades said that the policy of Demosthenes was the cause of all the evils, since after it came the war.[72]

- Another is by the omission of when and how. As the argument that Paris justly abducted Helen, since the choice was given to her by her father. But it was not the same at all times, but on the first occasion, for a father's jurisdiction only lasts that far. Or if one were to say that it is an outrage to strike free men, as it is not so always, but only when the attacking man begins the fight.[73]

- Again, just as in eristics, there arises an apparent syllogism from considering simply and not simply in a particular case. For example, in dialectic, the argument that the non-existent exists, since the non-existent *is* the non-existent,[74] and that the unknown is known, since the unknown is known to be unknown. Similarly, in rhetoric too, there is an apparent enthymeme from probability, not in general but of a particular kind. The latter is not general, as Agathon indeed says:

> One might indeed call probability
> That men meet many things improbable ...[75]

For the improbable happens, so that it is probable that the improbable will occur, but if that is so, then the improbable will be probable. But the probability is not general, but as indeed in eristics the omission of relation, aspect and manner produces the trickery, so in this case too it comes from the probability's not being general but particular. Corax's art is composed from this topic: 'If he is not likely to be guilty of the charge, for instance if a weakling is accused of assault (which is not probable) the topic comes in, and even if he is likely to be guilty, for instance if he is strong (for this is not probable, because it was likely to be thought probable).'[76] And it is similar also with the other cases; for a man must either be or not be likely to be guilty. Both possibilities seem probable, but the one is probability proper and the other not so absolutely but in the way mentioned; and this is 'making the weaker argument stronger'. Hence men's justified complaints against the claim of Protagoras; for it is both false and not real but apparent probability, and occurs in no other art than rhetoric and eristics.[77]

CHAPTER 2.25. REFUTATION

The long excursus on the forms of argument ends with a review of refutational enthymemes. Aristotle devises an ingenious definition of them, which makes clear their characteristic function of exposing hidden inconsistencies in the adversary's argument. The general approach is, however, once again illustrative rather than analytic.

CHAPTER 2.25

Now we have discussed both real and apparent syllogisms, the next thing after what we have said is to discuss resolution. One can resolve them either by reasoning against them or by bringing an objection. Now it is obvious that counter-reasoning can be done from the same topics. For some syllogisms are from accepted premises, and many accepted premises are mutually contradictory. And objections are brought in four ways, as in the *Topics*: either from the enthymeme itself, or from its like, or from its opposite, or from things that have been decided.

- By that from the enthymeme itself I mean that if the enthymeme was that love was a serious thing, the objection would *1402b* be in two ways: either by the general claim that all lack is evil, or by the partial claim that Caunian love would not be spoken of if there were not also evil forms of love.[78]
- An example of objection from the opposite would be, if the enthymeme was that a good man benefits all his friends, that a wicked man does not harm all his.

- An example of that from the similar would be, if the enthymeme was that those who have been treated badly always hate, that not all those indeed who have been treated well love.
- Judgements are those from famous men. For example, if someone gave the enthymeme that one should forgive drunkards since they commit their errors in ignorance, the objection would be that Pittacus is then indeed not to be praised, since if he was he would not have set greater punishments in the laws, if someone errs from drunkenness.[79]

And since enthymemes are derived from *four things*, and these four are *probability*, *example*, *proof* and *indication*, arguments concluded from things either being or being thought to be for the most part are *enthymemes from probability*.

- Those by induction from the similar, either one or several, whenever one takes the general point and deduces the particulars, are that by example. Those by necessity and what is always the case are those by proof, and those from the general or the particular, either real or not, are those by indication; and since probability is not what always happens but what happens for the most part, it is obvious that this sort of enthymeme can be refuted by bringing an objection, but the refutation is sometimes apparent and not always true; for the objector does not refute by showing that it is not probable but that it is not necessary. For this reason, one can always gain a greater advantage in defence than in prosecution through this trick. For the prosecutor demonstrates by probabilities, and it is not the same to refute something as being improbable and as not being necessary (and what is for the most part always admits of objection), but the judge thinks that if the argument is refuted in this way then it is either not probable or not for him to judge, and he is tricked, as we said (for he should not judge only from necessities but also from probabilities, since this is to judge by the best opinion), and it is therefore not sufficient to refute an argument as not being necessary but one must also refute it as not being probable. And this will happen if the objection is rather for the most part. And it can be of this kind in two ways, either in time or in the facts, but the best is if it is in both; for if more cases are this way and more often, then this is more probable.

- Indications are also refuted and the enthymemes spoken through them, even if they are given, as was said in the first book; for it is obvious from the *Analytics*[80] that every sign is non-deductive.

- Against enthymemes by example there is the same refutation as against probabilities; for if we have a single counter-instance, the argument is refuted as not necessary, even if more cases are otherwise or more often otherwise; and even if the majority and most cases are as claimed, one must contend that the present case is either not the same or not in the same way, or that it has some difference.

Proofs and proof-derived enthymemes cannot be refuted from their being non-deductive (we made this clear also in the *Analytics*),[81] but it remains to show that what is said does not apply. But if it is obvious that it does apply and that it is a proof, then the argument immediately becomes irrefutable. For all cases immediately become clear demonstration.

CHAPTER 2.26. AMPLIFICATION

The discussion of the common topics ends with an examination of the technique of amplification, which prepares the way well for the study of style that is to follow. Amplification and diminution are ancillary supports to the enthymeme, not constituents of it, and the same can be said for objection, as opposed to refutation proper. These exclusions make it clear that Aristotle cannot fairly be accused of attempting to fit all aspects of rhetorical argument into the strait-jacket of the enthymeme.

CHAPTER 2.26

Amplification and *diminution* are not elements of the enthymeme (I call topic and element the same thing, since the element and topic is what many enthymemes are brought under). But to amplify and diminish are enthymemes to show that something is large or small, as are others that it is good or bad, or just or unjust, and whichever of the other aspects. These are all the subjects of syllogisms and enthymemes, so that if not even each of these is a topic of an enthymeme, then neither are increase and diminution.

Nor are the refutational enthymemes a species other than the demonstratives; for it is clear that one refutes either by demonstration or by bringing an objection, and counter-demonstration is of the opposite. For instance, if a man demonstrates that it has happened, then his opponent shows that it has not happened; so that this would not be a difference (for they both use the same premisses, since they bring enthymemes that it is or is not the case), and the objection is not an enthymeme, but, as in the *Topics*, it is to mention some opinion from which it is clear that a deduction has not been made or that something false has been assumed.

And since there are three things that one should put into practice about the speech, let this much suffice us about *examples* and *maxims* 1403b and *enthymemes* and in general everything connected with the *intellect*, as to whence we may have an abundance of them and how we may refute them. It remains to go through *style* and *arrangement*.

SECTION NINE: STYLE

CHAPTER 3.1. HISTORICAL PRELIMINARY

The central business of rhetoric is the invention of proof, and this has been exhaustively dealt with in the first eight Sections of the work. At the start indeed it was announced that all other aspects of oratory were not properly part of the art of rhetoric. The position about this has, however, shifted during the course of the work and in the last two Sections Aristotle addresses the conventional, though by him initially repudiated, subjects of style and composition. His excuse for this is that rhetoric is a practical skill and that the study of presentation is therefore required by the baseness of the audience. In the first chapter of this Section, he is concerned to locate the study of style within both its historical context and the other aspects of oratory. There are in all three contributors to the effect of a speech: the content, to be produced by the processes of invention that have been outlined; the style, presently to be discussed; and the delivery. The last has not yet received a systematic treatment and is not to do so in this work, though its importance is stressed more than once. Style itself resembles delivery in being something carried over into rhetoric from the tragic stage. Thus its history is that of its gradual emancipation from its poetic origins. The peak of poetic influence on rhetorical prose style came in the era of Gorgias, and this approach, though discredited among connoisseurs, still finds favour with the uneducated. However, there is a very clear distinction between the virtues of poetic and of prose style. The former is treated in the Poetics (in a lost section) and the latter is to be dealt with here.

CHAPTER 3.1

There are, then, three things that must be worked on in connection with a speech. One is the *grounds* from which the proofs will be drawn, the second has to do with the *style* and the third with how one should *arrange* the sections of the speech. Now we have discussed the proofs, saying both from how many sources they are drawn and that these are three and giving the characteristics of these and explaining why there are only so many (all persuasion is either by the judges' being themselves affected in a certain way, or by their supposing the speakers to be of a certain character or by a demonstration's having been given). We have also explained the points from which the enthymemes should be drawn (some enthymemes are special, the others general).

The next task is to speak of *style*. For it is not sufficient to have a grasp of what one should say, but one must also say these things in the way that one should, and this makes a great contribution to the character that the speech projects. Our first enquiry, then, was about what was naturally first – what aspects render the facts themselves persuasive; but the second question to this is that of the stylistic deployment of these points; and the third of the enquiries – that which has the greatest effect, but has never yet been attempted – is that to do with delivery. Indeed this came late into tragedy and rhapsody. Originally the poets themselves delivered their own tragedies. So it is clear that this sort of enquiry has just as much to do with rhetoric as to do with poetics. And indeed various writers have dealt with it, including Glaucon of Teos.[1] The skill consists in the manner of employing the voice for each emotion, such as when one should use a loud voice, when a small, and when a middling one, and in the manner of using the accents, such as sharp and heavy and intermediate, and what speech rhythms should be used for each subject-matter. For there are three things that are investigated, and these are dynamics, harmony and rhythm. Experts in these more or less carry off the prizes at the contests, and just as in the case of tragedy actors now have more effect than the poets, so is it also in political contests, through the baseness of the citizenry. However, an art has not yet been composed on these aspects. Indeed, even the consideration of style developed late, and is thought to be rather 1404a crude – a justified assessment. But since the entire enterprise connected with rhetoric has to do with opinion, we must carry out the study of style not in that it is appropriate but in that it is necessary (the appropriate thing would be to investigate no more the manner of the speech than so as neither to cause pain nor delight). Justice requires contention from the facts themselves, so that all other aspects apart from demonstration are ancillary. Nevertheless, these have a great effect, as has been said, because of the baseness of the audience. (The study of style, however, has a certain necessity in all instruction; for it makes a difference for explanation to speak in one way or another – but not that much; all these things are rather mere display directed at the listener. That is why no one teaches geometry in this way.) The art of delivery, for its part, when it arrives, will have the same effect as that of acting. And some writers have tried to say a little about it, such as Thrasymachus in his *On Arousing Pity*.[2] Acting skill, also, is a natural capacity and relatively untechnical, while the art of style is a technical matter. Hence those who have this capacity, again, win prizes, as also orators with histrionic deliveries. For written speeches have more effect through their style than through their intellectual content.

It was the poets, as was natural, then, who first began to develop the study of style and delivery. For words are imitations, and we are equipped with a voice that is the most imitative of all our parts; hence arts have been composed, that of rhapsody and acting and other things. And since the poets, expressing inanities, were thought to have gained a certain fame from their style, it was for this reason that poetic prose style first came into being, such as that of Gorgias,[3] and still now most uneducated men think that such people produce the finest discourse. However, this is not the case. Argument, rather, and poetry have a different style, as can be shown by their outcome. For not even the writers of tragedy still use style in the same way, but just as they have changed from the tetrameter to the iambic line since this is most suited of all the metres to speech, so have they also abandoned words foreign to conversation, those with which the first writers adorned their works, and now even the writers of hexameters have done so. Thus it would be absurd to imitate those who themselves no longer employ that manner, so that obviously we do not have to be precise about everything that has to do with style, but only those things that relate to the sort of style of which we are speaking. We have discussed the other sort in the *Poetics*.

CHAPTER 3.2. CLARITY

*The prose of Aristotle's own, non-extant, popular treatises and dialogues
was much praised in antiquity, while that of the technical works that we
have is distinguished more by gritty concision than by eloquence. It is thus
not a great surprise that he begins the discussion of style with a definition
that enshrines clarity and propriety as the central virtues. The production
of the former is the province of the main verbs and nouns, that of the latter
of the ancillary words. Propriety, moreover, is tolerant of a certain restrained
exoticism. All these virtues are combined by judicious use of the device of
metaphor, and metaphor forms the central subject of the whole discussion of
style. In this chapter, the use of metaphor is reviewed from the perspective
of clarity, but Aristotle will later return to it under other headings.*

CHAPTER 3.2

1404b Let us then consider those points to have been surveyed and let us
lay it down that the virtue of style is to be clear (since a speech is a
kind of indication; if it does not indicate clearly it will not be
performing its function), and to be neither mean nor above the
prestige of the subject, but appropriate (the poetic style is doubtless
not mean, but it is inappropriate to a speech). Now it is the main
nouns and verbs that make the style clear, and this is made not mean
but ornate by the other words, as mentioned in the *Poetics*.[4] For an
unusual replacement for a word makes the style seem the more
lofty. Men in fact are affected in the same way by style as by
foreigners and compatriots. So the discourse must be made to sound
exotic; for men are admirers of what is distant, and what is admired
is pleasant. Now in metre many factors contribute to this effect, and
this fits in that context (for the subject-matter and the characters of
the discourse are more exceptional), but in prose far fewer. For the
brief is slighter, since even in poetry, if a slave or an exceptionally
young character were to speak in fine words, it would be rather
inappropriate, or if they were to do so about too trivial matters.
Even in verse propriety requires contraction and expansion. So one
must do this without being noticed and give the impression
of speaking not artificially but naturally (for the latter is persuasive,

218

the former the reverse; for men are wary of it as malicious, as
they are of mixed wines) and achieve the effect of the voice of
Theodorus by comparison with that of the other actors; for his
voice seemed to be that of the speaker, the others to belong to
someone else. But the technique is well concealed by drawing words
from normal idiom, which Euripides did and was the first to demonstrate.[5]

Since it is *nouns* and *verbs* from which the speech is composed,
and the nouns have as many species as were studied in the book on
poetry,[6] of these we should make little use and in few places of
exotic, compound and *artificial* ones (where we should will be given
later, and it has been said why this is so; they involve too great a
change from what is appropriate), and the proper noun, and pertinent noun and metaphor alone are useful for the style of prose. This
is shown by the fact that all speakers use these alone; for all men
conduct their conversations in metaphors and pertinent and proper
nouns. Accordingly, it is clear that, if one handles things well, there
will be something unfamiliar and it will be able to be concealed and
the meaning will be clear – and this we found to be the virtue of
rhetorical speech. (Among names the homonyms are useful for
the sophist – for it is by these that he does his mischief – and the
synonyms for the poet. I mean by proper words and synonyms such
cases as 'faring' and 'walking'; for these are both proper and synony- *1405a*
mous with each other).

What, then, each of these words is, and how many species there
are of metaphor, and that stylistic questions have the greatest effect
both in poetry and in prose has been asserted, as we said, in the
Poetics. But in prose we should take more trouble over them, in as
much as prose has fewer supports than poetry. *Metaphor* also pre-
eminently involves *clarity, pleasantness* and *unfamiliarity*, and it cannot
be drawn from any other source. But one must also make one's
adjectives and metaphors appropriate. And this will come about by
their being proportionate. If not, the effect will be inappropriate
through the fact that opposites are more apparent when juxtaposed.

● But one must consider what it is that suits an old man as a red
   coat suits a young one (for the same garment is not appropriate),

and if the orator wishes to ornament the subject, he must draw
the metaphor from the best species in the same genus, and if to
depreciate, from the worst. I refer to such cases as, when there
are opposites in the same genus, one says that the beggar be-
seeches and the beseecher begs, because both are requests, and
these have to do with what is being mentioned, as Iphicrates said
that Callias was a mendicant priest of Cybele and not a torch-
bearer, and he replied that Iphicrates had obviously not been
initiated, as he would not then have called him a mendicant
priest but a torch-bearer. Both positions are connected with
the goddess, but the one is prestigious and the other not.[7] A man
might also call actors the flatterers of Dionysus, while they call
themselves artists (these are both metaphors, the one abusive,
the other not), and pirates do actually call themselves purveyors
(which is why it is possible to say that the criminal made a
mistake, and that the man in error is a criminal, and that the
thief both takes and acquires). There is also the example in
Euripedes' *Telephus*:

By rule over the oar in Mysia landing . . .[8]

This is inappropriate, as 'rule' is too grand for the importance
of the subject; so the trick has not been concealed. There is also
error in the word forms, if they should not be expressive of a
pleasant timbre, as Dionysius the Bronzesmith described in his
elegies poetry as the 'scream of Calliope', because both screams
and poetry are vocal, but the metaphor is bad . . .[9] And again
the metaphor should be drawn not from remote things but
from those with affinity and of the same species, to name
things without name, which on being spoken immediately
reveal their affinity (as in the famous riddle: 'I saw man fasten
1405b   bronze on man with fire . . .';[10] for the occurrence has no
name, but since both are a form of addition, the riddler used
the word 'fastening' for the application of the cupping-glass),
and in general from well-composed riddles one can draw fitting
metaphors; for metaphors are cryptic, which shows that they
have been clearly drawn. And they should come from fine
things; the fineness of a word being, as Licymnius says, in its

220

sound or in its meaning, and similarly the ugliness.[11] The third aspect is that which refutes the sophistic argument; for it is not, as Bryson said, the case that none speaks shamefully, if it means the same to use one word instead of another. For this is false; one can choose a word that is more proper, similar and pertinent than another, to bring the matter before the audience's eyes. Again one word or another does not indicate the same thing under different conditions, so that in this way, too, one word should be allowed to be more beautiful or ugly than another; for both indicate beauty or ugliness, but not the way that they are beautiful or the way that they are ugly, or do this, but to a greater or lesser extent. So metaphors should be drawn from words that are beautiful either in sound or in effect or in image or to some other sense. There is a difference, for example, in saying 'rosy-fingered dawn' rather than 'purple-fingered dawn' or, even worse, 'red-fingered dawn'. With epithets the adjection can be made from fine or ugly things – 'the matricide', for instance – or can be made from better properties, as, for instance, 'avenger of his father'. And Simonides, when the man who won the mule race gave him a stingy fee, refused to write an ode, disdaining to sing the praises of half-asses, but, when his client gave him enough, wrote:

> Hail, daughters of the stormy-footed horse . . .[12]

Though they too were the daughters of asses. There is also in this vein the use of diminutives. And diminution is what makes something lesser, whether good or bad, as with Aristophanes' joke in the *Babylonians*, talking of 'goldlet' instead of gold and 'clothlet' instead of clothing, 'mocklet' instead of mockery and 'diseaselet' for disease.[13] But one must be on one's guard and in both cases observe what is moderate.

CHAPTER 3.3. FRIGIDITY

Exotic metaphorical clarity is the supreme merit of style, but the search for it is perilous and often leads into frigidity and flatness. Of this there are

*four species: the misuse of compounds, the use of outlandish expressions,
the injudicious choice of adjectives and the introduction of inappropriate
metaphors. All these lapses offend both against the principle of clarity and
against that of propriety, as Aristotle makes clear by an illustrative rather
than analytic account.*

CHAPTER 3.3

Frigidity occurs in four stylistic uses:

- First, in that of compound names, such as Lycophron's 'many-
faced heaven of the great-peaked land' and 'straight-corridored
shore', and those whom Gorgias named 'beggar-poet-flatterers
perjuring against a true swearer', and Alcidamas' 'soul full of
anger, eyes fire-hued'. Also he thought that the audience's enthusiasm would be 'end-bringing' and made the persuasion of
his words 'end-bringing' and made the surface of the sea 'blue-
coloured'; for all these expressions seem poetic because of their
conjunction.[14]

- This, then, is one reason for frigidity, and another is that of
using exotic words, as Lycophron called Xerxes an 'ogre of a
man' and Sciron was a 'ransacker-man', and Alcidamas coined
'toy of poetry' and spoke of the 'audacity of nature' and being
'honed by the unmixed anger of the mind'.[15]

- The third cause is the case of epithets, the use of either long
or untimely or too-frequent ones. Poetry is apt to say 'white
milk', but in prose this sort of thing is rather inappropriate.
These, if they are transparent, expose the artifice and make it
clear that it is so, although it is also right to use them (for it
varies the customary and makes the style exotic), but one must
aim for the mean, since failure to produces a greater disadvantage than speaking at random. The latter does not have stylistic
merit, but the former has demerit. This is the reason for the
frigidity of effect in Alcidamas. For he uses epithets not as a
sauce but as the meal, so frequent and large and blatant are
they. For instance, he does not talk of sweat but of 'damp
sweat', and of one going not to the Isthmia but to the 'congress
of the Isthmia,[16] and not of laws but 'laws, kings of cities', and

1406a

not by running but 'by the cursory urge of the soul', and not of
a museum but a 'museum of nature', and of the 'glowering
circumspection of the soul', and claims to be a producer not of
charm but of 'universal charm' and a 'distributor of the pleasure
of listeners', and that he hid not just in branches but in the
'branches of the wood', and did not cover his body but the
'shame of his body', and made the appetite of the soul 'counter-
imitative' (this is at the same time both compound and an
epithet, so that it becomes a piece of poetry), and similarly the
excess of baseness he called 'bound-transcending'. So by speaking poetically men produce an absurd and ridiculous effect
through the inappropriateness, and also obscurity through their
loquacity. For whenever a speaker overburdens someone who
knows the point, he destroys the clarity by overshadowing it.
And men tend to use compounds when the thing has no name
and the word is easily put together, such as to 'pass-time'; but if
it is done too much, it is always artificial. That is why com- *1406b*
pound diction is most useful for dithyrambic poets (for they are
wind-bags), and exotic words for epic poets (for they are solemn
and forceful), and metaphor for iambics (for this is what men in
fact use, as has been said).

• And there is yet a fourth source of frigidity – in metaphors.
There are also inappropriate metaphors, some through their
absurdity (even comic poets use metaphors) and some through
their being too solemn and tragic. They are also unclear if they
are drawn from too far afield, such as Gorgias' 'the affairs are
pale and bloodless', and 'you sowed in shame and harvested in
disaster', since they are too poetic. And as Alcidamas called
philosophy 'the bulwark of the law' and the *Odyssey* 'a beautiful
mirror of human life' and spoke of one 'bringing no such toy
to poetry'. All these are unpersuasive for the reasons given.[17]
Also Gorgias' remark to the swallow, when flying above him it
dropped its excrement, would have been excellent in a tragedy
– 'Shame on you, Philomela.' For to a bird it would not be
shameful to do what she did, but to a girl it would be. So he
berated her effectively by addressing her not as what she is but
what she was.[18]

CHAPTER 3.4. SIMILE

Simile is a species of metaphor. It is best suited to poetry, but it may be used in prose also, though with restraint, as is illustrated by a number of well-known instances.

CHAPTER 3.4

The *simile* is also a metaphor, as it is only slightly different.[19] For when the poet says 'and like a lion leapt', it is a simile, but when 'a lion leapt', it is a metaphor; for because they are both bold, he spoke of Achilles by the metaphor of the lion. The simile is also useful in prose, but only in small doses, since it is poetic. They should be brought in in the same way as metaphors; for they are metaphors, though differing in the way described.

Examples of similes are:

- The one that Androtion used against Idrieus, that he was like dogs fresh from the leash. They bite when they are set loose, and after his release from prison Idrieus was hostile.[20]
- And Theodamas' comparison of Archidamas to a Euxenus who could not do geometry – in proportion, for that matter, Euxenus will be an Archidamas with geometry.[21]
- Also the simile in Plato's *Republic* that those who despoil the dead are like dogs biting stones but not touching the one who throws them, and that on the people that it is like a strong but slightly deaf sea-captain, and that on the verses of poets, that they are like boys with bloom but without beauty; for when the latter lose their bloom, and when the former are broken, they are not comparable.[22]
- Also that of Pericles on the Samians, comparing them to children who receive scraps in tears and on the Boeotians that they are like oaks, as oaks are brought down by themselves and the Boeotians by fighting among each other.[23]
- And Demosthenes' simile on the people, that they are like those seasick on board.
- And in the way that Democrates likened orators to nurses who, having drunk the milk, anoint the children with spit.[24]

1407a

● And as Antisthenes compared the skinny Cephisodotus to incense, in that he gives pleasure by being consumed.[25]

All these we can give both as similes and as metaphors, so that all the ones that are given as metaphors will of course also be similes, and similes are metaphors that invite explanation. But one should always make the metaphor by analogy reciprocal and applying to each of the two members of one genus. For instance, if the goblet is the shield of Dionysus, then it would also be apt to call the shield the goblet of Ares.[26]

CHAPTER 3.5. PURITY

With superficial inconsistency we are now told that the first principle of good style is the speaking of correct Greek. This of course is an essential element of clarity, though Aristotle is unconcerned to spell out the formal connection. Linguistic purity is produced by five things: the correct use of connectives, the use of specific vocabulary, the avoidance of ambiguity and the observance of agreement both in gender and in number. Further, the phrase structure of the sentences must be easily parsed, even by the first-time hearer.

CHAPTER 3.5

The speech, then, is composed of these elements, but the prime principle of style is to *speak Greek*;[27] and this consists of five things:

● First, conjunctions. One should deploy them in the way that they are naturally constituted to be before or after one another, as some call for correspondence, as 'the one . . .' [*men*] and 'for my part . . .' [*egō men*] demand 'the other . . .' [*men*] and 'but for his . . .' [*de*]. But one must produce the reciprocation within the scope of the hearer's memory, and neither separate them by too great a distance nor introduce another conjunction before the reciprocating conjunction; for it seldom fits. 'For my part, when he said this to me (for Cleon had come begging and requesting), I went off and took them along.' In this case many intervening clauses are inserted before the reciprocating words; but if a great deal of sentence comes in before the 'went off', the effect is obscure. One aspect of good Greek, then, is the proper management of the connectives.

- And another is to use particular, not general, words.
- The third is to avoid ambiguity. And this if the opposite is not preferred, which men do when they have nothing to say but are pretending to say something. In poetry men say such things, as does Empedocles; for an extended periphrasis is deceptive, and the audience are affected in the way that the ordinary man is by oracles. For whenever these make ambiguous pronouncements, men nod along with them:

Crossing the Halys' stream will Croesus destroy a great empire . . .[28]

1407b And generally, through there being less error in generalities than in the matter itself, prophets speak like this. For in Odds and Evens[29] one would be more likely to be right by saying 'odd' or 'even' than by specifying how much, and also by saying 'it will be' rather than when, which is why oracle-mongers do not further specify the 'when'. All these things, then, are similar, so that if they are not required for some such reason, one should avoid them.

- The fourth element is respecting the way that Protagoras distinguished the genders of words, masculine and feminine and neuter; one must also make these agree correctly:[30] 'She, having come and spoken, went away.'
- The fifth is in correctly naming many, few and single things: '*They* came and struck *me*.'

In general what is written must be easy to read and easy to speak, which is the same. A long sequence of connections does not have this feature, nor do sentences which it is not easy to punctuate, like the remarks of Heracleitus.[31] For it is a hard task to punctuate the sayings of Heracleitus because of the obscurity about to what word another is attached, to the later or to the earlier, as in the very beginning of the collection; for his words are: 'Although reason exists for ever men are foolish.' The 'for ever' is obscure, as to with which it should be grouped. Another source of solecism is failure to reciprocate, if you do not connect two words with one that fits both: as with sound and colour, 'seeing' would not be common but 'hearing' would. There is also obscurity if you do not say at the start what you mean, intending to insert much material before the end: for instance, 'I was intending, having discussed with him and after such and such and so and so, as described, to go away . . .', and not, 'I was intending to talk with him and go away, and then such and such happened in such and such a way.'

CHAPTER 3.6. AMPLITUDE

Stylistic amplitude is quite distinct from rhetorical amplification. The latter, which has been dealt with earlier, is a means of increasing the impact of a rhetorical point, while the former is the mere generation of expansiveness in expression. The two might, of course, easily be combined, but their inherent roles are different. Amplitude is achieved primarily by the substitution of descriptions for names.

CHAPTER 3.6

A contribution is made by the following things to the *amplitude* of the style:

● Using a description instead of a noun, such as not 'circle', but 'edge equidistant from the middle'; and for concision the opposite, a noun instead of a description. And if the thing should be ugly or unseemly, if the ugliness is in the description, to use the noun, and if in the noun, to use the description. And to illustrate by metaphor and adjectives, avoiding the poetic. And to make singular things plural, as the poets do; there being but one harbour, they yet say,

> To the Achaean harbours . . .[32]

and,

> These are the many-leaved windings of the tablet . . .[33]

● And by not connecting up, but giving each word its article ('this wife of ours'); and if you want to speak concisely, the opposite ('our wife'). And to speak with connection; and if concisely, without connection but not with asyndeton. For example: 'having gone and having talked'; 'having gone, I conversed'. The trick of Antimachus is also useful, to describe something by what it does not have, which he does on Mount Teumessus,

1408a

There is a little windy hill . . .³⁴

For this will produce amplification without limit. This can be both for good and bad things, with the latter that they are not the case, and either way it would be useful, whence do the poets also take their words, the 'chordless' and 'lyreless' melody; for they draw them from negations; and this is a successful feature in metaphors by analogy, such as to say that the trumpet sings a lyreless song.

CHAPTER 3.7. PROPRIETY

Propriety is, along with clarity, the great hallmark of good style, as we were told at the beginning of this Section. It consists of the precise attunement of expression to content, to produce a certain proportionality between them. Failure to achieve this can often have a comic effect. Connected with this is the virtue of opportunity or timeliness, which requires the use of the right expression at the right moment.

CHAPTER 3.7

Style will have *propriety*, if it should be *emotive* and *characterful* and *proportional to the subject-matter*. And the proportion will be achieved if one neither speaks dismissively of things of some magnitude nor solemnly about funny things, nor should there be any decoration of a simple word. If not, it will seem to be a comedy, in the manner of Cleophon; for he says some things which are as though he were to say 'Lady Fig'.³⁵ Emotive too, if there has been an outrage, is the style of an angry man, and if the matters should be impious and shameful, to speak in the words of an indignant man who hesitates even to mention them, and if they should be praiseworthy, then rapturously, and if pitiable, then humbly, and similarly with the other subjects. Also fitting style makes the matter persuasive; for the mind is tricked as though the speaker were telling the truth, because with such things being so they are in the same mood that, even if things are not as the speaker is claiming, they think that they are, and the listener always empathizes with the man who speaks emotively, even if he is talking nonsense. Thus many speakers befuddle their listeners by kicking up a fuss. And character is also given by demonstration from signs itself, since a style is fittingly attendant on each kind and condition. By kind I mean by age, such as child or man or old man, and woman or man, and Laconian or Thessalian, and by habits, those things by which the character of a man's life is established; for life-characters are not determined by all habits. If then the speaker uses words appropriate to each habit, he will bring out character; for neither the same things nor in the same way would the peasant and the educated man speak. The audience are also affected to some extent by what speech-writers use unsparingly, as in 'Who does not know?', 'All men know'; for the listener agrees from shame that he should not share what everybody else enjoys.

Timely and untimely use[36] is common to all the genres of rhetoric. *1408b* The cure in the case of all hyperbole is that often recommended – one must castigate oneself in advance; for the exaggeration is then thought to be true as it is clear to the speaker what he is doing. Also one should not use all proportionalities together (for so the listener will be illuded). I mean if, for instance, the words should be hard, then not also with appropriate voice and expression; but if not, then it will be clear what each one is. But if one point is and the other is not, then the audience do not notice that they have the same effect. So if soft thoughts are said in a hard manner and hard thoughts softly, persuasiveness is produced. Compounds and many adjectives and exoticisms are especially suited to one's speaking emotively: it is forgiven to the angry man to call an evil 'as high as heaven' or 'gigantic', and whenever he is already in control of his audience and is making them respond either with praises or with criticisms or anger or friendship, as indeed Isocrates does at the end of the

Panegyricus – 'O fame and name' and 'whosoever dared bore it out'.[37] For men say such things in enthusiasm, so that the audience obviously accept them as they are in the same condition. This is why they are also suitable in poetry; for poetry is an inspired thing. One must, then, either use them thus or with irony, as Gorgias did and as happens in the *Phaedrus*.[38]

CHAPTER 3.8. RHYTHM

The discussion of style has so far concentrated on its lexical and syntactic features, those determined by the orator's choice of vocabulary and sentence structure, but the rhythmic flow of the chosen words also has a notable effect on the persuasiveness and charm of what is being said. Here again, a device that began in poetry has migrated to prose and prose rhythm has now, like prose style generally, achieved an autonomy in its own canons. The primary function of prose rhythm is to be neither wholly unrhythmical nor of full poetical metre. This is to be achieved by the employment of metrical units not found in verse.

CHAPTER 3.8

The form of the diction should be neither fully metrical nor completely without rhythm; the former is unconvincing (as it is thought to be artificial), and at the same time it is distracting; for it makes one expect the recurrence of a similar rhythmic pattern; just as children hearing from the heralds, 'Whom did the freed man choose as guardian?', chorus, 'Cleon!'[39] On the other hand, the rhythmless is unlimited, and the speech should be circumscribed but not by metre; for what is unbounded is unpleasant and unrecognizable. All things are bounded by number, and the number of the form of diction is rhythm, of which even metres too are divisions. So the speech must have rhythm, but not metre; otherwise it will be a poem. But it should not have precise rhythm; and this will be the case if it is only up to a point.[40] Now of the rhythms the heroic is lofty but does not admit of harmony of diction, while the iambic is itself the speech of the many (that is why people speaking most often utter iambi of all the metres), but in a speech loftiness must be produced and an elevation of the audience. The trochaic is too rumbustious, *1409a* as is shown by tetrameters; for the tetrameter is a bouncy metre. There remains the paean, which speakers have used from the time of Thrasymachus, but without being able to say which it was.[41] In fact the paean is a third kind of rhythm, with an affinity with those mentioned; for it is 3:2, and of the others one is 1:1 and the other is 2:2, and the paean's $1\frac{1}{2}$:1 is related to these two ratios. The other rhythms, then, are to be rejected for the reasons given and because they are metric; but the paean should be adopted; for it alone of the rhythms mentioned is not a metre, so that it is the most easily concealed. In fact speakers use one kind of paean both at the end and at the beginning, whereas the end ought to be different from the beginning. Now there are two mutually contrasting kinds of paean, of which one is suitable in the beginning, as speakers indeed use it; this is that of which the first syllable is the long and the three shorts are at the end, 'Delos-born or Lycian' and 'Golden-haired far-shooter, son of Zeus'.[42] The other is that from the reverse arrangement, in which the three shorts begin and the long is at the end:

> For after earth and sea, night hid the ocean . . .[43]

This makes an ending; for the short syllable, through being incomplete, makes it mutilated. The speech must be cut off by the long syllable, and the ending must be obvious not because of the writer nor the full-stop but because of the rhythm.

CHAPTER 3.9 SYNTAX

The rules of style also cover the structure of the sentence. It can either have a full syntax with copious subordinate clauses, or be more paratactic in character, relying on pithy and effective contrast. In the latter form of sentence structure, various forms of antithesis and anaphora give edge to the expression.

CHAPTER 3.9

It has, then, been said that the diction must have a good rhythm and not be rhythmless and what feet make good rhythm and in what arrangement. Now the diction must be either *extended and conjunctively united*, like the preludes in dithyrambic verse, or *antithetic*, like the antistrophes of the ancient poets.[44] Now the extended style is the ancient one (formerly all, now most, speakers use it), and by extended I mean the one which has no stop within itself, except when the matter spoken of should be completed. And it is unpleasant because of its unboundedness, as all men wish to see the end: runners approaching the turning-point pant and grow faint, whereas when they see the end they do not weary before getting there. This then is the extended style, but the contracted style is that in periods. By period I mean a clause having a beginning and end in itself and an

1409b easily surveyed magnitude. This is both pleasant and easily learned, pleasant through being in the opposite condition to the boundless, and because the listener always thinks that he has something and that something is being concluded for him, and it is unpleasant neither to anticipate nor to get through anything, and it is easily learned because it is easily memorized, and this is because the periodic style is numerical and number is the most easily remembered thing of all. That is why all men remember better verse rather than flat prose; for it has a numerical dimension by which it is measured. But the period must be completed, and not cut off like the iambics of Sophocles,

This is the land of Calydon, Pelops' realm . . .[45]

For it is possible to suppose the opposite because of the division, as in fact in the quotation that Calydon is in the Peloponnese.

The *period* is either in clauses or straightforward. Now a clausal style is that which is complete and partitioned and can be delivered without drawing breath, not in division but as a whole (the clause being one or other of its parts). By a straightforward period I mean that with a single clause. Now, both the clauses and the periods should neither taper away nor be lengthy. For a small clause often makes the listener stumble (for if, when he is rushing on to the eventual point and an amount of speech whose bounds he has in mind, he is tripped by the break, he comes a cropper, as it were, through the interruption); and a long clause makes him get stranded, as those turning in the outer track beyond the boundary also leave behind those running with them. Long periods become a speech and are like a prelude, so that there occurs what Democritus of Chios mocked in Melanippides who, instead of antistrophes, wrote only preludes:

> A man does himself ill who harms another,
> And for the bard long preludes spell calamity . . .[46]

For such a comment fits also for those who use long clauses. But if the clauses are too short, there is no period; so that they carry the listener along helter-skelter.

Of clausal styles there is *divided* and the *antithetic*.[47] An example of divided style is: 'I have often admired those who arranged large gatherings and instituted gymnastic contests'; and the antithetic style is that in which for each of a pair of clauses either opposite is juxtaposed to opposite or the same word is linked to both opposites. For example:

- 'They benefited both groups, both those who remained and those who accompanied them; for the latter they acquired more land than they had at home and for the former they left suffici-ent behind them at home' – 'remaining' and 'accompanying' being opposites, as are 'sufficient' and 'more';
- 'So that both for those in need of money and for those wishing to spend it' – expenditure being the opposite of acquisition.
- And again: 'It often happens in these cases that the wise come unstuck and the foolish are successful'; 'They immediately received awards for valour and not much later they took over the rule of the sea'; 'To sail through the mainland, to march through the sea, bridging the Hellespont and cutting through Athos;[48] 'And those by nature citizens were deprived by law of the city'; 'Some of them died wretchedly, others disgracefully survived'; 'Privately to use only barbarians as slaves, but publicly to acquiesce in the enslavement of many of the allies'; 'Which they will either have when alive or leave behind them when dead.'
- And the remark someone made on Peitholaus and Lycophron[49]

in the court, 'These men sold you when they were at home, but coming among you they are buying you.'

All these things produce the effect mentioned. And this form of style is pleasant, because opposites are very clear and all the more so when juxtaposed, and because it resembles the syllogism; for the refutational syllogism is conclusion from contraries.

Antithesis, then, is of this nature. Parisosis is when clauses are equal and paromoeosis is when each clause has the same last syllable; and this must either arise in the beginning or at the end, and in the beginning it is always in the words, and at the end in the last syllables, or in the cases of the same word or in the repetition of the word.

- In the beginning are such things as: 'He received from him idle land'; 'Men that take gifts were they and with words easily talked round.'
- And at the end, such things as: 'You would think not that he has produced a child but that he has become a child'; 'with very many worries and very few hopes'. Cases of the same word are such as: 'Does he ask for a statue in bronze, not being worthy of a bronze penny?' And repetition: 'You spoke ill of him when he was alive and now you write ill of him.' Resemblance of a syllable: 'What terrible thing would you have suffered if you had seen an idle man?' It is also possible for one sentence to have all of them at the same time and for the same period to be antithesis, parisosis and homoeoteleuton.[50] The principles of the periods are more or less all listed in the Theodectea.[51] There are also false antitheses, such as the one Epicharmus used to use:

Now was I with them, now was I amongst them . . .

CHAPTER 3.10. WIT AND METAPHOR

Even if the speech has achieved complete clarity in impeccably pure Greek, has been adorned throughout with exotic but appropriate metaphor and has flowed with a pleasing, but quite unpoetic, rhythm, it will still be lacking

*in impact unless it is seasoned with the salt of wit. This is notoriously not
a subject for prescription, but Aristotle interestingly suggests that the essence
of the enjoyment of wit is the recognition that it involves in the hearer. To
the discussion of wit is appended a survey of the species of metaphor, which
completes the considerable treatment that this subject has already received
throughout the Section. The species of metaphor being four in number, the
first and most arresting are those which rest on proportionality. Another
important task that metaphor should achieve is that of bringing the object
illustrated, as it were, before our eyes, and this concept is to be the subject
of the next chapter.*

CHAPTER 3.10

Since we have become clear about these things, we must say whence
witty and popular sayings come about. They can be produced either
by the natural wit or by the man who has trained, and to show
them is part of this method. Let us mention them, then, and list
them. And let this be our beginning: to learn easily is naturally
pleasant to all, and words mean something, so that those words that
produce knowledge for us are most pleasant. Exotic words are
unfamiliar, and pertinent ones we know, and so it is metaphor that
particularly has this effect. For when the poet calls old age a reed, he
produces understanding and recognition through the generic similarity; for both have lost their flower. The similes of the poets also
have the same effect; hence if one is good, it seems a witticism. For
the simile is, as has been said before, a metaphor differing in one
addition only; hence is it less pleasant, as it is more drawn out, and
it does not say that this is that, and so the mind does not think out
the resemblance either. Both style and enthymemes must be witty
that produce swift understanding for us; hence neither superficial
enthymemes are popular (by superficial we mean ones obvious to
everyone, and which it is not at all necessary to scrutinize) nor ones
that we do not understand when they are said, but either those of
which recognition occurs as soon as they are spoken, especially if it
had not pre-existed, or those in which the intellect of the hearer is
but a little behind; for there occurs a kind of understanding in this
case, but not with either of the other two. So by the intellectual

content of what is said this type of enthymeme is popular. Stylistically, popularity is achieved, on the one hand formally, if the points are spoken antithetically, such as 'thinking that the common peace of others was a war on their own interests', war being the opposite of peace, and on the other verbally, if there is a metaphor, and this neither foreign, as it is difficult to see, nor superficial, as it has no effect. Also if it puts the subject before our eyes; for we should see things being done rather than imminent. So we must aim for these three things: *metaphor, antithesis* and *vividness.*

1411a   There are four kinds of *metaphor*, but those by *analogy* are the most celebrated:

- Pericles, for example, said that the youth killed in the war had so disappeared from the city as if someone had taken the spring from the year.[52]
- And Leptines said of the Lacedaemonians that he would not acquiesce in Greece's becoming one-eyed.[53]
- And Cephisodotus, when Chares was hastening to render his account in connection with the campaign at Olynthus, was angry and asserted that having seized the people by the throat he now was trying to render his account. And once in summoning the Athenians to Euboea with provisions he said that they should come with their own provisions, as in the decree of Miltiades.[54]
- And when the Athenians had made a truce with Epidaurus and the coastline, Iphicrates was angry and said that they were throwing away their own journey-money.[55]
- And Peitholaus called the *Paralus* the cudgel of the people and Sestus the granary of the Piraeus.[56]
- And Pericles told the Athenians to destroy Aegina, the eyesore of the Piraeus.[57]
- And Moerocles said that he was by no means more wicked than one of the respectable men whom he named; for the other was wicked on 33 per cent, but he himself on 10.
- And the iambic of Anaxandrides on his daughters' delaying their marriage: 'My daughters are late for their own wedding.'[58]
- Also Polyeuctes' remark on the paralytic Speusippus, about his

not being able to be at peace though bound by fate in a disease of five stocks.[59]

- And Cephisodotus called the triremes colourful mill-stones, and the Dog called the Athenian taverns the messes of Attica; and Aesion said that the Athenians poured the city away into Sicily – for this was a metaphor and also graphic.[60] And 'so that Greece cries out' – this too is in a way a metaphor and vivid.

- And as Cephisodotus told the Athenians to be on their guard lest they create many assemblies.

- Also Isocrates' remark on those running together in meetings.[61]

- And the example in the funeral speech of Lysias, that it was right that on the tomb of those who died at Salamis Greece should cut her hair, as by their courage her freedom was secured; if he had said that she should weep, as her freedom was also buried, this would have been a metaphor and visual, but 'their courage . . . her freedom' has a certain antithesis.[62]

- And as Iphicrates said, 'My route of words is through the midst *1411b* of the works of Chares', this being a metaphor by analogy and the words 'through the midst' making it graphic.[63] Also to say that one summons danger to assist against danger is graphic and a metaphor.

- Also Lycoleon in defence of Chabrias: 'Not even shamed by his suppliancy, in a bronze statue.' This is a metaphor in the present, though not always, but still visual; for, in his danger, the statue begs for him, as a case indeed of 'animate become inanimate', it being the record of his deeds for the city.[64]

- And 'studying by all means to think small thoughts'; for to study something is to increase it. And that 'a god set the intellect in the soul as its lamp'. (Both illuminate something.) 'We are not ending the wars but deferring them' – both are for the future, both deferral and a peace of that kind. And to say that a treaty is a much fairer trophy than those erected in war; for the latter are over small things and a single outcome, but the former for the whole war, both being signs of victory. And that the cities render a great account before the criticism of men; for the rendering of an account is a kind of judicial punishment.[65]

CHAPTER 3.11. VIVIDNESS

It is important for a metaphor to have its full effect that it be able to conjure up before our eyes an image of what it describes. This is achieved by the use of graphic language, in the most literal sense. As with so many other features of style, this is something much more easily illustrated by example than by theory and Aristotle proceeds to present an impressive catalogue of successful employments of graphic speech.

CHAPTER 3.11

That witticisms are produced from both analogical metaphors and by vividness has been said. But we must say what we mean by vivid and how this is produced. I say, then, that vividness is produced by things that indicate actuality, as it is a metaphor to say that the good man is four-square (as both are complete), but this does not indicate actuality; rather 'having his prime in flower' creates actuality, and also 'you, like an unleashed animal', and:

With shooting feet the Greeks . . .[66]

For 'shooting' has actuality and metaphor, as it means 'swift'. And, as Homer's usage often is, making the inanimate animate through 1412a metaphor. In all cases popularity is achieved by creating actuality, as in the words 'again down to the plain the wretched stone would roll', and 'an arrow flew', and 'yearning to fly against them', and 'they stuck in the earth yearning to taste flesh', and 'the tip rushed eagerly through his breast'. In all these cases through the things' being made animate they appear to be actual; for to be shameless and eager or show the other emotions produces actuality. And Homer made these ascriptions by analogical metaphor; for as the stone is related to Sisyphus, so is the shameless man to the one shamelessly treated. There is the same effect even with inanimates, as in the famous similes:

Arching with foam at their crests, some vanwards, some to the rearguard.[67]

For he makes all things moving and alive, and actuality is a movement.

But one must also draw the metaphor, as has been said before, from related but not obvious things. For example, even in philosophy it requires speculative capacity to observe the similarity even in very mutually remote things, as Archytas said that an arbitrator and altar are the same, as the injured party takes refuge in them both. Or if one were to say that an anchor and a pot-hook were the same; for both are the same thing, but differ by being set upwards or downwards. And the equalization of the cities is the same in regard to what makes them very different from each other, the equality being in the cities' structures and capacities.

Most witticisms are also produced through metaphor and an additional illusion; for what the hearer hears becomes clearer to him through its being the opposite to what he thought, and the mind seems to say, 'How true, and I was wrong.' And witty apophthegms come from not saying what they mean, like that of Stesichorus that the cicadas will sing for themselves from the ground. And good riddles are pleasant for the same reason (for they involve learning and metaphor), and (as Theodorus says) to speak new things. This happens whenever the thought is paradoxical, and not (as he says) in accord with our previous opinion, but like things distorted for comic effect (which effect is also produced by jokes turning on a single letter, which are illusory), and also in poetry; for this line does not end as the listener expects: 'He went with, on his feet, chilblains', whereas he expected 'sandals'.[68] But this sort of joke must be clear as soon as it is spoken.

Jokes turning on a word make the sentence not say what one means but what changes the word, like the remark of Theodorus to the lyre-player Nicon, 'You will be worried', for he pretended to say, 'You are a Thracian?' and deceived him by saying something *1412b* else.[69] Hence it is pleasant to one who understands, since if the hearer does not know Nicon to be a Thracian, it will not seem to be witty. Also, 'You wish to destroy him.'[70] Both types of joke, however, must be said appropriately. And similar also are such witticisms as to say of the Athenians that control of the sea was not the beginning of evils; for it was beneficial. Or, as Isocrates did, to call the empire the beginning of evils for the city. For in both cases what no one would expect to be said is said and is recognized to be true; for to say that the empire is the empire is not at all clever, but Isocrates means the second use of the word not in the same sense but in another, and the other use does not deny what he has said expressly but in another sense.[71] In all these, if the speaker appropriately brings in the word either by homonymy or metaphor, then the effect is good. For example, 'Anaschetus is intolerable' is a contradiction of the homonym, but appropriately, if he is unpleasant. And, 'Do not become more foreign than you should be.' For 'no more foreign than you should be' means the same as 'the stranger should not always be a stranger'; for this too refers to something else.[72] The much-praised remark of Anaxandrides is the same:

> 'Tis good to die not earning it by deeds . . .[73]

For this is the same as to say, 'It is appropriate to die, not being appropriate to die', or, 'It is appropriate to die, not being worthy of death' or 'not doing things worthy of death'. The form, then, of these things is the same; but in so far as they are said more pithily and antithetically, by so much are they the more popular. And the reason is that understanding is made greater by contrast and swifter through happening in a short space. But there must in addition always either be a particular person of whom it is said or it must be rightly said, for the remark's being true and not superficial; for these circumstances can occur in separation, such as 'One should die having never sinned' and 'The right woman should marry the right man', though they are not witty; but there will be wit if both circumstances apply at the same time: 'It is worthy to die, not being worthy to die.' In so far as an expression has more features, so much does it seem wittier, such as if even the words should be metaphorical and metaphorical after the right kind and with antithesis and parisosis, and should have actuality.

The *popular similes* too are, as stated above, in a way metaphors; for they are always produced from two things, like the metaphor 1413a by analogy, such as, 'The spear,' we say, 'is the goblet of Ares', and, 'The bow is a lyre without a string.' In this way of speaking, then, the metaphor is not simple, while to call a bow a lyre or a spear a jug is simple. And men also make similes in this way, comparing, for instance, a flautist to a monkey, a man with short sight to a smouldering lamp; for both are compressed. But the good effect is achieved when it is a metaphor; for it is possible to compare the shield to the jug of Ares and a ruin to the tatters of a building, and to say that Niceratus is Philoctetes bitten by Pratys, as Thrasymachus compared him, when he saw Niceratus beaten by Pratys in the rhapsodic contest, still dirty and shaggy.[74] This is what especially counts against poets if it is not well done, and if it is well done distinguishes them; I mean when they produce an answering clause:

> He walks on twisted legs, quite parsley-like . . .
> Like Philammon with leather punch-bag sparring . . .[75]

And all such are similes. And it has often been pointed out that similes are metaphors.

And *proverbs* too are metaphors from species to species; for instance, if someone should introduce someone else, hoping to do well himself, and should then be harmed, they say, 'Like the Carpathian and the hare.' For they both underwent the misfortune mentioned.[76] So we have more or less given the cause from which come witticisms and why; and popular exaggerations are also metaphors, as that on one who has a black-and-blue eye, 'You would think that he is a basket of mulberries.' For the 'black eye' is something purple, and the mulberry basket is so on a larger scale.[77] Also 'as this or that' is exaggeration differing only in diction. 'Like Philammon sparring with the bag', or, 'You would think that he was Philammon sparring with the bag', or:

> He walks on twisted legs, quite parsley-like, . . .[78]

Or, 'You would think he has not legs but parsley, so twisted are they.' Exaggerations are also puerile, as they reveal vehemence. That is why men speak them most in anger:

> Not if he gave so much as is the sand
> And dust. Nor shall Atrides' daughter be
> My wife, not if she vied in beauteousness
> With golden Aphrodite and in works
> Even with Athena . . .[79]

That is why they are inappropriate for an older speaker to use. (The *1413b* Attic orators especially use this device.)

CHAPTER 3.12. SUITABILITY TO GENRE

Good style will enhance any form of oratory in any of the genres and is a universal feature, like the use of common topics. However, it can also be enriched by employing certain modifications appropriate to particular genres. These are explained in this concluding chapter of the Section on style. The distinction between styles can be thought of in terms primarily of descriptiveness and pugnacity. Deliberative oratory requires little accuracy of description, but forensic oratory rather more, to arouse the interest of the audience, but even more accuracy is required by display oratory. The combative dimension is derived from the stage and is most appropriate to the courts.

CHAPTER 3.12

But one should not forget that a different style suits each genre. For the style of written compositions is not the same as that of altercation, nor are political and forensic style the same. And one must know both; for the altercative involves knowing how to speak Greek, and the written involves not being forced to be silent if you wish to transmit something to others, which is the fate of those who do not know how to write. Now written style is most precise, but altercative most susceptible of delivery (of this there are two species: the ethical and the emotional); hence actors seek out plays, and poets actors of this kind. But readable playwrights also make an impact, such as Chaeremon (for he is as precise as a speech-writer), and Licymnius of the dithyrambic poets. And in comparison the speeches of the writers appear empty in trials, while those of the orators, when read, seem peculiar even in their own hands. The reason is that in a trial easily delivered speeches are appropriate. So when the delivery is taken away, they fail in their function and seem silly; for instance, asyndeton and the frequent repetition of the same word are correctly rebuked in written style, but not in the altercative style, and the orators often use them. For they are suitable for delivery. But one must change the expression when saying the same thing, since this, as it were, paves the way for a delivery: 'This is the man who has stolen from you, this the man who has tricked you, this the man who has tried to betray you at the end', as Philemon the actor did both in the *Battle of the Greybeards* of Anaxandrides,[80] when he said, 'Rhadamanthys and Palamedes', and in the prologue of the *Holy Ones* his 'I'; for if one does not act such things, it is a case of the proverbial 'man carrying the beam'.[81] And it is the same with asyndeta: 'I went, I met him, I begged.' For it is necessary to act them out and not, as saying one thing, use the same manner and tone. Also asyndeton has its special force; for in the same time many things seem to be being said; for the connection makes the many things one, so that if it is removed, it is obvious that conversely the one becomes many. Hence amplification is produced: 'I came, I talked, I besought . . .' (this seems many things) '. . . He ignored what I said.' This is also what Homer is trying to do in the lines: *1414a*

> Nireus again from Syme,
> Nireus son of Aglaea,
> Nireus, who is most fair . . .[82]

For the one about whom many things are said must also be often mentioned; so if the name is often mentioned, then it also seems that many things have been said, so that there has been amplification in a single mention because of the fallacy, and Homer has made him remembered, though saying nothing of him later.

Deliberative style, then, also completely resembles a rough sketch; for the larger the crowd should be, the more remote is the inspection, so that precision is unnecessary and gives a worse impression in both cases. But forensic style is more meticulous. And still more that before a single judge, as here the smallest amount of rhetoric is involved. For the peculiarities of the matter are more easily seen and what is not germane to it, and debate is absent, so that the judgement is pure. Accordingly, the same orators are not equally distinguished in all genres; but where there is the most delivery, there is there the least precision. And this is where there is a need for a voice, and especially a loud one.

The style of display is most suited to written composition, since its function is to be read. And the next most is forensic. But further to make specifications about style, that it must be pleasant and magnificent, is superfluous; for why so more than that it be prudent

and liberal and possess any other moral virtue? And obviously the
things mentioned will make it pleasant, if the excellence of style has
indeed been correctly defined; for for what reason must the style be
clear, and not humble but appropriate? For if garrulous, it is not
clear, nor even if too concise, but it is obvious that the mean is
suitable. And the things mentioned will also make the style pleasant:
if there is a good mixture of customary and exotic, of the rhythm
and of the persuasiveness from propriety.

Our discussion of style is complete, both in general about them
all and in particular about each genre; it remains to discuss composition.

SECTION TEN: COMPOSITION

CHAPTER 3.13. NARRATION AND PROOF

The study of composition had, like that of style, initially been repudiated as part of oratory. Here, however, in the final Section of the work, it too receives a summary but stimulating treatment. The present introductory chapter stresses that the two primary functions of the speech are to state the case and to prove it and that its composition should be structured accordingly. In fact the speech should have four parts: an introductory section, to dispel the prejudice that will have been built up by the opposition against the speaker or his case; the main narrative section; the proof of the claims made in the speaker's own narrative and the refutation of those made by his adversary; and finally a recapitulatory and perorative epilogue.

CHAPTER 3.13

There are two parts of the speech. It is necessary both to *state* the subject-matter and to *demonstrate* it. Consequently, it is impossible without having stated the matter to prove it or having stated it not to prove it; for one who proves proves something, and one who describes describes for the sake of proof. Of these two elements one is presentation and the other is proof, which is as though one were to distinguish them as on the one hand problem and on the other demonstration. But at present the division is absurd; for narration belongs in a way only to forensic oratory, and how can there be in display and political oratory narration of the kind which they describe, or a refutation of the adversary, or an epilogue in de- *1414b* monstrative speeches? And introductions, counter-comparisons and recapitulations occur in deliberative oratory on those occasions when

245

there is a speech of opposition. Also there is often indeed an element of prosecution and defence, but not as deliberation. The epilogue, on the other hand, does not even belong to all forensic oratory, for example if the speech is short or the matter easily remembered; for its characteristic is to contract the length of the narrative. So the *necessary sections* are *presentation* and *proof*. These ones, then, are the proper ones, but the maximum number are *introduction*, *presentation*, *proof* and *epilogue*; for the refutation of the adversary comes under proof, and counter-comparison is amplification of the speaker's own position, so that it too is a part of the proofs (for the man who does it is demonstrating something), but not the introduction, nor the epilogue, which are rather reminders. So if one should distinguish these sections, as among the school of Theodorus, there will be the narration as one thing and also the supplementary narration and the pre-narration and refutation and further refutation. But one should apply a term only in mentioning a species with a characteristic feature; if not, it becomes empty and futile, like what Licymnius does in his 'art', coining terms for *apourosis* and *apoplanesis* and *roots*.[1]

CHAPTER 3.14. THE INTRODUCTION

A rhetorical introduction resembles a dramatic prologue or a musical prelude. In display oratory its function is to establish, as it were, the home key of the speech as a whole. In forensic and deliberative oratory, the introduction should make clear what is to be the central point of the whole speech, what it has been written for. It is also necessary to arouse the interest, and, if possible, sympathy, of the audience.

CHAPTER 3.14

The *introduction*, then, is the beginning of the speech, which in poetry is the prologue and in flute music the prelude; for all these things are initiatory and, as it were, prepare the way for what is to follow. The prelude is similar to the introduction of epideictic oratory; indeed flautists, by putting in the prelude whatever they should be able to play well, connect it with the tonic key, and that is how one should write in display speeches, speaking out immediately what one wants to say and so setting the tone and connecting this with the subject, as in fact all speakers do. And an example is the introduction to Isocrates' *Helen*; for there is nothing in common between eristic arguments and Helen.[2] And even if one should digress from the subject-matter, that is suitable, and also the whole speech should not be of the same kind. The introductions of display speeches are derived from praise or blame (as Gorgias says in his *Olympicus*, 'You are worthy to be admired by many, O men of Hellas'; for he is praising those instituting the congresses; and Isocrates blames them in that they rewarded bodily merits with prizes, but have assigned no reward for those with wisdom), and also from deliberation (as that one should respect good men, which is why the speaker himself is praising Aristides, or those who are neither distinguished nor base, but are good, without its being known, like Alexander, son of Paris;[3] for to say this is to advise). They are also drawn from forensic introductions – that is, from appeals directed at the audience – if the speech is about something unexpected or difficult or widely bruited, so as to be forgiven, as Choerilus: *1415a*

> But now that all has been divided up . . .[4]

The introductions, then, of display speeches are drawn from these things – from praise, from blame, from exhortation, from dissuasion, from appeals to the audience; and the keynote should be either exotic or cognate with the speech. But one must realize that the introduction of a forensic speech has the same effect as the prologues of plays and the introductions of epic poems, while dithyrambic introductions are similar to those of display oratory: 'Through you and your gifts and plunder.' But in forensic and epic introductions there is an indication of the story, so that it may be known in advance what the tale is about and that the intellect be not in suspense; for what is undefined is digressive; the man who puts the beginning as it were into the hands of his audience produces the likely result that they follow the speech. Hence:

> Sing of the wrath, O Muse . . .[5]

and:

Tell me, O Muse, of the man . . .[6]

and:

Tell me another tale, of how from Asia's land
Came mighty war to Europe . . .[7]

In just this way tragic poets indicate what the drama is about — if not immediately, like Euripides, in the prologue, yet somewhere, as even Sophocles has:

My father was King Polybus . . .[8]

And similarly with comedy. The most necessary function, then, of the introduction, and special to it, is to show what is the purpose of the speech (hence if the matter should be trivial or obvious, one should not use an introduction); and the other species of introductory points that are used are therapeutic remarks common to all speeches. There are derived from the speaker and from the audience and from the matter and from the opponent, as regards himself and his adversary, such things as to dissolve or create prejudice (these are not done, though, in the same way: for the defendant the first task is to address the prejudice; but the prosecutor should do it in the epilogue, and why this is so is obvious; for when the defendant is to introduce himself, he must remove the obstacles, so that he must first dissolve the prejudice; for the slanderer, however, the slander must be given in the epilogue, so that the audience may remember it better). The appeal to the hearer is drawn from the method of making him benign or of making him angry, and sometimes from that of making him attentive or the opposite; for it is not always expedient to make him attentive, which is why many seek to lead the audience to laughter. But all things will conduce to sympathetic understanding, if one wishes, and to one's seeming respectable; for more attention is paid to such people. And men are also attentive to great matters, things affecting them, the astounding and the pleasant; so one must produce the impression that the speech is about such things, and if one wishes that they are not attentive, that it is trivial or irrelevant to them or unpleasant. But one should not forget that all such things are external to the speech;

for they are directed to a low-grade listener, who listens to things outside the matter; if he be not of this kind, there would be no need of an introduction, but only of so much as to summarize the matter, so that it has, as it were, a head to its body. Also to make the audience attentive belongs to every section of the speech, if it should be necessary; for at all places they are more relaxed than at the beginning; so it is absurd to assign this task to the beginning, when they are all listening especially attentively; so that when the time is right, one should say, 'And attend to me; for my case is no more mine than yours', and, 'I will tell you something more terrible and astonishing than you have ever heard.' And this is, as Prodicus said, when the audience are dozing off, to give them a fifty-drachma lecture.[9] But that the address to the listener is not to him as listener is obvious; for all speakers either produce prejudice or remove fears in their introductions:

My lord, I shall not say that moved by haste . . .

Why these preliminaries? . . .[10]

And those who have a bad case, or seem to have one, do the same; for it is better to dwell on anything other than the case, so that slaves do not say what they are asked but speak periphrastically, as in introductions. Now it has been said by what method one makes men benign, and in each of the other such states of mind. And since it was well said:

Let me as friend to Phaeacia arrive or as object of mercy[11]

one should aim at these two things. In display speeches, on the other hand, one must make the listener think that he is joined in the praise, either in himself or his family or in his practices or in some other way; for it is true what Socrates says in his funeral speech, that it is not hard to praise the Athenians among the Athenians, but it is among the Spartans.

The introductions to political speeches are drawn from those of forensic oratory, but by nature there are very few; for the audience know what the speech is about, and the matter needs no introduction, but it should either occur on account of the orator himself or of those speaking against him, or if the audience assume that he is not of an age to advise, but either too old or too young, so that it is necessary either to excite or to remove prejudice, and either to amplify or to diminish the subject. For these things an introduction is needed, or perhaps for the sake of decoration, as the speech will seem off the cuff if it does not have one. Of this kind is Gorgias' 1416a encomium on the Eleans; for without any preliminaries or preamble, he begins straight off, 'Elis, fortunate city'.[12]

CHAPTER 3.15. PREJUDICE

In order to arouse the sympathy of the audience, the speaker will very likely have to dispel the prejudice that will have been set in motion against him. A paradigm of this, of course, is the Apology of Socrates, where the claim of the prosecutors that Socrates is an impressive speaker is attacked and rejected. It may also be necessary to engender a prejudice against the adversary and this too is the business of the introduction.

CHAPTER 3.15

In connection with *prejudice*:

- One technique is that by which one might dissolve a hostile supposition (it makes no difference whether it has arisen by someone's saying something or not, so that this is quite general);[13] and another topic is how to reply to the point at issue, by claiming either that the allegations are wrong, or that what was done was not harmful or not to the adversary, or that it was not so great as made out, or that it was not harmful or not greatly so, or not shameful or not having importance; for controversy arises about these things, as that of Iphicrates against Nausicrates;[14] for he agreed that he did what was alleged and that it was harmful but not that it was unjust.
- Or one can redress the balance if one has done wrong by claiming that one's deed, if harmful, was yet noble, or that it was painful but useful, or some other such claim.
- Another topic is that it was an error or misfortune or necessity, as Sophocles said that he was trembling not, as the accuser was

suggesting, to seem an old man, but from necessity; for he did not want to be eighty years old.

- And one can interchange the motives, to the effect that one did not wish to do harm but only such and such, not what is alleged, and that the harm was accidental: 'It would be just for you to hate me, if I did the deed so that this should happen.'
- Another is if the alleger is compromised, either now or before, either himself or one of his friends. Another is if others are involved whom the prosecution agree to be innocent of the charge, such as that because someone is a fop he is an adulterer, then so forth.
- Another is if either the same man or another has also accused others, or if others without allegation have been assumed to have acted as one currently is assumed to have, and who have been shown not to be involved.
- Another is from counter-allegations against the alleger; for it is absurd if one who is himself incredible will be credited.
- Another is if a judgement has occurred, as with Euripides in his antidosis case against Hygiaenon, who was accusing him of impiety. This he allegedly did by encouraging men to forswear:

  My tongue and not my mind it was that swore[15]

  Euripides replied that Hygiaenon himself did wrong by transferring the judgements of the Festival of Dionysus to the law courts; for there he had given an account of these words, or would again if Hygiaenon wished to accuse him there.
- Another is from attacking the prejudice, again showing how great it is, and this because it distorts judgements, and does not support the facts.
- It is a common topic to both parties to mention tokens, as Odysseus says in the *Teucer* that Teucer is a relative of Priam; *1416b* for Priam's sister was Hesione; while Teucer said that his father Telamon was hostile to Priam and that he himself did not expose the spies.[16]
- Another topic for the producer of prejudice is to praise a small thing excessively and criticize a great one slightly, or present

many good things, and criticize the one thing relating to the case. These topics are the most skilled and unjust; for they seek to harm the adversary by his good points, by mixing them with the bad.

● It is common to both prejudicer and defender, since the same thing can be done from many motives, for the slanderer to be malicious and interpret them for the worse and for the defender for the better, as that Diomedes chose Odysseus, for the one speaker because he thought that Odysseus was the best man, and for the other, that it was not for this reason but because he would be the only one not to rival him because of his baseness.[17]

CHAPTER 3.16. NARRATION

As soon as the speech has been successfully launched, it is time to turn to the business of stating clearly the speaker's own version of the facts. This is, of course, of paramount importance in forensic oratory, but it might also play a part in deliberation. It is in narration that clarity and descriptiveness are most important.

CHAPTER 3.16

Let this much suffice on the subject of prejudice. *Narration* in display speeches is not continuous but sectional; for one must go through the actions from which the account is drawn; for the speech is composed on the one hand having a non-technical part (for the speaker is in no way responsible for the deeds themselves) and on the other a technical one; and this is to show either that the facts are the case, if this should not be believed, or that they are of a given kind or quantity, or even all of the categories. For this reason one should sometimes not narrate all the deeds in sequence, because a demonstration in this manner is harder to remember; so from one group of facts a man is shown to be courageous and from another wise or just. And this latter speech is relatively simple, but the other is varied and not plain. And one must mention only famous actions; hence most people do not even need narration, for instance if you wish to praise Achilles (for all men know his deeds), but one should merely exploit the deeds. But if you are praising Critias, then you must narrate his deeds; for not many people know them ... But at present it is absurdly held that the narration should be swift. And yet, as a man once replied to a baker's question whether he should knead the dough hard or soft, 'What? To knead it well is impossible, then?', similarly in this case; for one should not narrate at length, any more than the introduction should be at length, nor the exposition of the proofs. For no more in this case is the good effect swiftness or concision but the striking of the mean – that is to say, things which illuminate the matter, or make one suppose that it has 1417a happened or been harmful or wrong or of such a kind as one wishes, and for the adversary the opposite. One should tangentially narrate everything pertaining to one's own virtue (e.g. 'I warned him, always recommending just actions, not to abandon his children'), or the vice of the other man (e.g. 'But he replied to me that wherever he might be he would have other children', or what Herodotus says that the rebelling Egyptians replied),[18] or whatever is pleasant to the jury. For the defendant the narration is shorter; for his contentions are either that the thing never happened or that it was not harmful or unjust or not so much, so that one should not spend time on what is agreed, if it should have no bearing on the point that, if it has been done, it was not a crime. One should also claim to have been done things which undone bring either pity or horror; an example is the narration to Alcinous, got through in sixty hexameters to Penelope,[19] and as Phayllus contracted the epic cycle, and the prologue to the *Oeneus*.[20] And the narrative must have character; and this will be the case if we know what produces character. One thing, then, is to indicate moral purpose, the character being determined by that, and that being determined by the end. This is why mathematical arguments have no character, as they also lack moral purpose (as they have no motive), while Socratic dialogues do, as it is with such things that they deal. Other characterizing factors are features attendant on each character, such as that a man was speaking while he walked; this reveals audacity and boorishness of character. And one should not speak as though from intellect, as is currently done, but from moral purpose: 'Yet I wished;

253

for I chose it; and if I did not profit from it, it was still better.' The one is of the prudent man, the other of the good one; it is for the prudent man to pursue advantage and for the good one nobility. But if the claim should be incredible, then one should add the reason, as Sophocles does; and an example is the case of Antigone, that she was more concerned for her brother than for a husband or children; for the others could be replaced if they died, but

> My mother and my father being in Hades,
> Never might I receive another brother . . .[21]

But if you do not have a reason, you must still show that you are aware of saying incredible things, but that you are by nature of this kind; for men do not believe that anyone would do anything except for their own interest. Also from the emotional factors mention in the narration both the consequences which men know, and special features relevant either to yourself or the adversary: 'He went off 1417b glowering at me.' And as Aeschines says of Cratylus, that he was hissing aggressively and shaking his hands; for these things are persuasive, because the things that they know become tokens for what they do not know. And one can draw many examples from Homer:

> So did he speak, but the old woman held her face in her two hands . . .[22]

For those who are starting to cry cover their eyes. And immediately introduce both yourself as of a certain kind, that they may consider you as such, and also your adversary; but do it secretly. But that it is easy see from the case of men making proclamations; for from them we form an assumption about things of which we as yet know nothing. One should narrate in many places and sometimes not at the beginning.

Narration is least common in deliberative oratory, as none relates what is to come; but if there should be narration, let it be of past facts, so that in recalling them men may judge better for the future, either in slandering or in praise; this, however, is not to perform the function of the adviser. If it should be incredible, one should promise both immediately to give a reason and to arrange it as they want, as Jocasta, in the *Oedipus* of Carcinus, is always promising when the seeker of her son asks her questions, and as the Haemon of Sophocles does.[23]

CHAPTER 3.17. PROOF AND REFUTATION

After the statement of the case comes the proof. The invention of the subject-matter of this Section has of course been discussed at length, but it remains to make clear certain features of the arrangement of the argumentative section of the speech as a whole. The function of the section is, of course, both to establish the speaker's own case and to rebut that of the adversary, but the latter task presents no profoundly new problems from the perspective of composition.

CHAPTER 3.17

Proofs must be demonstrative. They must demonstrate, given that controversy turns on four questions, in a way that brings the demonstration to bear on the subject of controversy. For instance, if it is contended that the event did not happen, in the trial it is demonstration of this in particular that must be introduced, but if it is that the action did no harm, then of this; and demonstration that it was not so important as claimed, or that it was with justice, is similar to the controversy about its having happened at all. But it must be kept in mind that in this controversy alone should the other be wicked; for ignorance is not a reason for his disagreement, as it might be if the parties are at issue about the justice of the action, so that on this point we must dwell, but not on the others. But in display speeches most of the gist of the amplification is that the action is noble or useful; for one must take the facts for granted; and only to a small extent do orators bring in demonstrations of these too, if they should be incredible or if another should bear the responsibility. In deliberative oratory, one might either contend that something will not be the case, or that it will turn out as the opponent says, if they do so, but will not be just or useful or as significant as claimed. But one must also look to see if there is some false claim outside the matter. For such things seem an indication that the other claims too are false. Examples are more suitable to deliberative oratory and 1418a

255

enthymemes more to forensic, the former being about the future, so that one must draw examples from past facts, and the latter about things that are or are not, about which there is rather scope for demonstration and necessity; for what has happened has necessity. But enthymemes should not be said in sequence, but be mixed; if not, they impair each other. For there is indeed a natural bound to their quantity.

Friend, since your speech is as long as a man's who lacks not in prudence
. . .[24]

'As long', note, not 'as good'. And do not seek enthymemes about all matters; otherwise you will do what some philosophers do, who deduce conclusions better known and more convincing than their premisses. And when you produce an emotion, do not introduce an enthymeme (for it will either drive out the emotion, or will be wasted as an enthymeme; for simultaneous stimulations exclude each other, and make each other either disappear or become weak), nor when you are making the speech characterful, should you at the same time seek out an enthymeme; as demonstration has neither character nor moral purpose. One must, however, use maxims both in narration and in proof; for this gives character: 'I gave, and that knowing that one should not trust.' Or if you do it for emotion: 'And I do not regret it though I was done wrong; for he got gain, but I justice.'

Deliberative oratory is harder than forensic, naturally, because it is about what is to be, while forensic is about the past, which is already clear even to prophets, as Epimenides of Crete[25] remarked (for he gave prophecies about no things that were to be, but about things that had happened but were unclear), and the law is the subject-matter in forensic speeches: so that having the principle it is easier to find a demonstration. And deliberative oratory does not have many opportunities for delay, such as speaking against the adversary or about oneself, or making the speech emotional, least indeed of all if one does not digress. One must then, if in doubt, do what the Attic orators and Isocrates do; for even in advising he attacks, as in his *Panegyricus*, the Spartans, and, in his *Symmachicus*, Chares. In display oratory, one must vary the speech with episodes of praise, as Isocrates does; he is always bringing some passage in. And this is what Gorgias meant when he said that the speech does not desert him; for if he is talking about Achilles, he praises Peleus, and then Aeacus, and then the god, and similarly courage, which has such and such effects and is of such and such a kind.[26]

If, then, one has demonstrations, one must speak both character-fully and demonstratively, and if you have no enthymemes, then at least characterfully; and it is more appropriate for the respectable man that he seems good than that his speech seems meticulous. And *1418b* refutational enthymemes win more renown than demonstrative ones, as it is the clearer that what is refuting is syllogistic, as opposites are more clearly recognized when juxtaposed.

The *refutation* of the adversary is not some other species of proof, but rather one can refute some of the proofs by objection and some by deduction. Even in deliberative oratory and in court one must begin by giving one's own proofs, and then meet those of the opposition by dissolving them and tearing them up before they are made. If, however, the opposition takes many forms, then one must deal first with the opposite points, as Callistratus did in the assembly of the Messenians; for after first anticipatorily demolishing what the other side were going to say in this way, he then put forward his own case.[27] But if one speaks second, one must first address the opposite argument, refuting it and anti-syllogizing, and especially if it has gone down well; for just as the mind does not accept a subject of prejudice in advance, in the same way neither does it accept a speech, if the opponent seems to have spoken well. One must, therefore, make space in the listener for the speech to come; and this will be done by demolishing the opponent's case; thus, having put up a fight against either all or the greatest or most specious or easily refuted points of the opponent, one should move on to one's own persuasive points.

> First, then, the goddesses will I defend;
> For I think not that Hera . . .[28]

With these Hecuba first touched on Helen's weakest point.

So much, then, about proofs. As for *character*, since to say some things about oneself has either enviousness or long-windedness or contradiction, and about another either mockery or boorishness,

257

one should make the other speak, as Isocrates does in the *Philip* and in the *Antidosis*, and as Archilochus in his insults; for he makes the father speak about his daughter in the iambic line:

> There's nothing in the world that can be sworn
> To be impossible . . .[29]

And he gives the carpenter Charon the iambic line that begins:

> For me not Gyges' life . . .[30]

And as Sophocles makes Haemon speak for Antigone before his father by the device that others are saying what he says.[31]

One must also change the enthymemes and sometimes produce maxims, such as, 'Men with sense in prosperity should come to terms; so will they get the greatest profit', but enthymematically: 'If it is necessary, whenever reconciliations are most beneficial and profitable, that one should be reconciled, then so men in good fortune should be reconciled.'

CHAPTER 3.18. ALTERCATION

The presentation of proofs will normally be contested by the other side and this may well lead to altercation. For this, certain techniques can be used, even though the whole matter cannot be planned so thoroughly as other sections of the speech. In altercation, there is also scope for a certain amount of ribaldry, and this too is touched on in the present chapter.

CHAPTER 3.18.

About *altercation*, it is timely to use it most of all when the adversary 1419a has said the opposite, so that when one asks a single question further, absurdity results:

- As when Pericles asked Lampon about the initiation ceremony of the Goddess of Safety, and he said that he could hear nothing as a non-initiate. Pericles asked him if he knew them himself, and when Lampon said he did, he asked, 'How can you? You are uninitiated.'[32]

- A second example is when one thing is clear but it is obvious that the adversary will admit the other under question; having asked, then, one premiss, the speaker should not further ask the one which is obvious but give the conclusion, as Socrates did, when Meletus denied that he believed in the gods, but had said that he talked of some 'demon'. Socrates asked him if the demons are not the offspring of gods or some divine thing, and when Meletus said they were, he asked, 'Is there any man who thinks that there exist the offspring of gods but not gods?'[33]
- Also, whenever one will show that the adversary is contradicting himself or being paradoxical.
- A fourth example is when it should not be possible for the adversary to deal with the question except sophistically; for if the reply is of the kind that it is and it is not, or that some do and others do not, or in a way yes and in a way no, the audience will heckle him as in a muddle. Otherwise do not attempt altercation. For if the adversary objects, you will seem to have been beaten. For one cannot ask many questions, because of the weakness of the listener; hence one must also contract the enthymemes as much as possible.

One must reply to ambiguous questions by distinguishing their meanings by description and not concisely, and those that appear to force contradiction immediately dissolve in one's answer, before the adversary asks what is next or deduces his conclusion; for it is not hard to foresee in what the argument will consist. And both this and the solutions are clear to us from the *Topics*. And, if the question should provide conclusions, we should seek to give the reason for the conclusions:

- As Sophocles, asked by Pisander if he agreed, as did the other Probouli, to install the four hundred, said, 'What? Do these things not seem mischievous to you?' And Pisander said, 'Did you not do these wicked things?' 'Yes,' Sophocles replied, 'as there was no better alternative.'[34]
- And similarly a Spartan, under enquiry for his ephorate, was asked if he thought that the others had been justly put to death,

and said that he did. But his prosecutor said, 'Did you not pass the same laws as they?', to which he agreed. 'Then would you not justly also die?' 'Indeed not,' he replied, 'for they did these things after taking a bribe, but I did not, but rather from my policy.'[35] So one should not pose additional questions after the conclusion, nor make the conclusion an additional question, unless there is a great margin of truth.

1419b

About *jokes*, since they seem to have some use in contests – and Gorgias said that one must destroy the seriousness of the other with laughter and their laughter with seriousness, and quite rightly – we have gone through the species of joke in the *Poetics*,[36] of which some are suitable to a free man and some not, so that one may choose those suited to oneself. *Irony* is more liberal than *slapstick*; for the one makes humour on one's own account, but the slapsticker at the expense of the adversary.

CHAPTER 3.19. THE EPILOGUE

Finally, the speech must be rounded off with an effective peroration. This consists of four elements: favourably disposing the audience; amplifying and diminishing one's own or the opponent's material; inspiring emotion; and recapitulation. The actual ending of the speech must be crisp and effective, preferably asyndetic.

CHAPTER 3.19

The *epilogue* is composed of four elements: the *disposing* of the listener well towards oneself and badly towards one's adversary; *amplification and diminution*; bringing the listener to *emotions*; and *recapitulation*. For after one has shown that one is true and the other man false, it is natural accordingly to praise oneself, criticize the other and round off. But one should aim for one or two things, either to seem good for the present audience or in general, and make the opponent seem bad either for the present audience or in general. But the topics from which this can be achieved, we have mentioned, whence we must make people serious or base. After this, when the facts have already been demonstrated, one should naturally amplify or diminish them; for the facts must be agreed, if one is to specify the extent; as indeed the increase of bodies is from things that previously exist. The topics have been laid down earlier from which one must amplify and diminish. After these things, it being clear both of what sort the facts are and how serious, one should lead the listener to the emotions. These are pity and indignation, anger and hatred and envy, jealousy and strife. The topics of these have also been mentioned earlier, so that it remains to recall what has been said. And it is appropriate to do this at the end, not, as some say incorrectly, in the introduction. For in order to be clearly understood they urge frequent repetition. But at the start one must state the matter, so that it should be clear what the judgement is about, but in the epilogue the points, in summary, by which it has been demonstrated. And the first point is that one has done what one promised, so that one must say what one has said and why. And this can be done by a systematic comparison with the opponent's speech. One must compare either what each party has said on the same point or by the converse ('He said this about this *1420a* point, but I this, and for these reasons'), or by irony (for instance, 'He said that, but I said this', and, 'What would he have done if he had shown not that but this?'), or by interrogation ('What then has been shown?', or, 'What has he shown?'). Either thus by comparison can we sum up or naturally in the order in which the points have been made, first one's own, and again, if you wish, separately the points of the opposite speech. An asyndetic ending is appropriate for the speech, so that it should be a peroration, not an oration: 'I have spoken, you have heard, you have the facts, judge.'[37]

NOTES

INTRODUCTION (pp. 1–61)

1. Homer, *Iliad*, IX. 225–655. There are three contrasting speeches urging Achilles to return to the fray. Odysseus' is studiedly formal, Phoenix's digressive and Ajax's bluntly candid. They are balanced by the noble and profound rejoinders of Achilles.
2. Homer, *Iliad*, XI. 656–803. Nestor's speech is the longest in the entire poem, but he never loses sight of his objective, that of seizing this last chance of impressing upon Patroclus the urgency of the crisis.
3. Homer, *Iliad*, II. 211–77. Homer firmly predisposes us against Thersites by the graphic description of his ugliness. In Aristotelian terms, we might say that Thersites' failure was one of ethos-projection.
4. Anaxagoras of Clazomenae, one of the heroes of Presocratic physics, was born in *c.*500 BC and lived in Athens from 480 to 450. He was closely associated with Pericles, ten years his junior, and it was Pericles' enemies who accused him of impiety in *c.*450, at the height of Pericles' power. He withdrew to his native city, but his book, containing highly controversial cosmological speculations, remained readily available in Athens for the rest of the century (Plato, *Apology*, 22c).
5. The traditional 'founders of rhetoric' are the two Syracusans Tisias and Corax, but little is known of their lives or teachings. Tisias was apparently the pupil of Corax. See Kennedy, *The Art of Persuasion in Greece*, pp. 58–61.
6. Aristophanes, *Clouds*, 112–18. The phrase is pointedly echoed by the first section of Plato's version of Socrates' defence speech (*Apology*, 19b).
7. There are historiographical reasons for doubting that Thucydides lived long into the fourth century. They can be supplemented by stylistic ones, as the whole character of his narrative, quite apart from the speeches, is far removed from the limpid smoothness of Lysias and the clarity of Xenophon and of the earliest Platonic dialogues.

8. Thucydides, I. 23.

9. The disputed *Seventh Letter*, which, even if spurious, is usually accepted to offer a plausible account of Plato's youthful career, makes it clear that his first ambition was the political pre-eminence which was his birthright. There is no reason to doubt that he conceived his move towards political theory as essentially a more circuitous step in the direction of power. He has, indeed, as a man, much more in common with Lenin than with Hegel.

10. Jaeger, *Aristotle*. Many writers have followed in Jaeger's footsteps in the search for a more accurate account of the evolution of Aristotle's theories. The most notable of these remains Nuyens, *L'Évolution de la psychologie d'Aristote*.

11. Isocrates was born into a wealthy Athenian family in 436 BC, the eve of the Peloponnesian War. By its end he was more or less destitute and turned first to the writing of speeches for clients and then to the profession of the rhetorician, opening schools both at Athens and on Chios by 387 BC. By the middle of the century, he had made himself a very rich man. He died in 338, aged ninety-eight, and, when Aristotle founded the Lyceum in the following year, he must surely have been influenced by Isocrates' phenomenal success.

12. For the whole question of Aristotle's relations with the Macedonian court, see Grayeff, *Aristotle and his School*, pp. 38–43. It must be stressed, however, that Grayeff's conclusions are by no means accepted by all scholars.

13. Ostracism was a curious, but thoroughly characteristic, feature of the Athenian democracy. It was probably introduced, and certainly first used, at the time of the Persian Wars (490–480 BC). Every year, the Assembly would decide whether an ostracism should be held, and if the decision was in favour of an ostracism then the vote would be taken in the Agora, or market square. Each citizen could cast one *ostrakon* (potsherd) with the name of another citizen on it. If more than six thousand potsherds were cast, then the citizen whose name appeared on the greatest number would be required to leave Athens for ten years but would suffer none of the otherwise normal disadvantages of exile.

14. Since the reforms of Cleisthenes in 507, the *phylai* (tribes) were divided into *trittyes* (thirds), and each *trittys* was required to be in a different area of the state, so that in some ways the thirty *trittyes*, rather than the ten *phylai*, were the closest parallel with the modern constituency.

15. *Rhetoric*, 1365b31–2 (Chapter 1.8); *Politics*, 1273a18.

16. The Athenian judicial system of the classical period should perhaps not

be credited with a full distinction between civil and criminal law. Criminal prosecutions were brought in just the same way as civil ones, by the injured party, and he would be responsible for ensuring that the summons was served on the defendant. Thus the system of criminal justice was essentially a formalization of a series of private disputes, umpired, as it were, by the state, in the form of the presiding magistrate and the popular jury. There was no notion that the criminal had committed an attack upon society as a whole, though a defendant might well appeal to his services to the state as a mitigating factor to offset his misdemeanours.

17. See above, n. 4. Anaxagoras held that cosmic order was the product of a rotatory motion initiated by the primordial *nous* (mind), which is the cause of all creation. This picture had, of course, traceable influences on both the Academy and the Lyceum.

18. There is some reason to think that in making these developments in the theory and practice of prose style, Isocrates is being influenced by his arch-rival Plato. Certainly this is as least as likely as that there was any influence the other way.

19. See above, pp. 5–6.

20. Aristotle divides the whole of science into three types of enquiry: those whose objective is the acquisition of theoretical knowledge, which are the highest; those which study rational activity within the context of the city; and those which study and prescribe for various types of productive activity. Of these last, the two activities for which we have Aristotelian prescriptions are poetry and rhetoric. More generally, however, Aristotle takes over from Plato a wide conception of *techne*, which embraces our concepts of art, technique and skill, whether or not there exists a precisely defined method for the conduct of it.

21. See 'Tithenai ta phainomena' by D. L. Owen in Moravsic (ed.), *Aristotle*.

22. The article by Bayliss of 1892 on the medical construal of the doctrine of *catharsis* is still valuable. It is available in Barnes, Schofield and Sorabji, *Articles on Aristotle*, Vol. 1.

23. Aristotle offers the case of an Olympic victor as an example. It would be superfluous to point out that he had won a garland for his victory, as this reward was automatic, and therefore an enthymeme would eschew this step in any argument connecting the award of the garland with the athlete. This has sometimes been thought to be the true hallmark of the enthymeme, but in fact it is merely a characteristic effect of its greater informality as against the dialectical syllogism.

24. See Chapter 1.3.

25. The *De Anima*, Aristotle's central psychological text, is devoted to the idea that rationality is what marks off man from other animals, with whom his soul has a certain amount in common. Since the emotions are not paradigms of rationality (though they are also not things that animals can, in any obvious sense, have), the discussion in the *De Anima* tends rather to play them down. The emotions are also discussed in the *Ethics*, but in a normative, rather than descriptive, way. Thus the treatment in the *Rhétoric* has a unique place in Aristotle's emotional psychology. See *Nicomachean Ethics*, 1111b4 ff.

26. Barthes, in 'L'Ancienne Rhétorique: Aide-mémoire', perceptively praised Aristotle for refraining from the attempt to offer a deep construal of the emotions, preferring instead to produce a *psychologie classificatrice* of them, which conceives them, almost in structuralist style, as *des morceaux de langage tout faits*. This is an interesting example of how 'contemporary' Aristotle's approach often is, not only in Britain and America, but also on the European mainland. (Quoted in Vickers, *In Defence of Rhetoric*, p. 24n.)

27. See Chapter 2.2.

28. It is by no means clear that the tripartite schema of analysis works as well for the definitions of the other emotions as it does for anger. It might even be claimed that the schema becomes progressively less convincing as we work through the emotions, possibly because Aristotle is tiring of its rather artificial constraints.

29. He was, for instance, a close associate of the tyrant Hermias, whose daughter he married. Hermias was distinguished by the gallantry with which he resisted Persia but not by any notable liberalism in the treatment of his own subjects.

30. This view is put forth entertainingly by Grayeff, *Aristotle and his School*, pp. 46–7.

31. Aristotle, *Politics*, 1252a32.

32. It is regrettable that he does not pursue this speculation further. A possible cause for the angry man's not wishing the annihilation of the object of his anger might, on Aristotelian terms, be his desire to see the punishment that the object deserves extended indefinitely in time.

33. The main discussion is in *Ethics*, IX. Aristotle's approach has also often been praised for its sensitivity to the concept of political friendship, which is explored in *Politics*.

34. See e.g. Cooper, *Class*.

35. MacIntyre, *A Short History of Ethics*, p. 35. MacIntyre's whole attitude

to Aristotle is a curious mixture of admiration for his methods and detestation of his results.

36. This seems, at any rate, a reasonable inference from the remark in *Rhetoric*, 1371b36 (Chapter 1.11).

37. In Barnes, Schofield and Sorabji, *Articles on Aristotle*, Vol. 1. Fortenbaugh shows a remarkable sympathy for the relations between the *Rhetoric* and the intellectual atmosphere in the Academy at the time of its composition. In general, the advantages of so early a work for the tracing of Aristotle's development have never been fully exploited.

38. A good collection of ancient testimony as to the literary character of the exoteric dialogues is assembled in Ross, *Aristotelis Fragmenta Selecta*.

39. A clear example is the first book of the *Metaphysics*, where the whole range of Presocratic philosophy is surveyed, for all that Aristotle has little sympathy with much of it. Much the same can be said for the survey of earlier views of the soul in the first book of the *De Anima*.

40. Cope, *Introduction to the 'Rhetoric' of Aristotle*, pp. 277–82, and Kennedy, *The Art of Persuasion in Greece*, pp. 103–14.

41. Cope, consistently with his general interpretation, considers *saphēneia* ('clarity') to be the *arche* of diction and *hellēnizein* ('purity') to be that of syntax. More generally, we might say that *saphēneia* is pictorial, *hellēnizein* grammatical, accuracy. Kennedy, however (pp. 104–5), insists that *hellēnizein* is a concept connected with clarity not with purity. It is certainly the case that the interpretation of these two concepts is central to any interpretation of the structure of the whole discussion of style.

42. Cicero, *De Oratore*, III. 37–8.

43. Kennedy, *The Art of Persuasion in Greece*, pp. 104–6.

44. *Rhetoric*, 1410b10 ff., quoted by Kennedy (ibid.) at p. 112.

45. Notably *Poetics*, 1448b4–19. There are, of course, many passages on the pleasures of learning in the more specifically scientific works, such as the *The Parts of Animals*, 644b22–645a23.

46. *Rhetoric*, 1404b8–10 (Chapter 3.2).

47. *Rhetoric*, 1405a32–4 (Chapter 3.2). Ross, in the Oxford edition, obelizes the obscure words *tais asēmais phōnais* in the subsequent sentence, which is obviously intended to explain the fault of the metaphor.

48. *Rhetoric*, 1405b1 (Chapter 3.2). This strange line appears to indicate the operation of a cupping-glass. cp. Athenaeus, 452.

49. For Lysias' speech see Plato, *Phaedrus*, 230e–234c, and for Polus' affected conversation, *Gorgias*, 461b–463d.

50. Ancient Greek (and Latin) verse was quantitative rather than merely

rhythmical, so that the line had to be formed from precise patterns of long and short syllables rather than merely from the play of stress. These metrical units were known as feet, and the most important were the dactyl, the trochee, the spondee and the iambus, which were all used in the serious metres of epic and drama. The paean, by contrast, was rare outside lyric metres, and this is no doubt the reason why Aristotle feels that its use in prose will give a rhythmic, but not metric, flavour.

51. Kennedy, *The Art of Persuasion in Greece*, pp. 113–14.

52. Cope (*Introduction to the 'Rhetoric' of Aristotle*, pp. 401–57) provides just such a comparison for the two works as a whole, and definitively shows the enormous superiority of the Aristotelian text over its only surviving sophistic rival.

53. *Rhetoric*, 1391a20–b6. The term *stasis* (the singular form) is not, however, used by Aristotle in this context.

54. Whence his brevity. Litigious proofs, especially, which he seems mainly here to have in mind, have been discussed extensively in Chapters 1.10–15.

55. Kennedy, *The Art of Persuasion in Greece*, p. 113.

56. A notable early attack on the third book was Diels, 'Über das dritte Buch der aristotelischen Rhetorik'.

57. Demetrius ruled in Athens with the support of the Macedonian general Cassander from 318 to 308 BC. He was then deposed by his namesake, the king of Macedonia, and by 297 had become one of the first librarians at Alexandria. He was much admired by Cicero, who sought to emulate his blending of rhetoric and middle-brow philosophy.

58. Aristotle, *Politics*, 1290b1.

59. Grayeff, *Aristotle and his School*, pp. 65–8. It is a commonplace to contrast the ruthless Hellenic chauvinism of the *Politics*, conspicuously the justification of slavery, with the liberal generosity with which Alexander sought that fusion of the Macedonian and Persian aristocracies which probably led to his assassination.

60. e.g. Cicero, *Ad Atticum*, 1.16.

61. Sulla's sack of Athens is graphically and extensively described in Plutarch's *Life*. Plutarch preserves his famous remark, when the Athenians pleaded their glorious past in extenuation, that he had come to punish rebels, not to learn ancient history.

62. Cicero, *Orator*, 75.

63. The opinion of Quintilian, who may be taken as representative, was certainly very high: 'What of Aristotle? I cannot make up my mind

whether to think him more distinguished by his knowledge of the subject, the abundance of his writings, the charm of his style, the subtlety of his insights or the range of his achievements' (10.1.83). It is true that, in this famous judgement, Quintilian is talking of the philosopher's corpus as a whole – and indeed of the exoteric works that have not survived – but it is clear from the rest of the *Institutio Oratoria* that, as we would expect, the *Rhetoric* was the work of Aristotle with which he was most familiar.

64. Notably in his treatment of metaphor and simile in Book VIII.

SECTION ONE: INTRODUCTORY (pp. 65–70)

1. For the concept of *techne* (art) in Aristotle, see the Introduction, p. 14, and n. 20 (Introduction).

2. In many classical city states the founder and original lawgiver was accorded a heroic role in local cults. The paradigm case is that of Lycurgus at Sparta, but the conception would be familiar, and sympathetic, to the Athenian aristocrats with whom Aristotle shares so much of his political outlook.

3. This sentence is, of course, a particularly glaring contradiction of the principle which underlies the whole of Book II, that emotional persuasion is a legitimate part of oratory. This has induced some to doubt the integrity of the work as a whole, but for the case against such doubts, see the Introduction, pp. 21 ff.

4. Dialectic in Plato and Aristotle is a broad concept. It is first fully expounded in the *Republic* (531–9), where it forms the pinnacle of the philosopher's education. It might be defined as the science of winning arguments, since it proceeds by the examination of hypothetical, rather than certain, propositions and their consequences. The manual of dialectic in the Aristotelian corpus is the *Topics*, to which the *Rhetoric* frequently makes reference.

5. Aristotle, *Topics*, I. 2.

6. In giving this definition, which is to be amplified in the next Section into its full form, Aristotle is breaking with the sophistic conception of rhetoric and offering a more tempered and judicious account of the activity, which avoids any prejudgement of its practical value.

7. Rhetoric differs from dialectic in that it is in principle available for anyone to learn. It is a curious feature of the *Rhetoric* that it pays very little attention to the natural capacities of the would-be orator. By contrast, the Lyceum unquestioningly inherited from the Academy the

idea that only a fortunate intellectual élite could be true philosophers and dialecticians.

SECTION TWO: THE GENRES OF ORATORY (pp. 73–82)

1. These are the ethical (moral), emotional (pathetic) and logical forms of demonstration, whose trichotomy dominates Aristotle's whole conception of invention.
2. There is a textual difficulty here, but the sense must be more or less as rendered. This requires the insertion of a missing 'not'.
3. Once again the similarity with dialectic is stressed. It is tempting to conjecture that Aristotle laid such emphasis on the parallel with dialectic in order to win his readership round to the realization that, so far from being in tension with philosophy, as the proponents of both arts had sometimes claimed, rhetoric could in fact only properly be imparted by philosophers, since they alone understood its sister science of dialectic.
4. Aristotle, *Prior Analytics*, II. 23, and *Posterior Analytics*, I. 1.
5. Aristotle, *Topics*, I. 1.12.
6. *Rhetoric*, 2.20–24.
7. A syllogism (or an enthymeme) must take as its premisses propositions which we have some grounds for accepting as true. This can be either because they have been antecedently demonstrated by other syllogisms or because they are accepted as being self-evident parts of the received wisdom.
8. Aristotle, *Prior Analytics*, I. 8.13–14.
9. Pisistratus made three attempts to seize power in Athens in the 550s and 540s. The last of these was successful and he and his sons ruled for thirty-five years until they were expelled with Spartan assistance. Theagenes, one of the earliest of the Greek tyrants, seized power in Megara between 640 and 620 BC. The Dionysius referred to is Dionysius I of Syracuse, who won from the democratic constitution a position as presiding general in 406, which he was then able to convert into his sole rule.
10. 'Seize on characteristic arguments' is not an ideal translation for the Greek *mallon haptomenoi kata tropon*. The point of this rather obscurely worded passage is that, as soon as the orator takes as the premisses of his enthymemes the propositions of some established science, the course of the argument will be dictated by the rules of that science and not by those of oratory.
11. This final sentence of the section is, in effect, programmatic for the whole of the rest of the first book.

12. Again this is not an ideal translation of the Greek *telos*. The point, however, is sufficiently obvious for the infelicity not to be disruptive.

13. Homer, *Iliad* XVIII. 78–137. Thetis warns her son that, if he avenges Patroclus by killing Hector, then his own death must follow shortly thereafter. Achilles, consumed by remorse for having allowed Patroclus to be killed, heroically refuses to neglect his duty to his friend.

SECTION THREE: DELIBERATION (pp. 83–103)

1. By this he means political theory itself, of which what we would call ethics is a subsidiary study. See Aristotle, *Ethics*, 1181b12–23.

2. Aristotle has made a minor change in the subject description of this section. In fact, of course, ancient trade was heavily centred on food-stuffs and other primary agricultural products.

3. Illustrations from the snub nose are among Aristotle's favourites, even for abstruse points of metaphysics. No doubt some academic in-joke, perhaps referring back to Socrates himself, is involved here.

4. The doctrine here entirely coincides with that of the *Ethics*, in the first book of which the concept of happiness (*eudaimonia*) is subjected to a searching and fascinating critique.

5. The last four items in the list look suspiciously like a gloss derived from the discussion of the elements of happiness in the *Ethics*. They do not figure in the subsequent detailed analysis.

6. Yet virtue is not specifically defined in the discussion of epideictic invention (see 1366b23 f., Chapter 1.9).

7. Homer, *Iliad*, I. 255. From the comments of Nestor on the disastrous row between Agamemnon and Achilles.

8. Homer, *Iliad*, II. 160. Hera is pointing out to Athene – who, with her, supports the Greeks – what a rich spoil for Priam they would leave behind in Helen if, as they plan to, they were to abandon the siege and sail to Greece.

9. Homer, *Iliad*, II. 268. Odysseus, rallying the Greeks from their plans to flee, points out how shameful it would be to fail after so many years' effort.

10. It was, no doubt, especially galling to drop a water-jar on the very threshold of one's destination.

11. This seems to have been a misunderstanding between poet and patron. Commissioned to praise Corinth, the great lyric poet Simonides of Ceos echoed in this line the fact that the Corinthian hero Glaucus was honoured even by the Trojans, natural enemies of the Greeks,

since they accepted him as an ally. The Corinthians, however, seem to have taken the line as a suggestion that Glaucus had somehow betrayed Greece.

12. When, in 366, the Thebans occupied Oropus on the border with Athens, the Athenian politician Callistratus suggested that the Thebans should be given a rather generous deadline for departure. On this basis, his associate Chabrias entered into negotiations with the Thebans, but these backfired from the Athenian point of view. Thereupon, both Callistratus and Chabrias were prosecuted by Leodamas.

13. Pindar, *Olympian*, I. 1.

14. Homer, *Iliad*, IX. 592–4. Phoenix tells the story of Meleager's repentance as a moral example for Achilles. It was his wife Cleopatra who painted this dismal picture of the consequences of his continued pique.

15. Epicharmus of Cos (550–460) combined the writing of comedies with philosophy, unusually for his time. 'Composition' and 'construction' are technicalities of Academic logic, as is 'division'.

16. The epigram is ascribed to Simonides.

17. See n. 4 (Section Four).

18. Odysseus' bard Phemius claimed to be self-taught in *Odyssey* XXII. 347, and Pericles' famous remark was probably made after the fighting against the island of Samos in 440. It does not occur in Thucydides' great version of the speech delivered in 431 for those who fell in the first year of the Peloponnesian War.

19. The subject is dealt with at much greater length in *Politics* 1289a26. *The Constitution of the Athenians* is also certainly a work of the Lyceum, though not of Aristotle himself.

20. Aristotle, *Politics*, loc. cit.

SECTION FOUR: DISPLAY (pp. 104–10)

1. This list broadly corresponds to the list of moral virtues in Books III and IV of the *Ethics*.

2. Alcaeus, frg. 55.

3. Sappho, frg. 28. The precise circumstances of the exchange are unfortunately unclear.

4. About Iphicrates nothing is known, but he was presumably a self-made man, who adopted and made popular this rather polyptotic slogan. ('Polyptotes' means the use of the same word in more than one grammatical form, a favourite mannerism of the Greek and Roman writers, which, however, cannot be reproduced in a non-inflected language.)

5. cp. n. 16 (Section Three).
6. The last tyrant of Athens, Hippias, son of Pisistratus, married his daughter Archedice – the subject of this epigram – to Aeantides, son of Hippocles, who was tyrant of Lampsacus.
7. Nothing is known of Hippolochus, but Harmodius and Aristogeiton were the two young Athenian aristocrats who murdered Hipparchus, brother of Hippias, probably on purely personal grounds, and thus precipitated the democratic revolution of 511, and who were revered thereafter as heroes of the people. One of the most conspicuous posthumous honours that they received was the erection of a double statue in the Agora, a well-known Roman copy of which has survived.

SECTION FIVE: LITIGATION (pp. 111–35)

1. The Greek word *adikia* is rather wide in meaning. Conventionally translated as 'injustice', it really is closer in meaning to the idea of unjust *behaviour* or indeed *crime*. The latter would be a good translation in this context, but deference to tradition militated against it.
2. Pleasure is also discussed, in a more philosophical manner, in the *Ethics*, IX.
3. Frg. 8 of the sophist Evenus of Paros. Very little is known of his views, but he did contribute to the growth of sophistic rhetorical theory before Aristotle.
4. Euripides, *Andromeda*, frg. 133.
5. Homer, *Odyssey*, XV. 400–401.
6. Homer, *Iliad*, XVIII. 108.
7. Homer, *Iliad*, XXIII. 108 and *Odyssey*, IV. 183.
8. Euripides, *Orestes*, 234.
9. This conception is interestingly similar to the view put forward in the early pages of the *Poetics* to explain the pleasure involved in aesthetic experience. See Aristotle, *Poetics*, 1448b4–19.
10. Euripides, *Antiope*, frg. 183.
11. Unfortunately, the discussion of comedy, which we know from this and other passages to have been included in the *Poetics*, has been lost. Aristotle offers some thoughts on the subject of humour, or at least wit, in the section of Book III in which he deals with repartee (Chapter 3.18).
12. Carthage was on the edge of the Greek military horizon, so that if the Greeks were to attack her, there would be little danger of retaliation. This point applies, indeed, rather more to the mainland Greeks than to

their Italiote and Siciliote cousins, who fought long and bitter wars with Carthage before the rise of Rome. It is very possible that the expression originated in the debates connected with Athens' disastrous expedition against Syracuse in 415 BC, when we know that some of the wilder proponents claimed that Carthage as well as Sicily might fall to Athens or at least yield her booty. Thucydides, VI. 15.

13. The people of Mysia, for reasons that are not now entirely clear, were apparently regarded by the mainland Greeks as being too feeble to resist raids. This is not entirely borne out by their history.

14. Dion of Syracuse played a key role in the history of the Syracusan tyranny in the fourth century and of Plato's involvement with it. He originally brought Plato to Syracuse to educate Dionysius II, son of the first tyrant, to become a philosopher king. When this failed, Dion participated in the removal of Dionysius and effectively ruled himself for some years. He was eventually murdered by his henchman Callippus, who had formerly studied with him in the Academy. Callippus defended his action as being pre-emptive.

15. Aenesidemus and Gelon were Sicilian tyrants of the fifth century. It is unclear what city was the object of their rivalry, but it was probably either Camarina or Megara Hyblaea. The *cottabus* was a rather bizarre game played during the later stages of the Greek dinner-party (*sumposion*). The diners competed to cast the lees of the wine in their cups, which would be of a very heavy and viscous consistency, either into the central mixing-bowl (*krater*), which would have stood throughout the proceedings in the centre of the table, or into saucers floating on water within it. In the latter case, the objective was to sink the saucers with the injected lees. There were, it seems, still more elaborate variations. It is not known what prize was awarded to the winners, but the institution probably corresponds to that of the 'sconces' at the end of the undergraduate dinners of today.

16. Sophocles, *Antigone*, ll. 456–8. This is one of Aristotle's favourite quotations from the tragic stage.

17. Empedocles, frg. 135.

18. Alcidamas, a Peloponnesian by birth, studied rhetoric under Gorgias and, on the occasion of the eventual liberation of the Messenians from Spartan rule, after three centuries, delivered a celebratory speech, which became a model of epideictic oratory.

19. The point of this rather obscure comment is that a blow from a hand carrying a ring might well do more damage than one from a hand without a ring. However, it would not be equitable to take this as

making the crime more serious, since the ring would obviously not be being worn as an offensive weapon.

20. Callistratus was an important Athenian orator and statesman of the early fourth century. Nothing is known of Melanopus, but it is thoroughly characteristic of Athenian jurisprudence that the principle *de minimis non curat lex* should not apply in religious cases.

21. This is not Sophocles the poet, whose only known litigious performance was to contest an allegation of insanity by his son and consisted of a reading of one of the Odes from his *Oedipus at Colonus*.

22. Little is known of the judicial and penal system of the Argives, but their arrangements were probably fairly familiar at Athens in Aristotle's day, since Argos had tended to ally herself with Athens as a counterweight to the power of Sparta in the Peloponnese. The point here about the man responsible for the passing of a law's being punished is easier to grasp than that of the same principle's applying in the case of those for whom the prison was built, but we must remember that in ancient Greece imprisonment was not a form of punishment, so that the prison can only have been required for remand purposes. Thus the point seems to be that those who were suspicious enough to merit remanding in custody deserved, even if they were eventually acquitted, to be punished merely for the inconvenience and expense to which they had put the state.

23. The distinction between the technical and non-technical proofs is established at 1356b35 (Chapter 1.2). It became a standard part of rhetorical jargon. Cicero makes an interesting use of it, before an audience most of whom would have received at least some rhetorical training, in his defence of M. Caelius Rufus (*Pro Caelio*, 66).

24. Those quoted in Chapter 1.13. cf. n. 16 (this Section).

25. In the early sixth century a dispute between Athens and Megara for possession of the island of Salamis was settled, according to legend at least, by the Spartans in favour of Athens on the strength of a line in Homer (*Iliad*, II. 557–8).

26. Periander was the founder of the Corinthian tyranny in the sixth century and he was anxious to increase his city's influence in the vital Hellespontine area. Precisely what dispensations he made, however, and how they were later used is uncertain.

27. Solon, frg. 22. This line was used maliciously against the late-fifth-century politician Critias by his opponent Cleophon to discredit the former's claim to distinguished ancestry. In doing so, he almost certainly perverted the sense of the remark, but this by no means weakens its value as an illustration in this context.

28. When Xerxes' massive forces were converging on Athens, the citizens consulted the Oracle at Delphi as to their best course of action. They were told to trust to their 'wooden walls', and Themistocles interpreted this to refer to their newly built navy. They evacuated their city and defeated the Persians at the battle of Salamis. See Herodotus VII. 173.

29. Apparently this was a current Athenian proverb, but Greeks were in general rather disposed to be excessively deferential, though not necessarily generous, to the old.

30. Stasinus, *Cypria*, frg. 2.

31. Eubulus was the leader of the doveish faction in fourth-century Athens. We know nothing of the circumstances of the trial of Chares.

32. The point is obscure, but seems to be that, if the orator is arguing that his adversaries are lying out of a feeling of danger, then he can adduce distinguished contemporary testimony to the reality of the dangers that they are in, making his claim that they are lying all the more plausible.

33. This was a standard phrase binding Athenian jurors to use reasonable discretion in arriving at their verdicts.

34. The torturing of slave witnesses, though only with the consent of their owners, was standard practice in Greek, and, with restrictions, in Roman, courts.

35. In civil proceedings in an Attic court, either party could challenge the other to swear to the validity of their claims on whatever they held sacred. The other party had the right to reject the challenge. It might seem obviously in one's interest to challenge the other party to swear, but, on the other hand, he might be happy to perjure himself, he might be less willing to come to a settlement and he might, by accepting the oath, gain a credibility in the eyes of the jurors which he would not otherwise have had. Similarly, it is not always advisable to accept the challenge of the oath. There are also various ways of escaping from the consequences of oaths which are against one's interests.

36. It is not precisely certain to what incident reference is being made here, but Xenophanes, an Ionian by birth, spent much of his life in exile in the West and no doubt had considerable experience of litigation. The remark is a little curious, in that Xenophanes, a major figure of the sixth century, is usually thought of as something of a religious radical, notoriously attacking the anthropomorphism of the Homeric pantheon. It is thus surprising that he should raise the subject of his own piety in, of all places, a court of law.

SECTION SIX: EMOTION (pp. 139–71)

1. In the course of the actual discussion, Aristotle is in fact far more concerned to examine the state of mind of the audience than the character projected by the speaker. He would not, however, have held that these were in practice far removed from each other. Notionally, the discussion of the emotions pertains to the state of mind of the audience, while that of the characters pertains to the discussion of the impression made by the speaker, but this division does not really apply in practice.

2. The merits of the tripartite division are examined in the Introduction (pp. 16–17).

3. Homer, *Iliad*, XVIII. 109. Also quoted in 1370b12 (Chapter 1.11).

4. Homer, *Iliad*, I. 356.

5. Homer, *Iliad*, IX. 648. This is from the speech in which Achilles delivers his seasoned reflections on his row with Agamemnon.

6. Homer, *Iliad*, II. 196.

7. Homer, *Iliad*, I. 82.

8. Calming (πραοτησ, *praotēs*) is the most convincingly treated of the emotional opposites in the second book, perhaps because it is the one most likely to be of practical use.

9. The fates of both Ergophilus and Callisthenes illustrate the Athenian practice of trying generals for military failure. Both were unsuccessful in campaigns in northern Greece during the period of the rise of Philip of Macedon.

10. Homer, *Odyssey*, IX. 504. Odysseus taunts the Cyclops, whom he has just blinded, at considerable risk to himself and his men.

11. Homer, *Iliad*, XXIV. 54. The gods are shocked by the extremity of Achilles' persisting hatred of the dead Hector.

12. The Greek *philia* and its many cognates pose a particular problem for the translator, since the wide meaning of the word encompasses our concepts of *friendship*, *affection* and *love*. Preserving the connection with its verb forms is often impossible in English.

13. The point of the tag must, presumably, be that one potter is a rival to another.

14. Euripides, *Cresphontes*, frg. 457. It is interesting to compare this proverb with some modern thoughts on shame and modesty. See Scruton, *Sexual Desire*, pp. 140–9.

15. The scholiast offers as a gloss on this the highly improbable story that the poet was sent on an embassy to gain a Syracusan alliance and that he urged as a reason for making the alliance the sophistic point that the

Syracusans should be flattered by the very fact of having been asked. It is almost certain that Euripides neither went on any such embassy (which is in any case highly unlikely to have been sent) nor, indeed, took any other active part in the administration of Athens.

16. The precise circumstances were unclear, but after the defeat of the Samian attempt to secede from the Athenian Empire in 440 BC, the Athenians imposed on the islanders settlements of their own citizens (*klēroukhiai*) such as they had for some years been imposing elsewhere in the Aegean.

17. Antiphon was an Athenian orator, who was sent on an embassy to the court of Dionysius I of Syracuse. Legend has it that he provoked the tyrant by praising the Athenian tyrannicides Harmodius and Aristogeiton (see n. 7, Section Four), and was put to death.

18. Very obscure. Presumably some conspicuous act of charity to a destitute recipient which achieved renown in the Lyceum.

19. Pity was one of the areas of the emotions where we know of at least one predecessor, namely Thrasymachus of Chalcedon, who wrote a work entitled *Eleoi* (*On Arousing Pity*).

20. It is unclear why Diopeithes was to be rewarded by the Persian king.

21. Herodotus, III. 14. But the story is told there of Amasius' son Psammenitus. Aristotle frequently makes this sort of minor error in citations.

22. *Nemesis* is one of the key concepts in Greek tragedy, where it signifies divine punishment for human ambition. Later it became the name of a goddess.

23. Homer, *Iliad*, XI. 542–4. It is Cebriones who does not feel up to fighting with Ajax, one of the greatest of the Greek heroes.

24. Aeschylus, frg. 305.

25. See n. 13 (Section Six).

SECTION SEVEN: CHARACTER (pp. 172–9)

1. These words are in sympathy with the detailed account offered in the *Ethics* of virtue as a disposition to good actions. See *Nicomachean Ethics*, 1102a14.

2. The whole question of the Greek attitude to age has been well dealt with in Garland, *The Greek Way of Life*.

3. Pittacus was a statesman on the island of Mytilene, who for ten years wielded great power after the fall of the tyranny (*c.*590 BC). He was opposed by the poet Alcaeus and the rest of the aristocracy, and his rule was characterized by such measures as the suppression of alcoholic consumption. Amphiaraus is unknown.

4. The point seems to be that young men may be able to tell the noble from the base, but this is only because they have been properly brought up, not because they can yet judge for themselves. They realize this, and the realization gives them a certain bashfulness.

5. Chilon was the architect of Sparta's Peloponnesian League, which maintained the power of Sparta in Greece for more than a century. He was one of the canonical sages, and to him was ascribed the dictum written on the wall of the Temple of Apollo at Delphi, *mēden agan*, 'nothing in excess'.

6. The distinction between necessary and contingent assets, already well established in the fourth century, anticipates the still more familiar one between internal and external goods in the philosophical systems of the Hellenistic age.

7. Cimon, who died in 450 BC, was the son of Miltiades, the victor of Marathon. He was a prominent conservative in the first half of the fifth century at Athens, and contributed greatly to the rise of the Athenian Empire.

SECTION EIGHT: COMMON TOPICS (pp. 183–214)

1. The formal definition of the common topic is given at 1355a27 (Chapter 1.1). It is also discussed in *Topics*, I. 2.

2. See also *Topics*, loc. cit.

3. Agathon was the most prominent late-fifth-century Athenian tragedian after Sophocles and Euripides; it is to celebrate the first of his victories that the dinner party in Plato's *Symposium* is held. See frg. 765.

4. This looks as though it may come from one of Isocrates' rare sallies into forensic oratory.

5. The Greek settlements along the fringe of the Libyan coastline seem to have exploited the wealth of unfamiliar wildlife in the area in order to compose fables in the style of Aesop. See Quintilian, V. 11–20.

6. The Persians originally conquered Egypt in 522 under their king Cambyses. After the disturbances of the Ionian revolt (499–495), Darius, Cambyses' successor, had to visit Egypt to secure calm there before launching his punitive expedition against Athens and Eretria.

7. Phalaris, the notorious tyrant of Acragas (Agrigento) in southern Sicily, came to power in *c.*565 BC. Stesichorus was a choral lyric poet from Himera on the north coast.

8. Aesop lived at the beginning of the sixth century, at which time Samos, like many other of the Aegean islands, was rent with civil war between the landowners and the population at large.

9. Euripides, *Medea*, 296.

10. Ibid., 298–9.

11. Euripides, *Sthenoboea*, frg. 661.

12. Euripides, *Hecuba*, 858.

13. The fondness for quotations from Euripides well indicates the enormous popularity of that poet in the fourth century (and later).

14. Probably from Epicharmus. See n. 15 (Section Three).

15. Euripides, *Troades*, 1051.

16. See n. 9 (this Section).

17. Neither of these dicta can be definitively identified, but they may well come from Epicharmus or Euripides.

18. A favourite Aristotelian example of eloquently graphic metaphor. Epizephyrian Locri was an important settlement in southern Italy, frequently at war with the Sicilian states, with whom Stesichorus' sympathies would have lain.

19. Homer, *Iliad*, XII. 243. Hector's famous slogan as he prepares to breach the wall about the Greek camp.

20. Homer, *Iliad*, XVIII. 309. Hector refuses to accept that it would be prudent for the Trojans to withdraw to their city.

21. cp. n. 30 (Section Five).

22. Though Athens had herself played a heroic part in the defeat of the Persian invasions of the early fifth century, she subsequently embarked on the domination of many of the states who had fought with her. Aegina was forced into her empire in 447 and Potidaea was captured, at considerable cost, in 427.

23. Cycnus was a son of Poseidon. Since he was invulnerable, Achilles had to choke him to death, and his father then turned him into a swan (*kuknos*).

24. The speech delivered by Alcidamas of Elis on the occasion of the freeing of the Messenians from the Spartan yoke. See n. 18 (Section Five).

25. The fragment is probably from either Euripides or Epicharmus, though more likely the latter.

26. Euripides, *Thyestes*, frg. 396.

27. Tax-collecting in antiquity was standardly farmed out to the highest bidder by the state treasuries.

28. Theodectes was an important cultural figure of the fourth century, of whose work, which included both tragedies and an *Art of Rhetoric*, very little survives. The line is from Alcmaeon's reply to his wife Alphesiboea, who asked him whether he was not right to murder his mother Eriphyle.

29. It is not clear whether the cases of Demosthenes and Nicanor are connected. This Demosthenes is probably not the great orator.

30. Instances such as this are an interesting example of the fact that there must have been a kind of informal law report available to scholars in fourth-century Athens. Aristotle is often able to identify cases without specifying the parties.

31. Antiphon, *Meleager*, frg. 885.

32. Theseus abducted Helen, and the Tyndarids (Castor and Polydeuces) prided themselves on their beauty.

33. In the 340s Philip showed ruthless cunning in playing the Greek states off against each other. In particular, he used the Thebans to eliminate the Phocians, the main power of central Greece. These are some of the latest events referred to in the work.

34. The line from the *Teucer* of Sophocles is not actually quoted in the text as we have it.

35. For Iphicrates see n. 4 (Section Four).

36. Aristeides had a reputation for such unsullied integrity that any suggestion made against him would be transparently false.

37. Plato, *Apology* 27b–28a. In this famous passage, Socrates makes a mockery of the claim by his prosecutor Meletus that he does not believe in the gods. Meletus has conceded that Socrates believes in spirits (*daimonia*; *daimonion*, sing.) and he is also brought to admit that spirits are by religious convention a kind of god. Thus the prosecution's case in this item turns out to be elementarily self-contradictory.

38. For Harmodius and Aristogeiton see n. 7 (Section Four).

39. Polycrates, a sophistic rhetorician of fourth-century Athens, not the famous tyrant of Samos, wrote this as an epideictic treatment of the theme of Paris (the *Alexander*).

40. Mantias was forced by his mistress Plangon to acknowledge his paternity of her two sons by him.

41. It is not clear, in this case, why the mother's evidence should have been unquestioningly accepted, but this seems to have been so, as indeed in the affair of Mantias.

42. It is unclear whether Theodectes' *Law* was a work of rudimentary jurisprudence. See nn. 28, 50 (this Section).

43. This is effectively a roll-call of the great and good of archaic and early classical Greece.

44. Autocles was an anti-Spartan Athenian politician. The remark castigates Mixidemides for reluctance to stand trial before the Areopagus, which had, according to legend, once tried the Eumenides ('Solemn Goddesses') themselves.

45. Hegesipolis, king of Sparta, consulted the oracle of Zeus at Olympia as to whether he could invade Argos in contravention of a religious truce; when given a favourable reply, he turned to the oracle of Apollo at Delphi for confirmation. The point of the present remark was that Apollo, being Zeus' son, could hardly contradict him on so major a matter.

46. Such dubious characters as Helen, Paris and Euagoras could all be defended on the grounds of the apparent admiration shown for them by personages agreed to be serious. Euagoras was tyrant of Cyprus, to whom the Athenian general Conon fled when threatened with a death sentence at Athens.

47. Aristotle, *Topics*, 106a14. The point is that to anything to which a generic predicate applies there must also apply one of the specific predicates characteristic of that genus, since the species exhaust the genus. In this case, if the soul is a process, and if there are, as Aristotle held, only two kinds of process, a *kinesis* and an *energeia*, then the soul must indeed be either one or the other, but the argument, obviously, applies to all cases where the species exhaustively instantiate the genus.

48. Callippus of Cyzicus, an associate of Aristotle in the Lyceum, was primarily known for his work in astronomy. It is not clear whether it is he that is here referred to.

49. The equivalent of our 'chaff with the grain'.

50. The *Law* of Theodectes dealt primarily with the question of the enfranchisement of mercenaries.

51. Xenophanes was one of the most strikingly original of the Presocratic physicists.

52. Lysias, XXXIV. 11. The situation referred to is that of the civil strife that followed the fall of Athens and eventually led to a democratic restoration and the ejection of the thirty tyrants.

53. The fragment has not been identified, but is thoroughly Euripidean in spirit.

54. Antiphon, *Meleager*, frg. 2.

55. cp. Homer, *Iliad*, X. 218. The circumstance is the Greek raid on the Trojan camp which coincides with the espionage of the Trojan Dolon. Theodectes' play has not survived. For Theodectes' *Aias* see n. 58 (this Section).

56. No rhetorician by the name of Pamphilus is known. For Callippus, see n. 48 (this Section).

57. Just because something is the source of something else, it does not follow that it never stands in need of it. It may sometimes be right to send coals to Newcastle.

58. For Theodectes, one of Aristotle's favourite sources of quotation, see n. 28 (this Section). His *Aias*, unfortunately, like all his other works, is lost. The story presumably covered the details of the struggle between Aias and Odysseus for the arms of Achilles after that hero's death. In the traditional version of the story, as for instance presupposed in Sophocles' play, Aias deserves to have the arms on general grounds of heroic merits, and indeed consanguinity, since Achilles' son, Neoptolemus, has not yet arrived at Troy, but they are in fact won by the persuasive skill of Odysseus. Presumably, the point referred to here is typical of the sophistry that Odysseus used in Theodectes' version of the story.

59. Thrasybulus alleged that the name of his political opponent Leodamas had been written on the bronze plate on the Acropolis reserved for traitors to the city but that he had had it removed during the irregular government of the thirty tyrants. Leodamas replied that he would have had no motive for so doing, since the tyrants would have been more sure of his loyalty if there was evidence that he had betrayed the former democracy.

60. Leucothea ('the white goddess') was a human daughter of Cadmus, founder of Thebes, who was changed at her tragic death into a goddess, thereby posing a cult problem.

61. Theodorus of Cyrene, to whom this may be a reference, was a fifth-century mathematician and sophist.

62. Sophocles, *Tyro*, frg. 597. A pun on the name of Tyro's stepmother, Sidero, and *sidēros*, the Greek for 'iron'.

63. Euripides, *Troades*, 990, and Chaeremon, frg. 4. Aphrodite is close to *aphrosunē* ('mindlessness') and Pentheus to *penthos* ('grief').

64. Pindar, *Parthenia*, frg. 1. The point about the dog is by association, since dogs in general might be argued sophistically to have the same sort of importance as 'The Dog', i.e. either the Dog Star or the goat-god Pan, if the reference to Pindar is to be so interpreted. The point about mice, on the other hand, is a purer case of near-homonymy, since the Greek for mouse, *mus*, is very close to the word for the mysteries, *musteria*, secret ritual cults of the Goddess Demeter and of other deities.

65. This strange point is made at greater length in the *Sophistical Refutations* (20. 6). The fallacious argument runs: (i) you saw in Sicily the triremes that are now in the Piraeus; (ii) you see now in Sicily the triremes that were in the Piraeus; therefore (iii) you now also see in Sicily the triremes that are in the Piraeus. The fallacy arises from the ignoring of the tense-markers in the predicates.

66. This, again, is Polycrates the rhetorician, not the tyrant.

67. Theodectes, *Orestes*, frg. 5.

68. The fallacy rests on the false assumption of commutation between the sets of wicked men and thieves.

69. Polycrates panegyrized the mice who, according to the story, ate through the bowstrings of the Assyrian army attacking Egypt.

70. From a satyr play of Sophocles, in which, in a parody of the plot of the *Iliad*, Achilles is angry with the Greeks for their failure to invite him to dinner. See frg. 161.

71. See n. 39 (this Section).

72. This is one of the few references in the work to the great orator, Demosthenes, who, as an anti-Macedonian, was politically opposed to Aristotle.

73. These are both, presumably, standard debating points in topical dialectic.

74. This is the fallacy of confusing two senses of the verb 'to be'. The verb can be used both to ascribe a property (the *is* of predication) and to assert existence (the *is* of existential assertion), amongst many other uses. An example of the first use would be 'The coffee is cold', and of the second 'There is a God'. The fallacy, the basis of the ontological proof of the existence of God, arises from the fact that the assertion of the existence of a thing grammatically resembles the predication to that thing of some property, so that an assertion of existence, like a predication, appears to presuppose the existence of the very thing whose existence is asserted. This makes positive existence assertions tautological and negative ones contradictory, leading to such confusions as the thought here referred to, that even the non-existent must in some sense exist, since it can be the subject of a negative existential assertion.

75. Agathon, frg. 15.

76. For Corax, see n. 5 (Introduction).

77. Protagoras seems to have been the coiner of the notorious phrase about making the weaker argument stronger. It is certainly in line with his universal relativism.

78. 'Caunian love' is, apparently, a euphemism for incest.

79. For Pittacus and his attitude to wine, see n. 3 (Section Seven).

80. Aristotle, *Prior Analytics*, II. 27.

81. Ibid.

SECTION NINE: STYLE (pp. 215–44)

1. Nothing of Glaucon's work survives.
2. Thrasymachus is the main opponent of Socrates in the first book of the *Republic*. He was influential in the sophistic development of rhetoric, especially in connection with delivery, elocution, rhythm and sentence structure. Aristotle makes fairly extensive reference to his work *On Arousing Pity*.
3. The fragments of Gorgias that survive, notably those from the *Helen*, certainly bear out the description of his prose style as poetic.
4. Aristotle, *Poetics*, 22.
5. Aristophanes' *Frogs* is a brilliant satire on Euripides' strange combination of high-flown ideas and down-to-earth language.
6. Aristotle, *Poetics*, Chapter 21, 1457a31 f. Aristotle there distinguishes eight types of noun: proper noun, exotic noun, metaphor, decoration, artificial noun, extended noun, reduced noun and substitute. In the present passage, he is explicitly restricting the writer of prose to the proper noun, metaphor and decoration, since the exotic and artificial nouns are expressly discouraged and the term here translated as 'compound' seems to cover the extended, reduced and substitute nouns of the *Poetics*. Although neither here nor in the *Poetics* does he make it clear entirely what diction is appropriate to each form of writing, it is notable both that the present passage presupposes familiarity with the detailed doctrine of the *Poetics* and that metaphor is assigned a central role as the necessary supplement to clarity for the prose writer. The philosopher is also far more concerned in the ensuing discussion of metaphor to explain why it should have the effect that it does have, an explanation that is not paralleled by anything in the sections of the *Poetics* that have survived.
7. Iphicrates' denigratory remark about Callias hinges on the status of the *dadoukhos* ('torch-bearer') in the cult of the goddess Cybele. It was in fact more honorific than its title suggests.
8. Euripides, *Telephus*, frg. 21.
9. Athenaeus (XV. 669) tells us that this poet and rhetorician acquired his nickname from urging the Athenians to coin bronze money.
10. The solution to this riddle is that one man is applying a cupping-glass to another.
11. Licymnius of Chios was a rhetorician of the late fifth century, roughly contemporary with Gorgias.
12. Simonides, frg. 7.
13. This sort of diminutive coinage is extremely common in those plays of Aristophanes which, unlike the *Babylonians*, have survived.

14. Lycophron and Alcidamas were contemporary sophistical rhetoricians.

15. It is interesting that the two rhetoricians are once again mentioned together.

16. The festival of the Isthmia was one of the four great sporting and religious festivals of universal Greek cult.

17. It is quite unclear what is wrong with these last two metaphors of Alcidamas. See Introduction, p. 41.

18. Philomela, daughter of Pandion, legendary king of Athens, was raped by Tereus, husband of her sister Procne, who then killed Tereus in revenge and served him as a meal to their son Itys. The gods then turned them all into birds, Philomela into a swallow.

19. The discussion of the simile is never really developed as a separate category from metaphor in general. This no doubt partly reflects the subject-matter of oratory, which does not lend itself well to elaboration by means of simile in the poetic manner.

20. Idrieus was a Carian, and the occasion of his imprisonment, though uncertain, must be dated to the fourth century.

21. The same amount of geometry must be subtracted from Euxenus to bring him down to Alcidamas' level as must be added to Alcidamas to bring him up to that of Euxenus.

22. For the corpse-spoilers see *Republic*, 469d; for the deaf sea captain see *Republic*, 488a; for the boys see *Republic*, 601b.

23. The simile on the Samians suggests ingratitude for the benefits of Athenian rule, that on the Boeotians refers to the endemic strife among the Boeotian states, from which Athens profited considerably. This latter simile suggests either that oaks fall under their own weight, or that they fall, when cut, on other oaks.

24. The Demosthenes here mentioned is probably the fifth-century general; the remark of Democrates originates in Aristophanes, *Knights*, 715–18.

25. The point of the remark is obscure. Cephisodotus may be the sculptor, father of Praxiteles.

26. A favourite Aristotelian example of the metaphor of reciprocal analogy. It is also discussed in *Poetics*, 21.4.

27. For the distinction between this quality of style, *hellēnizein*, and the criterion of clarity, *saphēneia*, see the Introduction, p. 37.

28. Herodotus, I. 53. Croesus consulted the oracle on the advisability of launching a pre-emptive attack on the threatening empire of Cyrus. On receiving the prediction quoted, he assumed that the omen was favourable and attacked. Cyrus defeated him at the crucial battle of the river Halys. The empire that he had destroyed was his own.

29. This game presumably had a certain amount in common with modern roulette.

30. Protagoras' introduction of the terms of the grammatical genders and numbers reflects the growing interest in the machinery of language in the Greek world during his time. This paved the way for the growth of interest in logic in the next century.

31. These are notoriously obscure and were often accused of being deliberately so contrived to disguise their lack of real significance.

32. The use of the plural for the singular is, indeed, a standard device of amplification at all periods of Greek and Latin literature. The numbers, like the tenses, had a wider use than their primary function of indicating extent.

33. Euripides, *Iphigenia in Tauris*, 727.

34. Antimachus of Claros wrote a *Thebaid* in the mid fifth century, from which this reference to a Boeotian landmark presumably comes.

35. Cleophon was a tragedian of the late fifth century, who seems to have taken to extremes Euripides' mannerism of discussing lowly subjects in unduly high-flown style.

36. This is the only passage in which Aristotle specifically discusses propriety to context rather than to genre.

37. Isocrates, *Panegyricus*, 186.

38. Plato, *Phaedrus*, 238d, 241e.

39. An interesting echo of fifth-century politics. Cleon was a populist politician in the 420s, and he no doubt made a practice of taking on the legal patronage of newly freed slaves. So familiar did this become, that when the slaves were on the point of publicly declaring their choice, groups of small boys would anticipate it by calling out the name of Cleon. It appears that this was still proverbial in the fourth century.

40. The distinction between metre and prose rhythm is discussed in the Introduction, p. 43.

41. Thrasymachus of Chalcedon made a number of contributions to the study of prose rhythm and other aspects of style. See n. 2 (this Section).

42. These lines are in the paean rhythm in the original Greek.

43. Simonides, frg. 26b.

44. In early choral lyric, there is an elaborate rhythmic and formal symmetry between the sections of the odes, and it is probably this, rather than sentence structure proper, that Aristotle has in mind here.

45. Euripides, *Meleager*, frg. 515. The mistaken attribution is very characteristic of Aristotle, who probably made no habit of checking his references.

46. Democritus of Chios (Mullach, p. 91).

47. It is very possible that Aristotle is the originator of this distinction.

48. A favourite commonplace about the arrogance of Xerxes, who bridged the Hellespont, making the sea into land, and cut through the promontory of Mount Athos, making the land into sea.

49. Courtiers of King Alexander of Pherae in Thessaly.

50. 'Homoeoteleuton' is the ending of a section of a sentence with a word rhyming with the last word of the preceding section.

51. A work composed by Aristotle in honour of his deceased friend Theodectes, for whom see n. 28 (Section Eight).

52. cp. 1365a32–3 (Chapter 1.7).

53. Leptines was a prominent opponent of Demosthenes in contemporary Athens.

54. During the crisis of the Marathon campaign, Miltiades had ordered the Athenians to take with them their own provisions, which would normally have been provided by the state.

55. They should have used the proceeds of the sack of Epidaurus to launch an expedition in the north.

56. The *Paralus* was the flagship of the Athenian fleet.

57. Famously remarked in 447 BC, when Athens took the opportunity of war in the Saronic Gulf finally to annex Aegina, her long-term enemy and trading rival.

58. Anaxandrides, frg. 68.

59. The description does not permit us to speculate as to the nature of Speusippus' complaint. Polyeuctes was a minor politician of the period.

60. The Dog was the nickname of the fifth-century politician Cleon (see n. 39, this Section). Aesion's comment refers to the enormous material and moral losses to Athens that resulted from her defeat by the Syracusans in 413 BC.

61. Isocrates, *Philipus*, 12.

62. Lysias, XXXV.

63. For Iphicrates see n. 4 (Section Four). Chares was a fourth-century Athenian general, of greater military skill than political sagacity.

64. The kneeling statue of Chabrias could be seen by the jury at his trial, and his supporter Lycoleon skilfully exploited this fact to his advantage.

65. Isocrates, *Panegyricus*, 151.

66. Euripides, *Iphigenia in Aulis*, 80.

67. All these illustrations are taken from Homeric similes.

68. This is presumably a line from contemporary comedy.

69. This obscure pun turns on the fact that Nicon was a Thracian. The remark was '*thrattei*', literally 'You should worry', but the 'something else' for which it could be mistaken was '*thratt'ei*', 'You are no better than a slave girl'.

70. Here the pun seems to be between *Persai*, the Persians, and *persai*, 'to destroy'.

71. The pun is on the two senses of *arkhē*, 'empire' and 'beginning'.

72. None of these puns is easy to interpret, except that on the name Anaschetus (*Anaskhetos*), which simply means 'Unbearable'.

73. Anaxandrides, frg. 64.

74. Philoctetes, in his destitution after abandonment by the Greeks, was a byword for unkempt self-neglect.

75. Neither of these two references can be securely identified or interpreted with full confidence.

76. The island of Carpathus was once, supposedly, devastated by a plague of hares which grew from an animal introduced misguidedly by one of the inhabitants.

77. This may be a rare humorous essay of the philosopher's own.

78. See n. 75 (this Section).

79. Homer, *Iliad*, IX. 385, 388–90.

80. Anaxandrides was a middle-ranking comic poet of the fourth century who ten times won the comedy competition.

81. Apparently an expression for an awkward and gangling orator.

82. *Iliad*, II. 671–3.

SECTION TEN: COMPOSITION (pp. 245–61)

1. Nothing can be made of these technical niceties. For Licymnius see n. 11 (Section Nine).

2. See Introduction, p. 46.

3. This certainly seems a curious comment to make on the Paris of legend.

4. Choerilus was a fifth-century epic poet; the point of the line is to deplore the fact that all the great subjects of poetry have already been covered, leaving him only with the wars of Greece and Persia.

5. Homer, *Iliad*, I. 1.

6. Homer, *Odyssey*, I. 1.

7. Choerilus. See n. 4.

8. Sophocles, *King Oedipus*, 774.

9. This is presumably to dazzle them with a display of ready-made rhetorical tricks.

10. Sophocles, *Antigone*, 233, and Euripides, *Iphigenia in Tauris*, 1162.

11. Homer, *Odyssey*, VII. 327.

12. The date of this encomium is unknown, but it would be a very

characteristic theme for Gorgias, though the opening would certainly be unusual.

13. It is striking that Aristotle appears not to explain here in what way a slander is to be refuted, but in fact he is referring to his chapter (3.17) on refutation. The technique of refuting a slanderous presupposition is not, apparently, distinct from that of refuting a direct allegation.

14. For Iphicrates see n. 4 (Section Four).

15. Euripides, *Hippolytus*, 612.

16. Teucer used in his defence before the victorious Greek army against allegations of disloyalty while he was in Troy the fact that in Troy he had not betrayed the Greek spies that had entered the city.

17. This is a reference to the spying expedition that both heroes undertook against Troy.

18. Herodotus, II. 76.

19. In Homer, *Odyssey*, 23. 310–43, the hero, who has at last been recognized by his wife, gives her an account of his wanderings since leaving Troy. This is naturally presented at rather less length than the narration of the same material to King Alcinous on Scherie, but it is also noteworthy that Odysseus omits or edits many episodes, such as his stay with the nymphs Circe and Calypso and his encounter with the Princess Nausicaa, which he presumably did not think it helpful for his wife to hear.

20. A non-extant play of Euripides.

21. Sophocles, *Antigone*, 911–12.

22. *Odyssey*, XIX. 361.

23. Sophocles, *Antigone*, 683 ff.

24. *Odyssey*, IV. 204.

25. This is the originator of the famous liar paradox. He lived in the late seventh century and his most certain historical contribution was to purify the Acropolis at Athens after the murder on it of the would-be tyrant Cylon and many of his followers in 630 BC.

26. These are all the ancestors of Achilles.

27. The circumstances of the case are unknown.

28. Euripides, *Troades*, 969 f.

29. Archilochus, frg. 74.

30. Ibid.

31. Sophocles, *Antigone*, 690.

32. Pericles seems to have exposed Lampon's pretence to religious scruples to which he was not justified by initiation. This exchange is of some interest as being one of the few extant examples of Pericles' wit in altercation.

33. Plato, *Apology*, 27c. This was a famous example of the exposure of the self-contradictions of a prosecution during an altercation. Socrates, who affects to have no skill in oratory, turns the debating technique of the elenchus to good forensic account.
34. See Chapter 1.14.
35. A very characteristic example of Laconic wit.
36. A reference to the lost section of the work that dealt with comedy.
37. From the last words of Lysias' *Against Eratosthenes*.

BIBLIOGRAPHY

BARNES, J., SCHOFIELD, M., and SORABJI, R., *Articles on Aristotle*, Vols. 1–4 (Duckworth, London, 1979).

BARTHES, R., 'L'Ancienne Rhétorique: Aide-mémoire', *Communications*, 16 (1970).

BURNYEAT, M., 'Enthymeme: The Logic of Persuasion', in FURLEY, D. J., and NEHAMAS, A. (eds.), *Aristotle's Rhetoric* (Princeton University Press, Princeton, 1994).

CHAIGNET, E., *La Rhétorique et son histoire* (Gallimard, Paris, 1888).

COOPER, J., *Class*, new edn (Corgi, London, 1980).

COOPER, J. M., 'Rhetoric, Dialectic, and the Passions', *Oxford Studies in Ancient Philosophy*, 11 (1993).

COPE, E., in SANDYS, J. E. (ed.), *Commentary on Aristotle's 'Rhetoric'* (Cambridge University Press, Cambridge, 1877).

COPE, E., *Introduction to the 'Rhetoric' of Aristotle* (Cambridge University Press, Cambridge, 1867).

DIELS, H., 'Über das dritte Buch der aristotelischen Rhetorik', *Abhandlung der Akademie der Wissenschaft*, No. 4 (Berlin, 1886).

FURLEY, D. J. and NEHAMAS, A. (eds.), *Aristotle's Rhetoric* (Princeton University Press, Princeton, 1994).

GARLAND, R., *The Greek Way of Life* (Duckworth, London, 1989).

GARVER, E., *Aristotle's Rhetoric: An Art of Character* (The University of Chicago Press, Chicago/London, 1994).

GRAYEFF, F., *Aristotle and his School* (Duckworth, London, 1974).

HALLIWELL, S., 'Style and Sense in Aristotle's *Rhetoric* Book 3', *Revue Internationale de Philosophie*, 47 (1993).

JAEGER, W., *Aristotle* (trans. R. Robinson, Clarendon Press, Oxford, 1948).

KENNEDY, G., *Aristotle, On Rhetoric: A Theory of Civic Discourse* (Oxford University Press, Oxford, 1991).

KENNEDY, G., *The Art of Persuasion in Greece* (Longman, London, 1963).

LEIGHTON, S., 'Aristotle and the Emotions', *Phronesis*, 27 (1982).

MACINTYRE, A., *A Short History of Ethics* (Duckworth, London, 1974).

BIBLIOGRAPHY

MADDEN, E. H., 'The Enthymeme: Crossroads of Logic, Rhetoric and Metaphysics', *Philosophical Review*, 61 (1952).

MORAVSIC, J. (ed.), *Aristotle* (Macmillan, London, 1968).

NUYENS, F., *L'Évolution de la psychologie d'Aristote* (Université de Louvain, Louvain, 1948).

RAPHAEL, S., 'Rhetoric, Dialectic and Syllogistic Argument: Aristotle's Position in Rhetoric I–II, *Phronesis*, 19 (1974).

ROBERTS, W., *Greek Rhetoric and Literary Criticism* (Cambridge University Press, Cambridge, 1928).

RORTY, A. O. (ed.), *Essays on Aristotle's Rhetoric* (University of California Press, Berkeley/Los Angeles/London, 1996).

ROSS, W., *Aristotelis Ars Rhetorica* (Oxford Classical Texts, Oxford, 1959).

ROSS, W., *Aristotelis Fragmenta Selecta* (Oxford Classical Texts, Oxford, 1955).

RYAN, E., *Aristotle's Theory of Rhetorical Argumentation* (Les Éditions Bellarmin, Montreal, 1984).

SCRUTON, R., *Sexual Desire* (Duckworth, London, 1986).

SEATON, R. C., 'The Aristotelian Enthymeme', *Classical Review*, 28 (1914).

SOLMSEN, F., 'Die Entwicklung der aristotelischen Logik und Rhetorik', *Neue philologische Untersuchungen*, 4 (Berlin).

THOMPSON, W. H., 'Stasis in Aristotle's *Rhetoric*', *Quarterly Journal of Speech*, 58 (1972).

VICKERS, B., *In Defence of Rhetoric* (Clarendon Press, Oxford, 1988).

WEIDEMANN, H., 'Aristotle on Inferences from Signs (*Rhetoric* I 2, 1357b1–25)', *Phronesis*, 34 (1989).